8 YEARS OF
UNFORGETTABLE
HISTORY
EXECUTIVE OFFICE OF THE PRESIDENT OF THE UNITED STATES
OFFICE OF MANAGEMENT AND BUDGET

# 8 Years of Unforgettable History: The allure of America's Firsts

*Compiled by* Minister Phyllis Hodges CFT, LHM

Foreword by Annie Abrams

Printed in the United States of America

First Printing, 2018

ISBN 978-1-942022510

ISBN13: 1942022514

Cover Artwork: Laurence Walden

Researchers and Organizers:

Mica Wright
Lynda Cooper
Shirley Ferguson
Jade Crosby
Siony Flowers
Henri Linton

Photographers:

Victor Coates- Victor's Photography
Ca'Ron Watkins- Plan C Video Production
Stevey McCall Photography
Kimberly Pearson Photography

Publisher:

The Butterfly Typeface Publishing
PO BOX 56193
Little Rock AR 72205

# Dedication

This book is dedicated to the extraordinary men in my life:

My grandfather, the late great John Henry Bolden
(July 15, 1882 - December 18, 1971)

My beloved dad, the late James Lawrence Marshall
(May 17, 1919 - November 18, 2007)

These two special men didn't live to witness history being made on January 20, 2009, when former President Barack Obama became the first African-American president of the United States of America.

My loving husband, Byron Lester Hodges,
I'm grateful that God anointed me to be your wife.

My son, Bryan Adaris Hodges,
as your mother, I love praying for you daily.

My grandson, Ryan Adaris Watkins,
it blesses me when you call me Dearest.

You all lived a part of history,
which is what so many men and women fought and died for,
equal rights.

"You never really understand a person
until you consider things from his point of view...
Until you climb into his skin and walk around in it."

Atticus Finch, *To Kill a Mockingbird*

# Table of Contents

# Foreword

This book shares and shows how the contributors' life travels became a *first* in the history of Arkansas and the nation. Their family trees, their education, their racial status, both religion and political stances are different; but, what the contributors have in common is that they overcame the challenges which are mastered throughout the world.

Each living legend selected to be included in this book contributed to the title, *8 Years of Unforgettable History.* The number '8' is a Biblically scriptural number that is found throughout the Holy Bible. To understand the number '8' in the Holy Bible, we all need to go to it which will enable us to be a *first* also. The Holy Bible, in many chapters, explains that after the achievement of being a historic *first*; there always follows a new birth, a new creation, or a new beginning.

According to Evangelist Ed F. Vallowe's book, *Biblical Mathematics,* he enables us to understand the Biblical reference and sanctity of the number '8,' such as there were eight people carried over and beyond the flood in the Ark (I Peter 3:20). There we find a new birth, a new creation, or a new beginning.

With those eight people saved, the world was populated anew and had a new beginning. This book of Mr. Vallowe shares the marvelous things that happened to Jesus who rose from the dead in eight days from Palm Sunday to Easter Sunday. According to Mr. Vallowe, this number, '8,' is used eighty times in the Bible.

Former President Barack Obama, Phyllis Hodges and *The Carousel*, and I, Annie Abrams have moved on faith and courage using God's instructional book, *The Bible.*

As African-Americans, *first,* in our life's work of service to mankind, we all have added sprinkles of the power of love, the power of prayer, and wisdom from God.

When one becomes a *first*, they live on in the memory and hearts of people. The sharing of good will help overcome political unrest, racial injustice, and fighting because of economic distress. These *first* gather their strength to fight and to endure pressure, through a passion of dedication by strengthening their faith to achieve godly given purpose.

If you, the reader of this book, want to become a *first*, you have to be spiritually anchored in the Lord using your head, heart, and hands.

*Annie Abrams*
Civil Rights Activist & Historian

# Acknowledgments

There are a tremendous number of people who made it possible for this project to come alive and to include the 8 Arkansas First (World Changers):

- Chief Master Richard E. Anderson.
- Martha Dixon
- Jeffery Henderson
- Pamela Huff
- Janis Kearney
- Thelma Mothershed-Wair
- Lottie Shackelford
- Judge Joyce Elise Williams Warren

my inner circle, prayer warriors, and women of God whom I call friends. They keep me undergirded and prayed up: Gwendolyn Porter-Cole, Mary Gorden, and Alice Polite.

I would like to give special thanks to Iris M. Williams and her team at *Butterfly Typeface Publishing* who saw the vision and patiently provided a wealth of knowledge to assist in making the dream come alive.

Thanks to Laurence Walden, my personal artist, whom I've never met personally, but only spoken with by phone and social media. You're such a professional, ordained and taught by God to create and design as you do. I'm thankful for this gifted man who was able to listen to my vision over the phone, put it on canvas, and turn it into a book cover.

To my amazing Mom, "Rose Wright," my best friend, confidant, angel in disguise, chief advisor, prayer warrior, mentor, and hero, you love, support, and encourage me. God has richly blessed me to be able to call you Mom.

Highlights and thanks to my Spiritual Mothers:

- The Late Mother Velma Johnson aka Big Mama
- Mother Odessa Stribling
- Mother Alveretta S. Lynch
- Mother Gladys Mae Calhoun

the BEST Grandmother in my world, the late Clara Bolden aka Other Mama and

the Family Matriarchs, my late great grandmothers *American Bolden* and *Elizabeth Armstrong*.

Thank you to the Pastors who imparted spiritual wisdom and prayers into my life, helping me to become the woman that I am today: The Late Rev. Sherman Abraham, The Late Rev. Banks, The Late Rev. Broadnax, and Bishop Silas Johnson.

Thank you to four professional business women who believed in me from the beginning of my professional walk: Albessie Thompson, Carmalita Smith, Christine Patterson, and Christal Cleaver.

To my sisters, Pamela Huff and Ann Williams, I thank God for you both. You all make me smile during the times I feel like crying. Thanks for being my 'sissies.'

My Chicago family: Dorothy Jean, Vivian, James, and Dallas, our love for each other is the real deal.

My brothers: James Marshall Jr. aka Mr. Marshall, Tony Wright, Terry Wright aka T-BONE, and Kenneth Marshall, thanks for being my brothers. All girls need brothers.

To the rest of my family and friends who believe there's nothing I can't do, thank you.

I must close by acknowledging my daughter and my two beautiful granddaughters:

My beautiful daughter, Candince, my firstborn, looks like me and generates a lot of my energy. As my firstborn, I thought I knew how to be a mother, but when you blessed me with two beautiful granddaughters, I had a second chance to get it right.

Ca'Ron, my firstborn granddaughter, you are so smart and the first generation of graduates in the family to hold a B.A. in Mass Communication.

Jade (aka Dr. Jade, my *mini-me* granddaughter), has the same smart genes that are taking her to the medical field as an aspiring Anesthesiologist.

All three of you ladies have blessed me to strive to be the best mom in the world. Although I wear a lot of hats, I thank God for the hat that's titled, MOTHER.

Laurence Walden aka "Blinky" is a native of Chicago. He now resides in Jacksonville, Florida. He is a self-taught visual artist as well as an accomplished jazz vocalist, playwright, and historian.

As an honorably discharged United States Air Force Veteran, Walden served as a technical illustrator and was the featured vocalist with the Air Force jazz band during the Vietnam Era.

While in the Air Force, he created costumes and album covers for Isaac Hayes, The Bar-Kays, and Jimi Hendricks.

He has received many honors for his art worldwide. As a jazz vocalist, he has opened for and/or performed with Cab Calloway, Jimmy Smith, Nancy Wilson, Willie Bobo, Dolly Parton, Dionne Warwick, Gerald Albright, Sammy Davis Jr., Billy Eckstine, Arthur Prysock, Dorothy Donnegan, Maurice Hines Sr., and Lena Horne.

Laurence Walden also directed the Gospel Choir at Philander Smith College in Little Rock, Arkansas, and in 1980, he performed in more than 3,000 shows as an opening act at Disneyland in Anaheim, California.

As a playwright, Walden wrote and starred in a historical and musical tribute to Billy Eckstine, Sarah Vaughan, and Duke Ellington, of which he has received several awards.

One of Walden's visual art rendering specialties is creating decorative masks out of fine dining silverware and other found objects, in addition to rendering abstract paintings, mixed media collages, murals, and portraits. He also designs and creates wearable art accessories including clutch purses, steampunk hats, t-shirt designs, and jewelry.

Laurence Walden believes that great art is the result of collaboration between GOD and the artist.

"Our Father Who ART in Heaven"

# **Credits** *(Special Thanks)*

---

This project was funded in part by a grant from the Black History Commission of Arkansas.

I am also thankful for the many newspapers I referenced from across the world:

- Arkansas Democrat-Gazette
- The Washington Post
- U-T San Diego Pensacola News Journal
- Los Angeles Times
- The Punch (Nigerian daily newspaper)
- Detroit Free Press
- Chicago Sun-Times
- Arkansas Times
- Chicago Tribune
- The Times (Illinois Edition)
- Southtown Star (Chicago Sun-Times Publication)
- The Little Rock Sun
- USA Today
- The Wall Street Journal
- The Florida Times-Union
- The News-Star
- Sync
- The Baltimore Sun
- New York Post
- The Washington Times
- The Commercial Appeal The Courier - Journal Amandala - Belize
- Courier-Index Marianna, Arkansas News Stand
- Bash Magazine

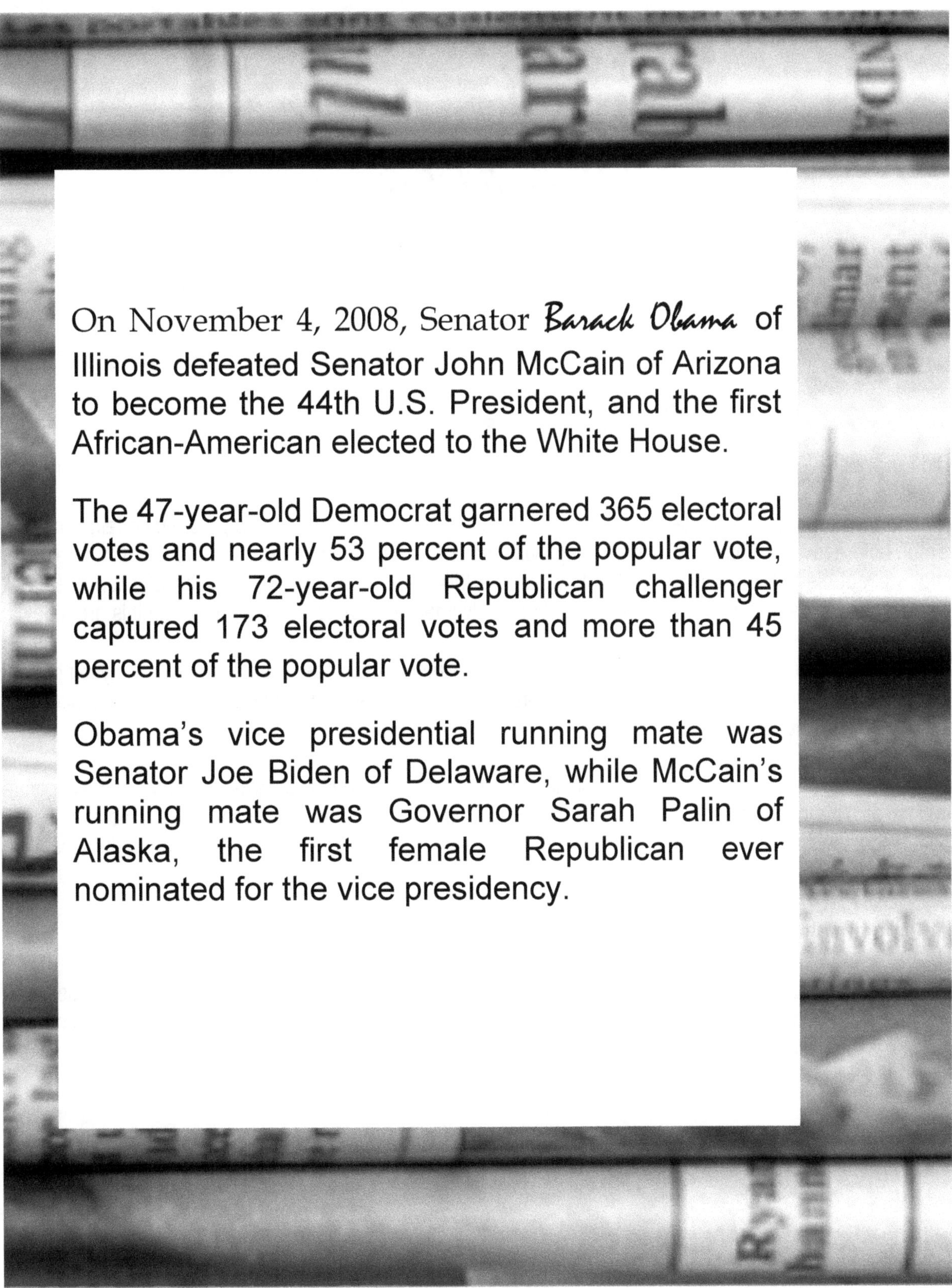

On November 4, 2008, Senator *Barack Obama* of Illinois defeated Senator John McCain of Arizona to become the 44th U.S. President, and the first African-American elected to the White House.

The 47-year-old Democrat garnered 365 electoral votes and nearly 53 percent of the popular vote, while his 72-year-old Republican challenger captured 173 electoral votes and more than 45 percent of the popular vote.

Obama's vice presidential running mate was Senator Joe Biden of Delaware, while McCain's running mate was Governor Sarah Palin of Alaska, the first female Republican ever nominated for the vice presidency.

# Preface

## Barack Obama

---

*First African-American President of The United States*

Did I ever believe that there would be a black president? Well maybe... one day, but not in this century.

My dad, James Marshall Sr. died at the age of 86. He was an entrepreneur and a prophet; certainly, he was a man before his time. Dad would share things with me before it happened regarding the world, but he never spoke about his political views. He didn't live to see this great moment in history, the election of Barack Obama as president of the United States, but I can only imagine how he would have felt on this great day.

I remember not being able to attend the inauguration of President Barack Obama, so I glued myself in front of the television and took pictures as though I was there. All news stations, local and international, aired this history-making change.

Years later, as the Obama Era ended, I couldn't help but feel an obligation to take ownership in making sure that we as a people (and especially our youth) are fully made aware of his significance as a trailblazer. I want people to know that those who go before us are the beacon many of us seek to pull us from a darkness that threatens to hinder our progress.

It is my prayer that this book *lures* you to your path of greatness.

Please allow Barack Obama, myself, and those who have so graciously contributed to this book to serve as your bait to greatness. Dreams do come true! Just because something hasn't been done before, doesn't mean it is impossible. The standard has been set, and the urgency is real. Learn, reference, and go make it happen!

Change is *inevitable;* allow it to **REEL** you to your destiny!

Phyllis Hodges

# Who Cares...

## *What is important about being the first?*

As I collected the many newspaper copies from different parts of the country, I smiled and thought about all the history I was holding in my hands. I knew there would come a day that I would sit down on the floor with my grandchildren and maybe even some of their friends and share these stories about the historic moment when Barack Obama became the first African-American president (In actuality, he was the first biracial president).

Among the countless conversations, there were many people *still* talking about Obama's mixed heritage. I continue to wonder why people who are born of a mixed race that includes an African-American father or mother are always considered black. During my research for this book, I found information pertaining to the 'one drop rule' which states that all you need is a drop of African blood to be considered black. This law was passed in 1911 when the Arkansas legislators passed its concubinage law.

The omission of his entire ethnicity bothered me so much because it was as though part of his family was omitted. I could relate to this story well because my children are biracial. My husband, their father, is Caucasian, and I'm African-American. I know firsthand how important it is to acknowledge the entire lineage of a person.

I found myself wanting to share this story with not only my children but the world's children. I had no idea I would end up compiling a history book from those newspapers and my life experiences.

Years later, I would find myself sitting in the middle of my king-size bed surrounded by newspapers from across the country referencing that historic moment!

There is significance in being the first. Barack Obama's unique life story inspired a message of hope and change, change that altered the world.

## *Front Page News*

Newsstands from Seattle to New York quickly sold out of newspapers declaring Barack Obama the nation's first African-American president. Jubilant customers picked extra copies as keepsakes.

In Obama's hometown, *The Chicago Tribune* and *The New York Times* were among papers that restarted their printing presses to produce hundreds of thousands additional copies across the country. In Little Rock, *The Arkansas Democrat- Gazette* sold all but about 60 copies of their newspapers by 4 pm!

It was said that lots of requests were being made; people were requesting 5-6 copies for keepsakes. Special printing of about 5,000 more copies of Wednesday's paper were printed; this addition would be on sale in the lobby of the *Arkansas Democrat-Gazette* headquarters for 50 cents, and photo-quality prints of the front page were also sold for 50 cents. The only other occasions for which *Democrat-Gazette* officials remembered such sales were editions covering the September 11, 2001, terrorist attacks, the 1992 election of Bill Clinton as president, and the deaths of Elvis Presley and NASCAR driver, Dale Earnhardt.

Entrepreneurs were seeking as much as $200 for the New York Times on eBay! Owning a piece of history is what most people were thinking. So, by chance, if you are reading this book and thinking, "I should have saved my newspaper or maybe even purchased a newspaper," don't fret. The majority of information gathered here is from my very own private collection, and I'm all too pleased to share it with you!

Obama said his election, "sent a message to the world" that the nation has "never been just a collection of individuals or a collection of red states and blue states." He said, "We are and always will be the United States of America." Obama acknowledged the difficult task awaiting him, noting the nation's long-fought wars and eroding economics.

For him, it was yet another task in the final days of his nearly 2-year quest for the White House. While he stood by his wife and two young daughters, he looked to the room packed with supportive voters and said, "I voted."

## Global High Spirits

Obama's ancestral Kenyan village declared that day a national holiday. Barack Obama's father grew up in the village of Kogelo where the people first heard the news of this unbelievable, life-changing event. Their emotions brought on hugging and dancing which carried on all through the night. Prime Minister Raila, who also came from the same area and the same tribe as Obama's father, was quoted of saying, "This victory was a Kenyan one." Sarah Hussein Obama, Obama's Kenyan grandmother, was spotted fellowshipping with other villagers while enjoying a feast of goats and chickens.

The Pope sent a personal note saying he would, "Pray for God's blessings." People across the globe called Barack Obama's election a victory for the world and a renewal of American's ability to inspire. People from all over the world, from Paris to Brazil said, "Obama's election made them feel more connected to America." Barack Obama was called the first global U.S. president. There were so many people who were excited about this election that said, "This was the first election that made them determined to vote." Many said, "Out of all previous years of elections this was the one they really remembered." It was also confirmation of the phrase, "I hereby declare that all men are created equal from the U.S."

Among the many congratulatory letters received was one from Nelson Mandela, South Africa's first black president which read, "Your victory demonstrated that no person anywhere in the world should not dare to dream of wanting to change the world for a better place."

Colin Powell, former secretary of state during the Bush Administration, endorsed Obama and became emotional during an interview with CNN from Hong Kong. He stated that he and his family wept when the networks declared Obama the victor.

In my opinion, these were the emotions shared by most African-Americans across the world. I am reminiscing about the moment I heard this great news. There are no words to describe how I felt. President Bush pledged complete cooperation in the transition and called Obama's victory "a triumph of the American story."

## Inherited Challenges

Some of the challenges that Barack Obama inherited from previous administrations included economic down fall, war on Iraq, and the healthcare crisis. When he was still senator, Barack Obama said in a speech, "In six days, we can choose hope over fear, unity over division, change or status quo. In six days, we can come together as one nation and as one people and choose our better history."

Obama asked Illinois Representative Rahm Emanuel, former political and policy advisor to President Clinton, to be his White House chief of staff. Receiving the victory over Republican Senator John McCain, Obama earned expanded security clearance, and the nation's top intelligence officials planned to give him top-secret daily briefings. They provided him with the most critical overnight intelligence that he had not been allowed to see as a senator or a candidate.

When Obama became president on January 20th with Delaware Senator Joe Biden as his vice president, Democrats took control of both the White House and Congress for the first time since 1994. Obama drew a record-breaking 700 million to his campaign account. He was also the first Democrat to receive more than 50 percent of the popular vote since Jimmy Carter in 1976.

He is the first senator elected to the White House since John F. Kennedy in 1960. Obama scored an Electoral College landslide. He won states that reliably voted Republican in presidential elections, Indiana and Virginia. Indiana and Virginia hadn't supported a Democratic candidate in 44 years. Ohio and Florida also went to Obama as did Pennsylvania; 52.3 percent of the popular vote went to Obama, and McCain received 43.6 percent. The count in the Electoral College was more lopsided favoring Obama 349 to 162. The turnout of voters was at an astronomical high which hadn't been seen in the last 40 years. Millions of Americans picked their president and waited long hours in long lines.

Obama and the vice president-elect met in Chicago with their panel of 17 economic advisors. After the meeting, Obama held his first news conference since winning the election over Republican Senator John McCain. Obama and his wife, Michelle, met at the White House with the Bushes to discuss transition issues where he cautioned the people that his election would not be a quick solution.

He warned that the nation faced the challenges of a lifetime and pledged that he would act urgently to help Americans devastated by lost jobs, disappearing savings, and homes seized in foreclosure. Obama said, "The number one priority is to get Congress to approve an economic stimulus plan that would extend jobless benefits, send food aids to the poor, and dispatch Medicaid funds to states and spend 10's of billions of dollars on public work projects."

# Celebration Throughout Churches

Here in Arkansas, I noticed the Little Rock churches were extraordinarily full that Sunday. The spirit was high. It was like everyone had found new hope. I was very concerned; I found myself praying more because it appeared to me that people had put the president-elect on a pedestal. I feared they thought he had the power to do the impossible. Still, we needed to remember Obama has to go to God just like all other believers. He was a man leading our country, and he needed a support team.

Let us be mindful and keep a sense of trust with all whom have worn the uniform of the United States of America; that America will serve you as well as you have served your country. Obama said, "As your next commander-in-chief, I promise to work every single day to keep that sacred trust with all whom have served."

While thinking about the history at hand, I can't remember reading about or watching any other of our presidents being so hands on or approachable. Obama had an *in your face* aura, whether it was a smile or just reaching out and hugging someone with obvious love in his heart for the people.

This moment in history was pivotal for me as a business owner and a leader. I was so intrigued by whom the nominees would be because I knew that to lead any business, you must have the right team, and Barack Obama was about to lead our country.

There was so much excitement, pride, and hope permeating through the pews and the pulpit in predominantly black churches across the nation.

So many things happened the first Sunday following Obama's election:

Dignitaries and celebrities could be spotted throughout the churches.

The Reverend Shirley Caesar-Williams was quoted saying, "God had vindicated the black folks."

The eldest sister of slain civil-rights leader the Reverend Martin Luther King Jr. attended services Sunday at Ebenezer Baptist Church.

Nation of Islam Minister Louis Farrakhan said, "God's divine plan for the world explains why Obama won the election and God would make sure Obama has the vision needed to guide the country through current economic and current social woes." Farrakhan gave a speech at the national headquarters on Chicago Southside, titled *American New Beginnings*.

President-Elect Barack Obama warned the packed audience that having a black president would not mean the end of racial inequality in the United States.

Black and white Christian clergy's members asked God to give Obama the wisdom and strength to lead the country out of what many considered a wilderness of despair and gloom. Local ministers, prayer warriors, and I prayed daily for our new president, and we also encouraged others to keep the first family covered and lifted up.

# Presidential Pastimes and Policies

President-Elect Obama, and his wife, Michelle, pulled up to the White House diplomatic entrance in an armored black limousine, a more formal transport than his usual sport utility vehicle. On this visit to the White House, the Obamas were greeted by the president and the First Lady, Laura Bush. They shook hands and smiled for the cameras. President Bush and President-Elect Obama visited in the oval office. The Bushes welcomed the Obamas during the visit which lasted nearly two hours. The new family explored the place that would soon become their residence for the next four years, 1600 Pennsylvania Avenue or the White House of the United States of America. President Bush and President-Elect Barack Obama talked war and financial crisis, while First Lady Laura Bush and Michelle Obama spoke about raising daughters and the nation's most famous house.

After a Veterans Day ceremony in Chicago, President-Elect Barack Obama was photographed hugging Tammy Duckworth and Iraq War veteran, who now is the Illinois governor's veterans affairs director. One week after winning the presidential election, Obama took a brief break from his primary task of planning his administration and monitoring the economic crisis to mark Veterans Day at the Bronze Soldier's Memorial between the Field Museum and Soldiers Field in Chicago.

The Wednesday before Thanksgiving, President-Elect Barack Obama received hugs as he, his wife, Michelle, and their daughters, Sasha and Malia helped out at a food bank at St. Columbanus Catholic Church on Chicago Southside. The President-Elect was in a jovial mood, calling out Happy Thanksgiving and telling everyone, "You can call me Barack." The Obamas wanted to show the girls the meaning of the holiday; especially when so many people were struggling.

President-Elect Barack Obama held a news conference on Monday, December 1st in Chicago where he announced the members of his national security team. He promised "A new dawn of American leadership."

He formally introduced his national security team, led by Senator Hillary Rodham Clinton, as his nominee for secretary of state. For defense secretary, Obama announced Robert M. Gates, and General James L. Jones was to be national security adviser. Governor Janet Napolitano of Arizona was to be secretary of homeland security. Susan E. Rice was to be ambassador to the United Nations and Eric H. Holders Jr. to be attorney general. Obama had then selected half of his cabinet including the high-profile jobs at the state defense, justice, and treasury departments. A week later, he named his economic team, led by Timothy Geithner as treasury secretary, and soon, he planned to announce New Mexico Governor Bill Richardson as commerce secretary and former secretary majority leader, Tom Dascale was announced as health and human services secretary.

President-Elect Barack Obama indicated that he wanted to use a significant portion of 700 billion dollars in financial bailout funds to help struggling homeowners avoid foreclosure. People were losing their homes to foreclosure and automotive companies such as Chrysler and Ford Motors were facing bankruptcy. Three of Arkansas' four publicly traded banks announced decisions to apply for participation in The Capital Purchase Chase program: Simmons First National Corp., of Pine Bluff (in the amount of $40 million), Little Rock based Bank of the Ozarks (between $25 million- $75 million), and Home BancShares Inc. of Conway ($50 billion dollars).

Most Americans were asking the question, "Would it be a bailout or tax increase?"

## Biography

Courtesy of Metro Creative Service

# Obama's Path to the Presidency

Barrack Hussen Obama II was born on August 4th, 1961, in Hawaii to Ann Durham and Barack Obama Senior. The Elder hailed from Kenya where he worked as a goat herder with his father who was a domestic servant to the British. President Obama's mother grew up in Kansas, where her father worked on oil rigs during the Great Depression. Mr. Durham enlisted in the armed forces during World War II, and eventually, through the federal Housing program, the family settled down in Hawaii. Durham and Obama Sr. met in Hawaii at the University of Hawaii. Durham was a student there, and Obama Sr., had won a scholarship enabling him to move from Kenya to pursue opportunities in America. They married and had Barack. After several years of marriage, Durham and Obama Sr. divorced, and he moved back to Kenya. Durham remarried when her son was six, and the family moved to Indonesia. He attended school briefly in Jakarta in Hawaii.

Obama moved to New York during his college years and graduated from Columbia University. He had plans to attend law school and enter the corporate world, but he put those plans on hold to make a difference for underprivileged communities following the lessons of empathy his mother had taught him growing up.

Obama relocated to Chicago in 1985; he became a community organizer with a church-based group seeking to improve the living conditions of poor neighborhoods plagued with crime and high unemployment. Although the group had some success, Obama desired for change on a greater level and decided upon a life of public service. Obama earned his law degree from Harvard in 1991. He returned to Chicago where he practiced as a civil rights lawyer and taught constitutional law. The path eventually brought him to run for the U.S. Senate, to which he was elected in 2004. He became the third black man to be elected to the Senate. The senator decided after four years of service to try his hand at a bid for the presidency period after a long presidential campaign with running mate Senator John McCain as the Democratic nominee. He is the first black United States president.

Obama is married to Michelle, whom he met while the two worked at the law firm of Sidley Austin in Chicago. Obama was a summer intern. The couple wed in 1992. Michelle and Barack Obama have two daughters, Malia and Sasha. The family resided on the south side of Chicago until Obama was elected as the 44th president of the United States. They then moved into their new residence at the White House. Barack Obama was virtually unknown outside of Illinois at the time. He delivered the keynote address at the 2004 Democratic National Convention in Boston and became the president of the United States of America in 2009.

## Accolades

- Rescued the country from the Great Recession, cutting the unemployment rate from 10% to 4.7% over six years
- Signed the Affordable Care Act which provided health insurance to over 20 million uninsured Americans
- Ended the war in Iraq
- Ordered for the capture and killing of Osama Bin Laden
- Passed the $787 billion America Recovery and Reinvestment Act to spur economic growth during the Great Recession
- Supported the LGBT community's fight for marriage equality
- Commuted the sentences of nearly 1200 drug offenders to reverse "unjust and outdated prison sentences"
- Saved the U.S. auto industry
- Helped put the U.S. on track for energy independence by 2020
- Began the drawdown of troops in Afghanistan
- Signed the Deferred Action for Childhood Arrivals allowing as many as 5 million people living in the U.S. illegally to avoid deportation and receive work permits
- Signed the Dodd-Frank Wall Street Reform and Consumer Protection Act to re-regulate the financial sector
- Dropped the veteran homeless rate by 50 percent
- Reversed Bush-era torture policies
- Began the process of normalizing relations with Cuba
- Increased Department of Veteran Affairs funding
- Signed the Credit Card Accountability, Responsibility, and Disclosure Act
- Boosted fuel efficiency standards for cars
- Improved school nutrition with the Healthy Hunger-Free Kids Act
- Repealed the military's "Don't Ask, Don't Tell" policy
- Signed the Hate Crimes Prevention Act, making it a federal crime to assault anyone based on sexual or gender identification
- Helped negotiate the landmark Iran Nuclear Deal
- Signed the Lilly Ledbetter Fair Pay Act to combat pay discrimination against women
- Nominated Sonia Sotomayor to the Supreme Court, making her the first Hispanic ever to serve as a justice
- Supported veterans through a $78 billion tuition assistance GI bill
- Won the Nobel Peace Prize in 2009 "for his extraordinary efforts to strengthen international diplomacy and cooperation between peoples"
- Launched My Brother's Keeper, a White House initiative designed to help young minorities achieve their full potential
- Expanded embryonic stem cell research leading to groundbreaking work in areas including spinal injury treatment and cancer

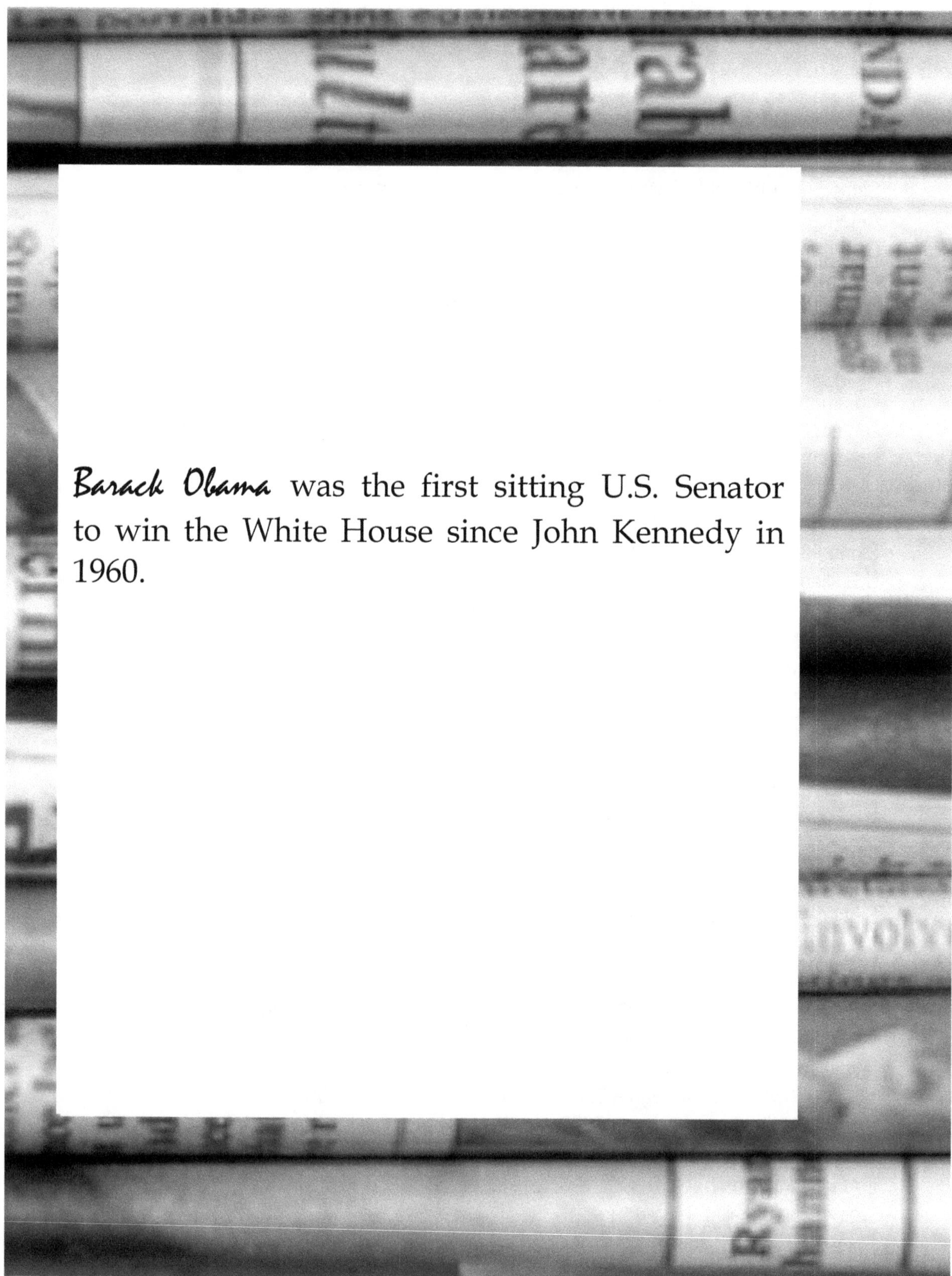

*Barack Obama* was the first sitting U.S. Senator to win the White House since John Kennedy in 1960.

# Introduction

## Phyllis Hodges

First African-American Trailblazer

## Similarities...

### My Life: A Reflection

I believe it is our similarities that help us to connect with one another. If you can connect with a person and find common ground, then you can bridge gaps. When we realize that at our core, we are all the same, we can let go of prejudices and find ways to better our lives and the lives of others.

In the 80s, I was a young wife. I worked part-time at various jobs (Magic Mart, Kentucky Fried Chicken (KFC), Equal Opportunity Agency (E.O.A.), and Employment Security Division (E.S.D).

I decided after those various careers, it was time to become the entrepreneur I always dreamed of becoming. My husband built me a beauty salon on the back of our home, and I truly loved working for myself as a cosmetologist and nail tech. I modeled, in those days, for many retail stores, but as I was working for someone else, I decided I would open up a modeling agency and combine my talents as a cosmetologist and model. I enjoyed this tremendously.

The *Gold Shears Beauty Salon* and the *Ms. Phyl. and Company Modeling Agency* were designed to help the community as well as to teach and to employ the youth. As a model and an agent, we would receive many requests to appear on local radio and talk shows.

This exposure caused me to get the media bug. I knew I could host and produce my own shows. It started with BET the local Black Entertainment show which was such a hit. I was fortunate to move the show to another high rating station, TV 38. At this time, advertisers were purchasing air time with me. I decided as a mover and shaker entrepreneur that I could sell my talk show ideas to KATV Channel 7, a local station, and it worked!

The first and only talk show owned and operated by a young black woman in the 80's, *"30 Plus talk show"* was aired locally for several years. We were interviewing local and international guests!

On January 23, 1991, we received a letter from former Governor Bill Clinton, congratulating us on our affiliation with KATV 7. Then, on January 28, 1991, we received a letter from Washington, DC the United States Senator Dale Bumpers with more congratulations.

Wow!

Another letter came from Washington D.C., on January 23, 1991, from Senator David Pryor.

January 21, 1991 was proclaimed "30-Plus Variety Talk Show Day" by the City Director Lottie Shackelford.

In 1992, another blessing happened. I became the first African-American female Assistant Director for War Memorial Fitness Center. This position was a fabulous move of God for about seven years, but eventually, that entrepreneurship bug hit again.

I started traveling internationally as a missionary and a licensed ordained minister of the gospel and finally decided to open up the only faith-based Health and Fitness Wellness Center in the state of Arkansas, *Carousel Fit 4 Life Wellness Center.*

How ironic it was that when President Obama became president of the United States, I was watching it all from my office at *The Carousel*!

President Barack Obama became the first biracial chief executive in history (Please understand that I identify President Obama as biracial, giving due respect to all of his diverse heritage)!

It's been stated that there were more than 1 million people in attendance, millions of television viewers, and thousands more lining the streets. I was one of those who watched the inauguration on television.

Reminiscing back to the Million Man March in Philadelphia, I never gave it a thought that years later we would be celebrating a man of color being president.

I can't help but think about many of my ancestors who labored in decades past, those who were involved in the Civil Rights Movement and the walkers and marchers on the Selma Bridge.

Barack has inspired many people. For me, that inspiration runs deep and so much so that I find myself wondering about my ancestry.

I'm in the process of researching my maiden name, Marshall. Could I be related to Thurgood Marshall?

Could I have been related to those who could not eat at the lunch counter or the ones who could not ride in the front of buses?

Does my family tree include those who could not enter in through the front doors of public places? Were they forced to use bathrooms and water fountains marked 'colored only'?

What about my marriage to the man of my dreams, a white man (or should I be politically correct and say Caucasian or European) which was once considered against the law?

I'm so thankful to be able to have a sound mind to write these words, to freely think these thoughts, and even to be able to read newspapers and to view historical moments.

God has allowed me to witness and to be a part of history in so many areas of my life. And yes, we all should know where we came from, whom our ancestors are, and that we all have a story to tell.

# Who Cares...

## *Your Life: A Revelation*

I didn't always care about history. I thought it was boring, and I didn't see the reason to study it. However, while Barack Obama's presidency did a lot for our country, it did a lot for me personally in many ways.

One way is that it opened my eyes to the significance of history.

Why is it important? Why should I care? Why should you care?

By finding the common threads in the lives of great people, I think we can better see and appreciate the greatness of all people.

In this book, I've compiled a group of eight people whom I believe are great. Like Barack Obama, they have all been trailblazers in their fields. They each have similarities to the life and legacy of Barack Obama.

These prominent Arkansans, firsts in many areas, have a thing or two to say about why you should care about history and the role you play in it.

Did you know that all of us are living and creating history right now?

What will your life say about you?

Who will care and why?

If you don't like the answer to these questions, perhaps, you will glean some inspiration from the authors in this book in a way that will prompt you to make positive changes.

It is never too late to rewrite your story.

Who cares?

I care, and so should you.

# What's Going On?

*Marvin Gaye (1971)*

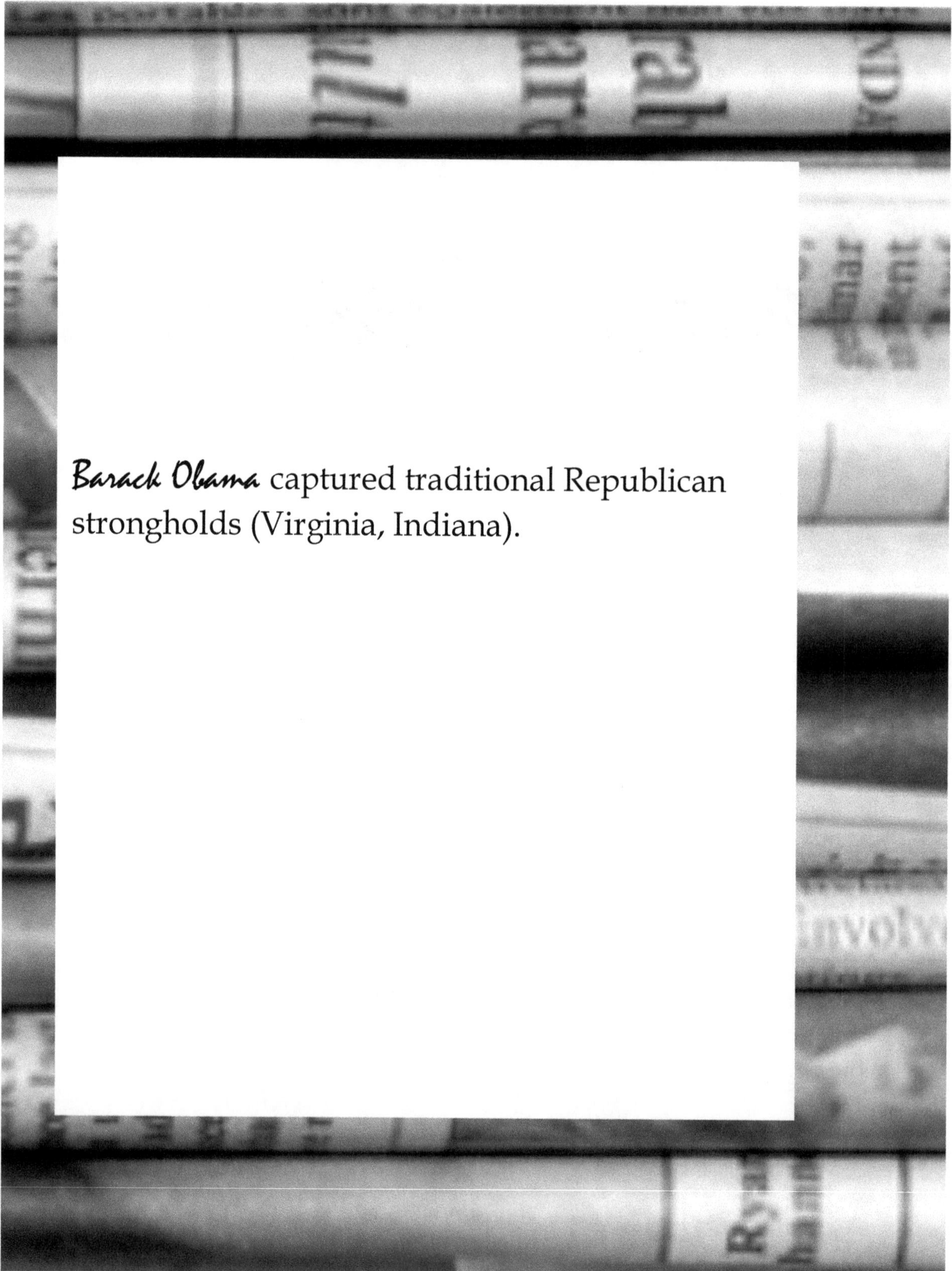

*Barack Obama* captured traditional Republican strongholds (Virginia, Indiana).

# Chapter 1 Endurance & Determination

## *Chief Master Richard E. Anderson*

First African-American Male 8th Degree Blackbelt

## Similarities ...

### *Life as a High-Ranking Black Man in the World's Largest Martial Arts Organization*

As the highest ranking African-American in the world's largest martial arts organization, Chief Master Richard Anderson has had to face a number of rewarding experiences as well as a number of challenging experiences. The experience of being a high-ranking black man has afforded Chief Master Anderson the opportunity to make a very positive impact on black youth and on the community at large. His position as a strong black role model has enabled him to make connections with people who share his vision and are willing to step in and aid him with his mission of cultivating positive, successful youth. With his ambition and experience, along with the assistance of other capable individuals, he has been able to give the young people in his community an alternative to gangs and drugs. Some of these youth, whom had been counted out by others, have now become leaders and positive role models themselves in their Taekwondo classes, in their schools, in their communities, and in their states.

Chief Master Anderson's status in the world of Taekwondo has made him a role model to all who have worked with him and even those who have simply heard of him. His name precedes his works. He is highly respected and known for his ability to positively change the minds of young people, especially young black males, who have no other positive role models that look like them. His influences as a high-ranking black man in martial arts have motivated many people and organizations in the city of Little Rock to work together to support the efforts and successes of the youth throughout the city. One example is Chief Master Anderson's collaboration with the officials of the city of Little Rock. This collaboration has led to the city supporting Chief Master

Anderson's Taekwondo students in regional tournaments at the University of Arkansas at Little Rock (UALR). The support of the university includes discounts on the rental of the gymnasium and the provision for dinner rooms for special guests. The city also assists the Taekwondo students with funding trips to world and national championship tournaments in Las Vegas and Orlando.

Because of these successes, Chief Master Anderson feels empowered to go back to school himself to complete his bachelor's degree. He plans to continue to grow and to learn as he helps others do the same. He has the influence to make things happen, not only because he is a successful high rank, but also because he is extremely passionate and vocal about positive change. He speaks with an air of optimism and confidence, which shows up in his encouraging method of teaching his Taekwondo students.

He compares his experiences as a high-ranked African-American Taekwondo instructor to a complicated maze that he, as a black man, had to go through in order to receive his high-ranking status. There were many facets that he had to understand and accomplish while moving up the chain in martial arts. He had to understand that most martial arts are based on many areas of discipline and on a military ranking system. In other words, the more rank a person has, the more respect others give him for achieving that rank. However, no explanation is required if an instructor is denied promotion to the next rank. He states, "The concern is that a black man has a problem in receiving higher rank and respect in a white man's martial arts organization in the United States."

Chief Master Anderson felt that in the early years of martial arts, many oriental martial arts instructors did not believe that the black man is capable or worthy of the learning disciplines of martial arts and therefore, is not a candidate to be honored or respected. However, Chief Master Anderson was fortunate enough to have an oriental martial art instructor who believed differently. He was cut from a different cloth. Throughout his life, Chief Master Anderson was blessed and fortunate to have black Taekwondo instructors when he started his training. These men have already gone through the process and broken some of the barriers to prejudice.

Starting from the bottom and moving up, Chief Master Anderson had to work very hard to matriculate through the ranks of martial arts. He moved through eleven belts from white to black. All belts below the black belt are recognized by grades, with the lower ranks representing the higher grades. They are designed so that the students advance up to first grade. Moving from bottom to top: white belt is ninth grade, orange belt is eighth grade, yellow belt is seventh grade, camouflage belt is sixth grade, green belt is fifth grade, purple belt is fourth grade, blue belt is third grade, brown belt is second grade, and red belt is first grade.

After these belt colors have been mastered, a candidate is qualified to become a black belt. Instead of grades, the black belt is honored by degrees, which starts with First Degree Black Belt. The average time that it takes a person to become a First Degree Black Belt is approximately two and a half years, during which time he engages in promotional testing every two to four months. Afterwards, testing slows down, and training is intensified. Unlike the grades for the lower colored belt ranks, the black belt degrees increase with rank. Therefore, the second series of testing is for Second Degree Black Belt. Students entering this level must train for one additional year before they are eligible to test for Second Degree Black Belt. To test for Third Degree Black Belt, a student must train for two additional years in order to become eligible for testing. Fourth Degree Black Belt requires three additional years of training to become eligible to test.

Chief Master Anderson was quite expeditious in excelling through the first four degrees of black belt. Conversely, fate had a different outcome for him where the Fifth-Degree Black Belt was concerned. To become a Fifth-Degree Black Belt, one has to meet the requirement of four additional years of training to become eligible to test. The first time Chief Master Anderson attempted to obtain this degree, he was held back. In his personal opinion, he was held back to keep his non-black counterparts with lower degrees from having to answer to him, a black man.

# Who Cares ...

## *Why know the history of Martial Arts?*

Normally, there is a five-year training period and a year of Mastership studies in order for an instructor to become a Sixth-Degree Black Belt. The individual is then dubbed as Master Instructor. This is when the honor and respect really come into full bloom. However, Chief Master says that this did not happen for him and some of the other black instructors.

He, along with some others, were held back for one additional year even though he had completed the requirements. Moreover, this happened once or twice for each of the other new black belt ranks that he achieved. To acquire his Seventh-Degree Black Belt, he was obligated to train for six additional years in order to be eligible for the testing. The Eighth-Degree Black Belt mandated him to train for seven additional years to be eligible to test.

The Ninth-Degree Black Belt requires an instructor to train for eight additional years. Then that instructor must wait one more year to be dubbed Grand Master, which is the highest level that one may achieve in Taekwondo. Chief Master Anderson is in his seventh year of the eight-year waiting period. He will be eligible to test for Ninth Degree Black Belt in 2018.

Chief Master Anderson states that many African-American black belt instructors were forced out before achieving their goal of Ninth Degree Black Belt, thereby losing the opportunity of one day being dubbed Grand Master. Chief is only one degree away from that title. He became an Eight Degree Black Belt in 2009 and was dubbed Chief Master in July of 2010. He is hopeful that the prejudice and envy will decline and that he can reach his goal of becoming a Ninth-Degree Black Belt with no dilemmas.

To know the History of Martial Arts is to move forward and train in this field. You must know the origin of Martial Arts in order to achieve your highest goal and ranks.

## Biography

Chief Master Richard Elijah Anderson was born to Jimmie and Mary Lee Anderson in Cass County, Michigan, on March 3, 1951, as the sixth of seven children. At six-months-old, a tumor formed on Chief Master Anderson's voice box and grew large enough to close his windpipe, so he had to undergo a tracheotomy. It was reported that he was the youngest baby at the University Hospital to have ever had this type of operation performed. That was the beginning of his first challenge to overcome the odds. After being in the hospital for his first two years of life, he had to overcome the challenge of living with his brothers and sisters who had become strangers to him.

Later in life, he became a boy scout in an all-white troop, which was another challenge. However, he had a great experience, and those camping days were some of his fondest memories. At the age of 14, he became the first junior counselor and the first black volunteer with the scout. Chief Master Anderson attended E. Root Fitch Camp during the summers. The dinner prayer that he learned at the Fitch Camp is the same one that he presently requires his students to recite at Anderson's Taekwondo Center. At the age of 16, he became the first black Waterfront Instructor at Fitch Camp.

During his senior year in 1969, he was All-State Defensive Corner Back. He also lettered in football, basketball, and track during that same year. He attended Southwestern Michigan Junior College, where he earned an A.A.S. Degree in Business. Chief Master Anderson graduated in 1969 from Union High School in Dowagiac, Michigan. While in high school, he was an All-State Defensive Back for Dowagiac's football team, coached by the late Jack McAvoy. He later became a counselor at Fitch Camp with the Olympic wrestler, Chris Taylor. He was the first person in his family to go to college.

Chief Master Anderson got his start in Benton Harbor in 1972 at a martial arts school under the instruction of Alvin Smith, a 1st Degree Black Belt in Taekwondo and a 3rd Degree Black Belt in Kung Fu. They worked in the factory at Whirlpool together. Chief remembers that the way Alvin Smith carried himself placed him in a position to get the nicer jobs. "When he opened a school, I was his first student. It was in the basement of a church with a marble floor. I'll never forget that. I was there every night. I lived in Dowagiac, drove to Benton Harbor, and worked out for two to three hours every day." Chief always had a knack for self-defense and martial arts, and he expected to acquire a career as a hand-to-hand combat instructor in the army. All of this changed with Alvin Smith. Chief's mind was so in tune with martial arts that he did not date for a year.

In 1975, he opened his first martial arts school in his hometown of Dowagiac, Michigan. He was one of the first black men to open a business in Dowagiac. There were some people who were unhappy about his success. "I put my flag out each morning and kept my storefront cleaner than the rest of the stores," he said. In six months, his sublease had come to an end. He then bought a building in that same year. That was the beginning of Anderson's Taekwondo Center Camp Positive, Inc. By 1987, he had two schools and three clubs with over 300 students. His daughter, Rashena Janea Anderson Johnson, followed in his footsteps and is a 2nd Degree Black Belt. Chief also has three grandsons who practice Taekwondo.

When Chief Master Anderson visits his mother in Dowagiac, Michigan each Thanksgiving, he does so with the assurance that he kept the promise he made to her when he was nine-years-old. He said that someday the family name would be up in lights. That did happen. In the 1980s, Chief Master Anderson operated five martial arts schools in Niles, Michigan; Decatur, Michigan; Buchanan, Michigan; Cassopolis, Michigan; and Mishawaka.

Chief Master Anderson, who is currently an 8th Degree Black Belt, has been a black belt for more than 40 years. In a newspaper interview, he humbly states, "It took me a year and 16 months to make Black Belt. Back in those years, you could skip a rank if your abilities allowed it." His interest in martial arts grew out of playing "I Spy" with Jerry Parker, one of his best childhood friends.

Mohammad Ali was one of his idols, and he always emulated Bill Cosby.

"Jerry and I got all of the books out of the library and studied kicking and punching," Chief Master Anderson recalls in an interview.

"Jerry's dad was in martial arts in the service, so he would show us a kick or two." "The Green Hornet" with Bruce Lee as Kato, a newspaper publisher's valet, was another early influence for Chief. He goes on to say, "We were very poor, so I could not afford to go to an established school," such as Kim's Karate Academy on U.S. 31 just across the state line between Michigan and Indiana. He later had his Niles school on the same highway just inside Michigan by 1984.

Chief grew up in a neighborhood where all of the adults raised the children. He said that that type of support system kept kids in line. He gives credit to some very special mentors who helped him succeed in school and life: his oldest sister, Betty Anderson Brown; his coaches, Jack McAvoy and John Lewis; his teacher, Annabelle Neidlinger; the neighborhood pastor, Rev. Charles E Wilson; and his principal (later mayor of Dowagiac), James Mosier. On the other hand, he has been a great mentor himself. Chief Master Anderson has impacted young lives like Sinbad when he was a Fitch Camp counselor long before he arrived in Arkansas. Chief Master Anderson knew Sinbad, aka future comedian David Adkins, from the McKinley neighborhood. "His dad baptized me," Chief Master Anderson said.

Chief Master Anderson started life in poverty. His family used to wait behind the grocery store for the food that was not fit to sell just so they could eat. However, he did become very successful, and it seemed like everything he touched turned into gold. Chief left the Michigan-Indiana area in 1989 for Arkansas. He said that he did not choose Arkansas, but that Arkansas chose him. One day, at which time he was living in a comfortable place in Michigan, Chief received a call from Arkansas. He owned several Martial Arts facilities, and he was comfortable financially. He said, "This is the type of call you answer! You don't hang up, and you don't ignore it. I knew where that call came from."

He went on to say, "I woke up early one morning about 3 o'clock with my hair standing up on my head. The hair on my arms was raised up, and I heard a spiritual voice telling me I needed to go to Arkansas. 'My children are killing themselves over red and blue colors.' I told my mother and she said, 'That's God talking to you. You've got to listen.' I wasn't going to go to Arkansas, but it happened a second and third time."

Chief Master Anderson knew that he would be working with children in poverty, children with small dreams, and children who were in gangs. However, succeeding in the South as a black man meant a lot to him.

Once in Arkansas, Chief (as he is fondly called) had a brilliant idea of how to organize and construct a judging certification program for the martial arts. He felt that one of the biggest problems in tournaments at that time was that judging seemed to be unfair. He said that if you were a Black Belt, you were a judge, whether you knew how to judge or not. Consequently, that caused a lot of bad calls and upset, crying students. Tournament hosts and the organization were getting bad names. Chief had a plan laid out in his mind that was everything his Taekwondo center needed.

"We staged a tournament in Chicago and brought the Grandmaster," Chief Master Anderson said. "It ran so smoothly that the Grandmaster brought me to Little Rock, where I became the first African-American executive vice president of the organization."

Currently, Chief has two schools, one in Little Rock, Arkansas, at Moody Chapel AME Church and one at Pine Bluff, Arkansas, at the Pines Mall. The Pine Bluff Center is run by Florence Wright and her husband Freddie Wright, both Black Belts.

The first six months after Chief Master Anderson arrived in Arkansas, he was broke. He would accept kids into his program only to have the parents drop out in a couple of months because they could not afford to keep their children in the program. Therefore, Chief Master Anderson began working with the kids without pay, figuring out ways to bring dignity to the kids and parents by giving them tasks and jobs to complete as compensation. He gave students who would otherwise be in gangs a new outlet with the opportunity to travel outside of the city, some for the first time. In 2010, the Taekwondo Center had 140 students.

One of his students' mottos is "College Bound, Sir," which is indicative of his strong conviction that they can be successful.

Furthermore, Chief runs an eight-week Camp Positive program in the summer to keep children off the streets. In this program, students can learn martial arts and academics as long as they keep a good record and follow the rules at school. Therefore, he visits the schools to monitor his students' progress.

He feels that martial arts change a person's nature – the way one looks, the way one walks, and one's mannerisms. Despite the fact that Chief Master Anderson is not one to reckon with, he has a calm, gentle demeanor. He gives selflessly. Chief has taught students as young as one and a half.

He seeks to develop a balance and to develop their minds so that they are not leaning towards gangs and other negative activities. His mission is to avert that negative behavior and to inspire in his students a desire to love school and learn necessary skills.

He is a firm believer that kids need to keep God in their hearts and know who He is. That is why each belt color represents a specific Biblical scripture. Chief Master Anderson readily acknowledges that the kind of respect and discipline he imparts would not be possible if he were a conventional classroom teacher instead of a martial arts instructor.

Chief Master Anderson has had to depend on the kindness of others and the grace of God to supply needs for his facility in Little Rock.

Why would any person continue in a place where he has to pay to help students succeed?

According to Chief Master Anderson, "If you see a child's eyes go from dark to light, all of a sudden, he can win a trophy and all of a sudden he becomes a Black Belt. That is why!" He has given many children and families in Little Rock an avenue to change their own destination and destiny.

In 2010, he earned the title of Chief Master Anderson, which is a very prestigious honor that can only be attained after one becomes an 8th Degree Black Belt. He earned this title not only because of his martial arts ability but also because he has and continues to do noble work in the community.

He has been awarded "Arkansan of the Year" twice. Oddly enough, most of his services do not come with any type of monetary compensation.

Chief Master Anderson is the highest-ranking African-American out of almost 400,000 members of the American Taekwondo Association (ATA), World Traditional Taekwondo Union, and Songahm Taekwondo Federation.

Chief Master Anderson is the pulse behind Anderson's Taekwondo Center Martial Arts Camp Positive. This camp is a non-profit martial arts school, which runs a high-profile program with approximately 120 members. Camp Positive offers an outlet to inner-city youth and their families, which strengthens them through the moral standards of the ATA. The emphasis at Camp Positive is its motto: "Go to Church on Sunday, Practice Free on Monday."

As evident in the creation of Camp Positive, Chief Master Anderson has dedicated his life to helping inner-city youth and children from all walks of life. His school consists mainly of students from single-parent homes or are being raised by grandparents or guardians with little or no income. He provides them with a positive path to gain self-confidence and a stable support system in their lives. Chief Master Anderson and the instructors at Anderson's Taekwondo Center (ATC) reach out to youth and families and give them life lessons. They are then able to teach other children and those around them that there is a positive alternative to the streets. In the last two years, Anderson's Taekwondo Center has had 63 students to graduate from high school and college.

Chief Master Anderson and his staff specialize in counseling youth with a lack of discipline, low self-esteem, and low school achievement. He teaches discipline through Taekwondo, and he stresses the importance of academic achievement by encouraging good grades and a "Yes I Can" mindset. Chief Master Anderson is not only concerned with children graduating from high school but also with them aspiring to graduate from college and becoming active contributors to society and their community. He specializes in working with families that may have children diagnosed with ADHD or Oppositional Deficit Disorder and children who are doing great and need to remain that way.

ATC provides a nurturing, responsible, licensed, and safe childcare facility with a great after-school component (Better Beginnings) that supports the emotional, social, intellectual, and physical needs of school-aged children through a strong, disciplined Taekwondo program. Every year, Chief Master Anderson attends three major martial art tournaments with his students (Las Vegas, Orlando and Little Rock).

It is Chief's plan for each child to become a productive member of his/her community and to gain confidence and discipline through a well-thought-out plan that is dedicated to community service. The after-school and summer programs are open on Monday through Friday and offer a safe environment. These programs are DHS approved, and vouchers are welcomed. ATC is child-focused, using the researched-based Conscious Discipline Initiative. The students receive tutoring in reading and math, and they are taught skills in anti-bullying awareness and prevention. Moreover, the after-school and summer program participants receive training in Taekwondo as a form of discipline.

Chief Master Anderson's Taekwondo Center has faced and overcome a number of challenges, including a fire that destroyed one of his buildings. Consequently, the Center has had several locations in Little Rock. It is currently located at Moody Chapel AME Church. Moody Chapel is one of Chief's very important sponsoring partners. Chief Master Anderson said that he has the best parents for which any instructor could ask and that his instructors are second to none. Moreover, he feels fortunate to have students who are willing to listen and learn.

The future of ATC is bright because of the past, which has made the Center strong and has made Chief appreciative of what he has. He is looking forward to a profitable and successful future where he and his staff will continue to save the lives of inner-city youth. According to Chief, the Center has acquired a grant writer who will assist with funding, and the board members will continue to be active in leading ATC forward. He is very optimistic that ATC will continue to be a light for the city of Little Rock.

## Accolades

- ∂ Promoted to Chief Master status in the world's largest martial arts association in 2010
- ∂ Named "Arkansas of the Week" by KATV Channel 7 in 2008
- ∂ Appointed commissioner of the Arkansas State Athletic Commission by Governor Mike Beebe in 2008
- ∂ Received Gold Collar for testing over 6,000 students per year in 2002
- ∂ Given November 3rd as a declared date for "Senior Master Richard E. Anderson Day" by Mayor Jim Dailey of Little Rock, Arkansas in 2001
- ∂ Promoted to Senior Master status in the world's largest martial arts association (180, 000 members) in 2001
- ∂ Received title of the highest ranked African-American in the world's largest martial arts association in 2001
- ∂ Inducted into the Martial Arts Hall of Fame for the Diamond Life Achievement Award and the Most Outstanding Martial Arts School of the Year in 1999
- ∂ Received the KARK TV Community Service Award in 1998
- ∂ Founded and Created Camp Positive Summer Program in 1991
- ∂ Founded and Created the "Go to Church on Sunday and Practice Free on Monday" Training Program in 1991
- ∂ Given November 21 as the proclaimed "Chief Master Richard E. Anderson Day" by Governor Mike Beebe
- ∂ Given March 12th as a declared date for "Master Richard E. Anderson's Day" by Mayor Alfred Boals of West Memphis, Arkansas

# A Change is Gonna Come

*Sam Cooke (1964)*

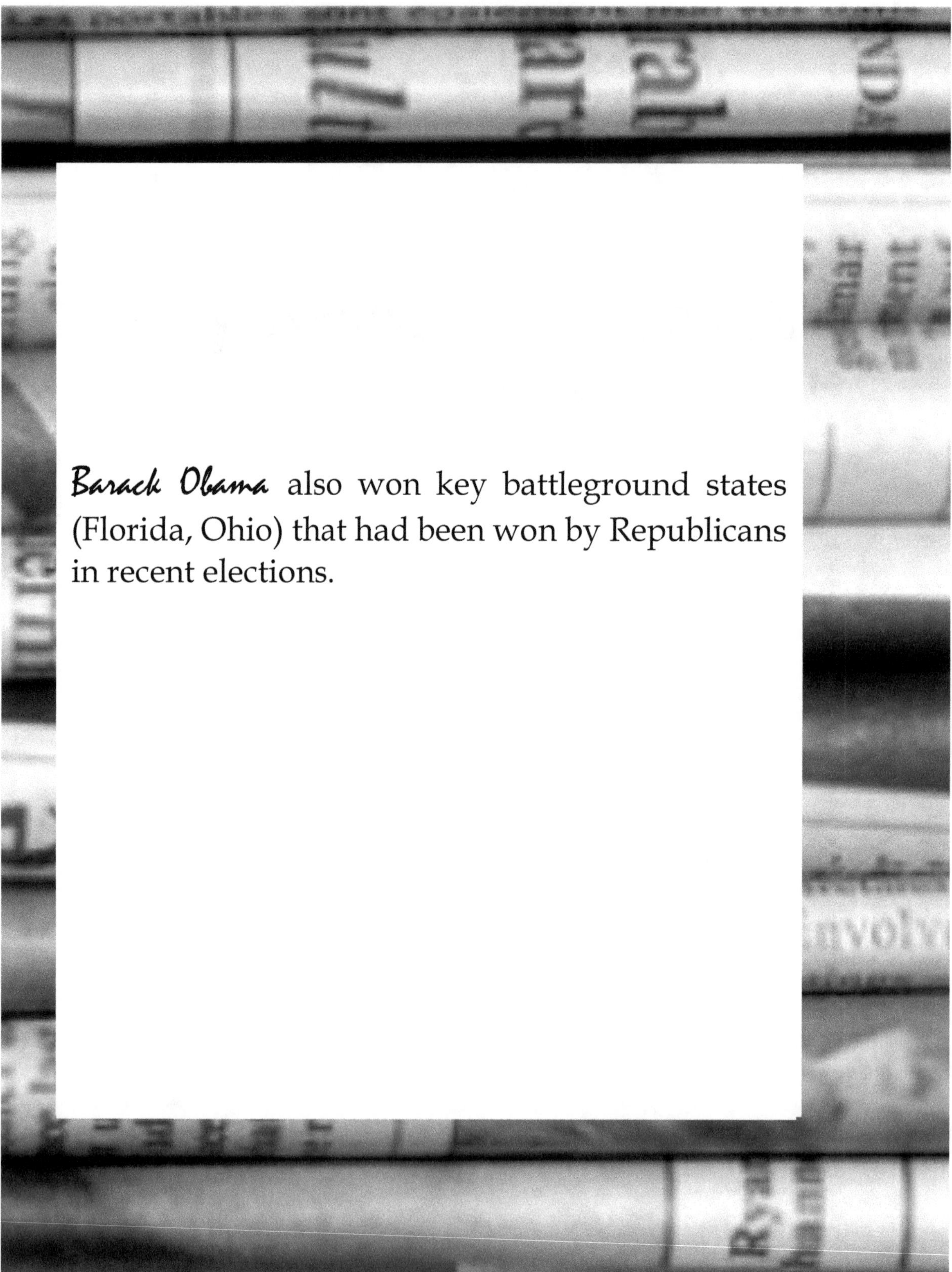

*Barack Obama* also won key battleground states (Florida, Ohio) that had been won by Republicans in recent elections.

# Chapter 2 Economics

## Martha Dixon

First African-American Fashion Designer for Former First Lady of the State of Arkansas and Former First Lady of the United States of America, Hillary Rodham Clinton

## Similarities…

### Never Be Surprised About Anything

Upon arrival to her first day at Princeton University, Catherine Donnely was surprised to discover that her roommate was an African-American. Confused and distraught, Catherine quickly told her mother that she was outraged at sharing a room with an African-American female. Her mother quickly went to the campus housing office and requested that her daughter be moved.

Little did either woman know that the young African-American female would someday become the First African-American Lady of the United States married to the Commander and Chief of the United States, Barack Obama.

All things are possible!

I worked hard and overcame a lot. There were things that happened that made me realize just how far I had come.

In the process of hiring employees, for example, I was very surprised to learn that one of my white neighbors had applied for a sewing job. When I was a child and not in the fields picking cotton, one of my jobs was cleaning this woman's mother-in-law's house.

How could I ever dream back then that someday that woman's daughter-in-law would be working for me?

Tragically, I faced a shocking disappointment; my thriving business *Martha's Manufacturing* caught fire and burned to the ground.

My mental health was challenged, and if not for God, family, and friends, the devastation would have consumed me. I had a lot of hard decisions to make.

After many days of prayer and family support, I decided not to rebuild my factory.

In the wake of the country's devastation, part of President Barack's plan for creating a better America; he implemented numerous programs starting with an economic plan called the "Stimulus Package." This package was designed to help stimulate the economy. He also created a healthcare plan called the Obama Care/ Affordable Care Act.

I think this was a good plan. There were things that Obama implemented like free cell phones for individuals who were economically challenged.

I think this is great, but at the same time, I think it could be a disadvantage too because too many people try to take advantage of the system. However, I think his health plan is one of the best things the United States could have received because everyone needs insurance, but everyone cannot afford insurance.

I learned a lot, starting my own business. One thing was never to say never or to be surprised about anything!

# Who Cares ...

## *Why know the history of entrepreneurship?*

It is never easy to pursue a dream and even harder if you're a trailblazer!

Even Barack Obama had help. He had people who not only believed in him, but they also demonstrated their support. Some of these notable people included Warren Buffet (investor and the richest man in the world), Chris Hughes (co-founder of Facebook), Jane Fonda (actress and political activist), and Caroline Kennedy (daughter of John F. Kennedy).

Starting my own business was not an easy thing to do especially living paycheck to paycheck. If it weren't for the city of Arkadelphia and Henderson State University who believed in me, this venture probably wouldn't have been possible. However, much like Barack, there were those who supported and invested in my dream too.

Majeed Nahas (a manager of a sewing plant in Hot Springs, Arkansas), Dr. David Luck (a leader in the community and a business owner for over thirty-five years) and Senator Percy Malone (a friend who went to bat for me in so many business areas) were a few of the ones who took a chance on me.

I had an opportunity and wisdom to select people on my board who were knowledgeable enough to guide and to lead me. In 1985, I owned and operated *Martha's Designs* which provided clothes for Hillary Clinton, and as time passed, I was able to merge *Martha's Designs* with *Martha's Manufacturing*. I was blessed to start my company with only fifty thousand dollars and three investors.

It's important to know your history because if you don't know your history, you will repeat it. You should know who you are and where you came from. It is also important to know that there are people who will support you!

Once you begin, never stop!

Crawl, stand, walk, run, fly, and soar beyond measure.

## Biography

The daughter of a poor sharecropper turned highly acclaimed fashion designer, businesswoman, and political advocate, Ms. Martha Dixon conquered adversity early and emerged as a fashion icon designing dresses for Hillary Clinton as First Lady of Arkansas and later as First Lady of the United States.

Martha was recognized as one of the "Top 100 Women of Arkansas" by Arkansas Business Magazine and the recipient of numerous awards for her entrepreneurship, political work, and community service.

Martha Dixon rose from poverty to the height of her profession. She was connected to the largest meat company in the world, Tyson Food. She made smocks for their meat producers' employees. Martha also did business with the Walmart stores throughout the country, making public and private school uniforms through this corporation.

She was a national committeewoman for four years representing Arkansas as a superdelegate. Martha served on many boards at the state and national level.

Ms. Dixon was the Founder of *Dixon Manufacturing* as well as other successful enterprises such as *Martha's Designs*. Ms. Dixon's career took her all the way from the cotton fields to the Lincoln bedroom, the White House, and beyond. Ms. Dixon wrote her autobiography in her latest book, "Triumph Beyond Measure" which is forwarded by Former U.S Secretary of Transportation Rodney E. Slater.

Ms. Dixon (as the dressmaker and designer of a presidential gala gown for former First Lady Hillary Clinton) is proud to say her original gown is on display at the Truman Library.

Ms. Dixon attended Henderson State University and majored in business. She also attended Little Falls School of Fashion in New Jersey for three years. Ms. Dixon is married to Huie L. Dixon. They have one son, Christopher L. Dixon.

## Accolades

- ∂ Owner Martha's Designs
- ∂ Owner Martha's Manufacturing plant
- ∂ Designer for First Lady of Arkansas Hillary Clinton
- ∂ Designer for First Lady of The United States Hillary Clinton
- ∂ Author: "Triumph Beyond Measure"
- ∂ Board member, Baptist Area Agent on Aging

# God Bless America

*Covered by Celine Dion (1980)*

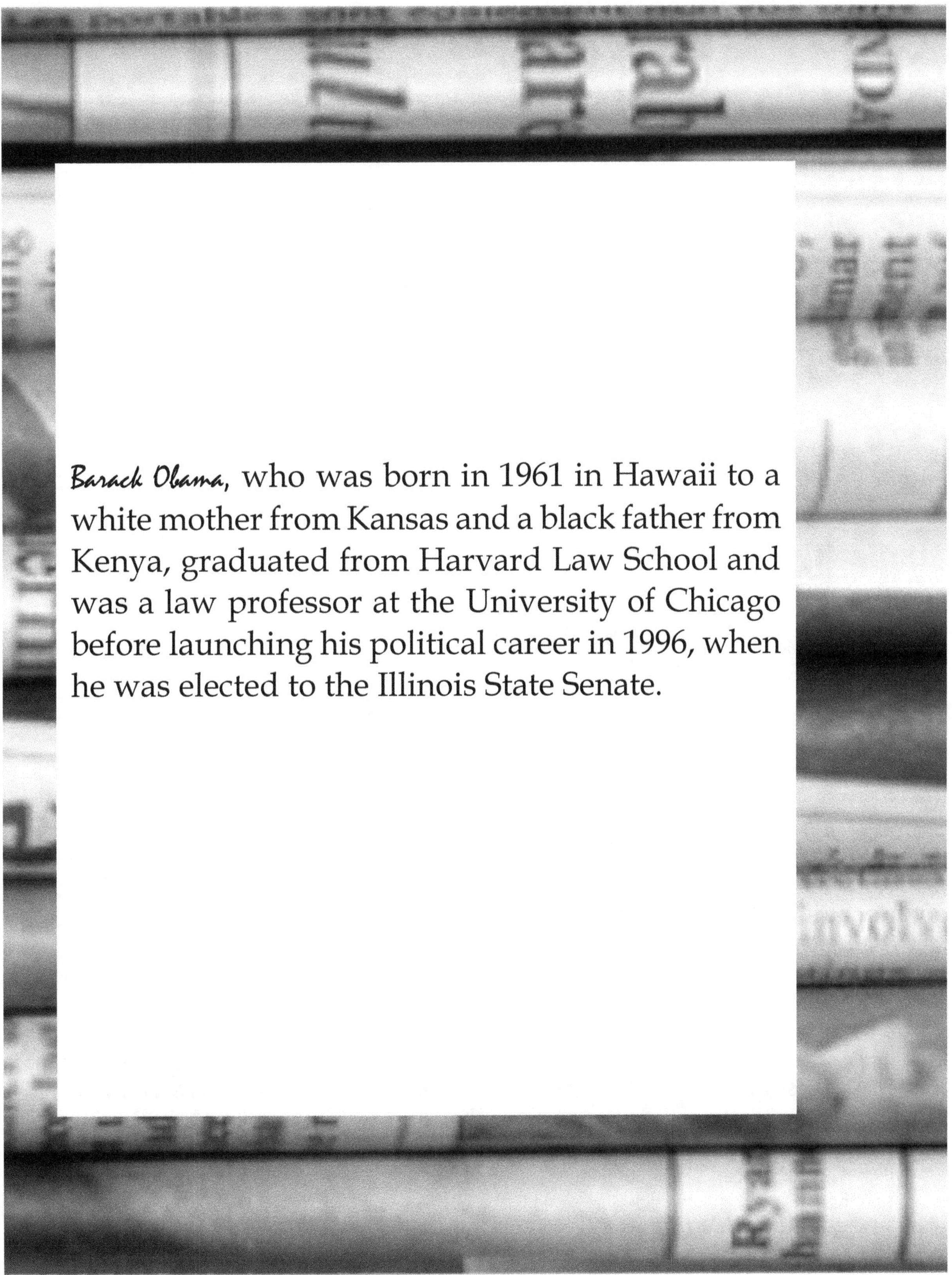

*Barack Obama,* who was born in 1961 in Hawaii to a white mother from Kansas and a black father from Kenya, graduated from Harvard Law School and was a law professor at the University of Chicago before launching his political career in 1996, when he was elected to the Illinois State Senate.

# Chapter 3 Family Values

## Jeffery Henderson

First (and only) Olympic Gold Medalist in Track and Field
(North Little Rock, AR)

## Similarities ...

### Embracing and Adapting to Change

In the beginning, I always remembered my family being close and tight with one another. Not that we aren't close now, but we all know how becoming adults will allow us to drift apart slightly. I feel it is a good thing for the most part. I am the youngest of six. Yes, I am the baby, and my mom did spoil me because of it. But, she also made sure that I always represented not only the family, but myself in the best way possible, and for that, I am beyond grateful. My dad worked two and sometimes three jobs to support us when my mom became a stay at home mom. It just made sense that she took on that role due to the number of children in the home and to be honest, we all loved it.

With my dad working as much as he did, we rarely got time to see him, but he always made sure his presence was felt in the best way possible. Coming from McAlmont, Arkansas, you had to work hard to make it. Many people don't, nor will they ever know or visit there, but it is where I will forever call my home. My dad instilled in all of us that you must work hard for everything you want in life, and no matter what the circumstances are, always give it your best shot. My mom did the same, but she did it with LOVE. She always made sure that we put our hearts into all that we did. She would tell us all, "Put your heart into it; if you do that, you will LOVE any and everything you do. LOVE will carry you, even when your body gives out." That belief sticks with me to this day, and that's what motivates me to continue to do what I do and to be able to give my all.

The fact that my mom was present in the house so much made not only myself but all my siblings, gravitate and cling to her. We needed her love, her support, her presence, and most importantly, HER. She was our rock, lifeline, and greatest supporter in anything and everything that we did; she still is, and that was the main reason I gave her my GOLD medal. I didn't win it; it was hers because of LOVE and how she passed it to me that won the medal in Rio. I owe my mother so much more, and as long as I have breath in my body, I will continue to give it to her.

She deserves that and so much more, and for me to see her battling Alzheimer's, going against what the doctors have said and told my family, it only makes me put my heart into what I am doing even more. I truly believe the reason she is still here, defying the odds, is mainly because of her LOVE for her family. She is strong, always has been, and always will be. Because of that, again, I will always put my heart and love into, not only track and field, but everything that I do.

It humbles me to be included and allowed to be compared to former president, Barack Obama. What he has done for our country, including every person of color, goes beyond what was at one point in time considered inconceivable. In my mom and dad's day, seeing a black president and a black family in the White House, was something only dreamed of, but he made it a reality. He wasn't elected once, but twice, and I am sure if it were possible, he would have been elected once more. I know I would have voted for him, hands down and without question.

President Obama and his family are the living examples of handling everything with poise and grace. The Obamas didn't have any scandals, mishaps, or anything that was major in the way of negativity. I strive to do these things. That is why I run not only my charity, "The Jeff Henderson Project," but also my management and finance company, "JH & Associates," the same way. President Obama and my family have a few similarities, and although only a few, they are still very great. He leads his family in the public eye, as well as behind closed doors, as my father did for us, and in turn, I will do one day in the future with a family of my own.

The First Lady, Mrs. Michelle Obama, carries herself just as my mother carried herself in my eyes, with grace, elegance, and poise. She and my mother ultimately did the same things when it came to carrying and holding up the family in adverse conditions. In the beginning and all throughout President Obama's terms in office, he dealt with great adversity which only made him stronger and his family closer as things progressed. I can relate to this in ways most might not understand.

As my mother battles Alzheimer's, it has brought about battles my family and I have had to overcome. We are just as any other family. That means we don't always agree upon everything at any given time, but we always have love and respect for each other and one another's decisions. The major decision maker in our home was my mother; she made sure everything was in functioning order. In many ways, the first lady did the same.

As President Obama ran the country, my mother ran our home, just as the first lady did. Our home basically ran like a well-oiled machine while my dad worked and became the leading provider for our family. We always made sure to work with one another and to make sure things ran smoothly. We didn't want to cause double work on my mom. Or at least we would try not to, but hey, we were children. I am more than sure, the first lady has had her fair share of double work, having Malia and Sasha running, playing, learning, and growing up in the White House.

I see now that it is all a part of growing and having a family. Just as the Obamas had to adjust to situations at any given time, so did my family and I. We weren't expecting for our mother, who was the backbone of our family, to get sick at such a fast pace. But, we made it work. We made the adjustments, and so did she. To me, this is what all families do and have to deal with on a regular basis. It might not be as vast as running an entire country, dealing with any form of disease, or even death, but we all have to change and must adapt to it as best as we can.

# Who Cares ...

## *Why is sports history important?*

President Obama's legacy will live on forever, just as his family's legacy will as well. To me, that comes from how you were and are raised. He came from a very tight knit family. He was close to his mother, grandmother, his father, and even his side of the family who was in a completely different country. This all goes back to how his mother raised him. It was because of LOVE. He was able to maintain close relationships with everyone in his family, and it was because of how his mother and grandmother raised him. It wasn't done out of anything but love because love is the one thing we all hold sacred, just as we hold our families.

Anyone who feels differently about the love he holds and has shown to each and every one with whom he has come into contact, can just take a look at how he interacts with his family as a whole. He is always showing his wife public displays of affection. He is always showing and telling his daughters how much he loves them and how proud he is of them and everything they have done and become. This, in my eyes, is how it should be done. You should not only tell someone that you love them, but you should show them.

My mother did just that, and I am more than certain that if my dad were around more, he would have done the same, but he worked a lot. Most of the time, he came home late from work after going in early and working seven days a week. This is the way he showed us he loved us, by working so hard for us tirelessly, and for that, I am more than appreciative of what he did and has done. President Obama always makes it a point to tell everyone how proud he is of his family and places a firm voice on how important family is. All in all, he is what a family man should be and stand for: understanding, love, compassion, strength, etc.

I could go on and on, but this is my point of view and comparison on the POTUS, family, my family, and myself. I wish to be all that he is and better in not only the values of family, but how I carry myself and how I transfer my energy to everyone with whom I come in to contact.

THANK YOU, PRESIDENT BARACK OBAMA & FAMILY, you have shown not only America what a true family looks like and how it should be conducted, but you have shown the WORLD.

The importance of knowing one's history, in my eyes, is a very simple question to answer. You have to know where you came from to know where you are going. A lot of the time, we repeat the past because we never knew that it had already been done. As an African-American coming from the south, many things of our past as black people are long forgotten because of how harshly we were treated. In a sense, because we fail to talk about it, we continue to live it.

We can look at how some of us live, our education systems within our neighborhoods, and to some of our overall ways of life. It isn't the best, but I will say this about my people; we make the best out of the worst situations. We have to; look where we come from. Schools refuse to educate us about our history and all of the great leaders we have had who paved the way for us. We shouldn't only speak about the bad, but we need to spend more than the month of February discussing the greatness of what my people, black people, did. For me, our history, as well as our future, is an everyday thing.

I feel deeply that we should not only talk about and teach our own children, but we should teach the children of other races to love, to respect, and to acknowledge the greatness of what Africans, as well African-Americans, have brought to the table of America and its construction. Good or bad, we all need to take responsibility when it comes to discussing this. We should open our minds to receive new and vast amounts of information. All our youth deserve that much, if not more. It starts and ends with us, and when we deliver the information, we should do it in love and love only.

As I stated earlier, my mother instilled in my family to do everything in love.

## Biography

"The difference in winning and losing is most often not quitting" (Walt Disney). As effective as that quote sounds, it has been that same philosophical view which has applied much pressure to the life of Jeffery Todd Henderson. Delivered on February 19, 1989, Henderson became the youngest of six siblings to be born to Laverne and Debra Henderson. Being raised in McAlmont, Arkansas did not equate to many athletic opportunities, but Henderson dared to dream further than his surroundings. His inner drive to simply be the best he could be has created a distinctively impactful story.

Henderson spent most of his youth exploring his talents as an athlete. With his undeniable passion for football, Henderson gained quite the confidence in his abilities as he participated in youth football leagues and played with friends and family throughout his community. Becoming more engulfed in his athletic capacity, he picked up baseball for a couple years, only to realize that his athleticism was far more superior than that sport.

Henderson continued to play football as he transitioned into his days as a Sylvan Hills High School Bear. Here is where Henderson began to capitalize on his natural talent – his speed. It did not take much time before Henderson began to focus his attention more on track and field rather than football. During his junior year of high school, Henderson started making greater efforts in the weight room which resulted in a drastic change in his quickness. As he began to claim title after title, his work ethic was incomparable. Henderson quickly came to the athletic forefront in his community after winning a Class 6A State Championship in the long jump and triple jump, the Arkansas Meet of Champs in the long jump, and triple jump at Sylvan Hills High School.

By the time Henderson's senior year rolled around, he realized that his quickness and endurance were motivating him not to settle for anything less than a championship status.

Challenges held more depth as Henderson looked toward life beyond high school. In 2007, Henderson underwent the devastation of his mother being diagnosed with Alzheimer's disease. After this life-changing declaration, his determination to succeed became driven by something much bigger than himself. It's no secret that Henderson struggled with Attention Deficit Disorder (ADD), but that never hindered him from getting a step closer to fulfilling his desires.

After careful consideration of his circumstances, Henderson discovered the best plan to move forward. Being that his grades were too low for a major college track program, Henderson was forced to attend a community college. He went on to attend Hinds Community College in Raymond, Mississippi. There, he won three National Junior College Athletic Association (NJCAA) long jump titles in 2008 and 2009 (outdoor and indoor), and one in the 400-meter relay.

Continuing on with his education and athletic endeavors, Henderson attended Florida Memorial University in Miami Gardens before transferring to Stillman College in Tuscaloosa, Alabama. Henderson's credentials continued to enlarge as he claimed the NCAA Division II title in the 100 meter and the long jump in 2013. In addition to that, he was named an All-American athlete.

Graduating from Stillman in 2013 with a degree in education, Henderson moved to San Diego, California where he began training. He trained at the U.S. Olympic Training Center in Chula Vista, California, just southeast of San Diego. Henderson had already been working with the infamous Al Joyner prior to the U.S. Olympic Training Center, but once this move occurred, Al Joyner became his full-time coach working with him solely on the long jump. Al Joyner is an NCAA All-American from Arkansas State University and a 1984 Olympic triple jump gold medalist. Not to mention, he is the husband of the late Florence Griffith Joyner. Joyner's expertise has brought much value to Henderson's career, and his motivation has helped Henderson soar to new heights.

Henderson went on to win the USA Track and Field National Outdoor Championships in 2014. Then, in 2015, Henderson won a gold medal at the Pan American Games in Toronto. His intense efforts have led him to his most current victory as a gold medalist for long jump in the 2016 Rio de Janeiro, Brazil Olympic Games.

Going into the 2016 Rio Olympic Games, Henderson had many sources of motivation uplifting him to come out on top. Joyner gave his personal gold medal to Henderson to wear as a source of motivation before the event. To feel the weight of the gold around his neck and to imagine being in the same category as legends before him, was enough influence to give the gold medal back to Joyner because Henderson was on the way to claiming his own. Before leaving to participate in the 2016 Rio Olympic Games, Henderson promised his mother, Debra, who was bedridden for the past four years due to her health implications, that he would win the gold medal and bring it back home to her. His confidence did not fall short of doing what he said he would do.

Henderson tapped his feet three times, as he normally did as part of his pre-jump ritual, raced down the runway, and flew past the record to beat landing with a jump of 8.38 meters (27 feet, 6 inches). It was just one centimeter better than Luvo Manyonga of South Africa. Henderson had become the first American to win gold since Dwight Phillips in 2004 and just the second to win since Lewis retired after the 1996 Olympics. This win would account for the country's 22$^{nd}$ gold medal in the long jump, and the 999$^{th}$ gold won by an American.

Many fans watched and supported Henderson as he made his way to victory, but nothing excited him more than to get back to Arkansas to share his accomplishment with his mother who's battling the late stages of Alzheimer's. Since his homecoming in mid-August of 2016, Henderson has been devoted to using his recent fame as a source for increasing Alzheimer's awareness.

He has become involved with the Alzheimer's Association, even playing a key role in the Alzheimer's Association and Arkansas Chapter's recent Walk to End Alzheimer's fundraiser in Little Rock. Having such a personal impact from the disease, Henderson went a step further to create his very own charity, "The Jeff Henderson Project" as well as to assist in healing his family by starting a foundation in the name of his mother, "Jeff and Debra's 999." With this organization, Henderson and his team envisioned providing a quality community and facility-based adult day healthcare with an emphasis on Alzheimer's and Dementia related diseases.

He wants loved ones to feel like they are home. The mission is to support and to educate Alzheimer's caregivers and their families at little to no cost. In addition to his efforts of increasing awareness for Alzheimer's, Henderson manages to stay involved with other community projects through work with the Jacksonville Community Center and the all-girls youth basketball team, the "Hustle Hearts."

Jeff commits himself to building a future for the future by providing additional opportunities for growth. His desires go hand in hand with his Adidas endorsement, which is to stand tall in making a difference in the community and to send the message that a resilient work ethic never fails.

## Accolades

- ∂ Philanthropist
  - o J. Henderson & Associates LLC was initiated to support Henderson's growth with Arkansas business endeavors, in hopes of branching out beyond the U.S. with regards much greater than the sports industry.
  - o As an initial effort towards long-term goals, the Jeff Henderson Project has been started as an opportunity to give a voice to the voiceless.
- ∂ Designer
  - o Henderson is currently in the works of building his own apparel line appropriately named "JH" Brand. They are clothes that are both comfortable and stylish. Recent designs of upcoming apparel have sparked much interest, so there is no doubt that the brand possesses the potential to go far.
- ∂ Competitor
  - o As the world-renowned Olympic gold medalist continues to train for the 2020 Tokyo Games and other events preceding that one, his sustaining efforts will give the world so much more by which to remember him.
- ∂ Resilient
  - o Coming from humble beginnings, Jeff has remained motivated by his dreams as he has effortlessly overstepped many obstacles. His resiliency to beat the odds will always be admired.

# Keep Me from Going Under

*Furious Five – Remix (Year)*

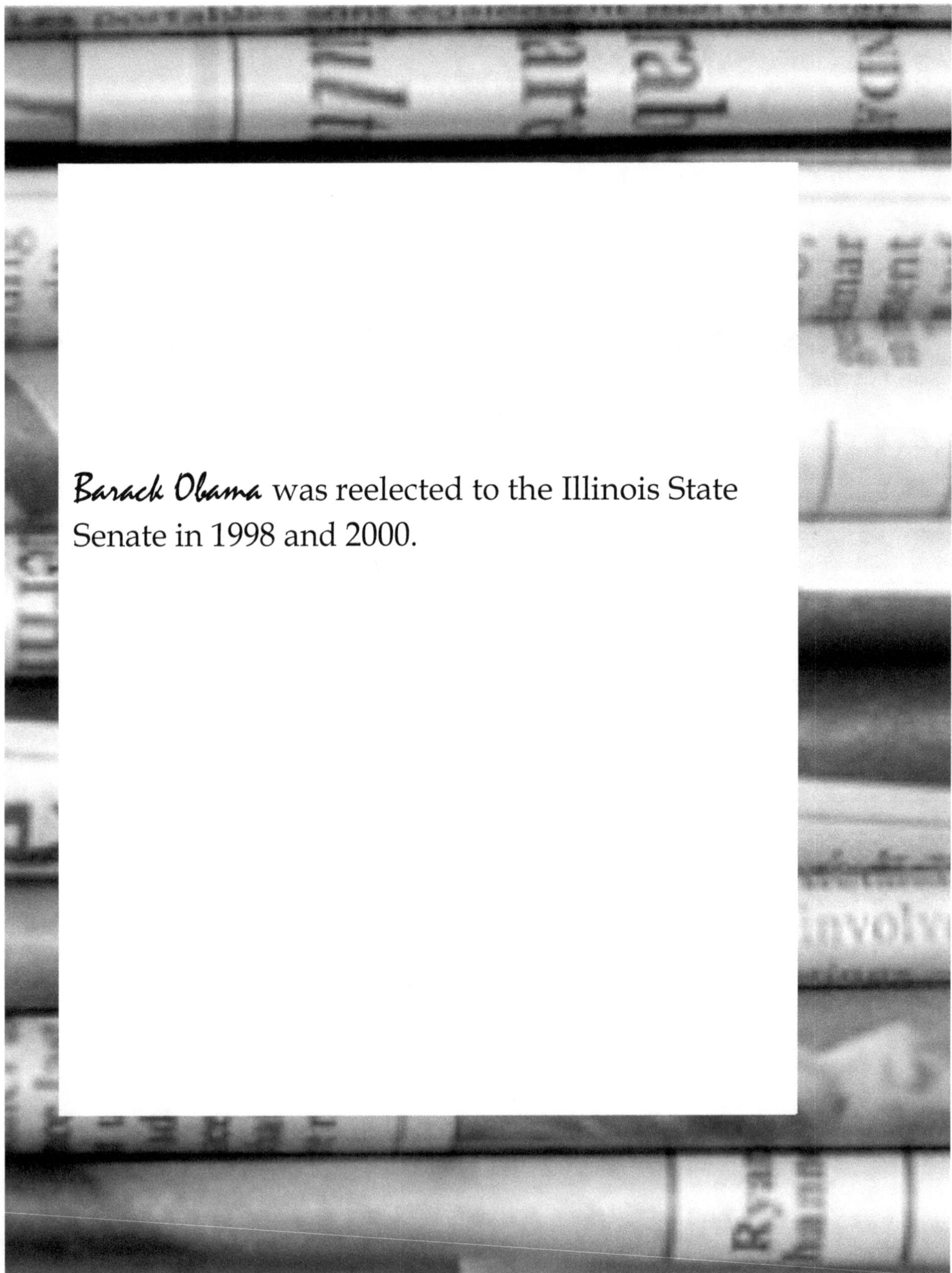

*Barack Obama* was reelected to the Illinois State Senate in 1998 and 2000.

# Chapter 4 Wars and Rumors of Wars

## Pamela Huff

First Female and the First African-American Female Chief Warrant Officer Five (CW5) in the Arkansas Army National Guard

## Similarities ...

### In Service to Country

The history of black women serving, fighting, and dying for a country that we are part of but still often rejected by is a long one. One of the earliest documented examples of black women serving in combat is the story of Cathay Williams who was pressed into service by Union Forces after being freed from a Missouri plantation. More than 80 years before women were allowed to enlist in the peacetime army officially, she disguised herself as a man and enlisted in November 1866 as "William Cathay" for two years until she fell ill, and her disguise was discovered. She served as a Buffalo Soldier with the 38th U.S. Infantry Regiment. Her story is a tragic one. She (as William Cathay) was denied disability, even though there were hospital records and proof. Women served as nurses, of course, and there is documentation for black women who served in the Civil War. Black women also served as nurses in the Spanish-American War, which was not without risk.

World War II would spawn the Women's Army Corps (WAC), and MAJ Charity Adams was the first black officer. She commanded the first all-black female unit, the 6888th Central Postal Directory Battalion.

In June of 1948, President Truman signed the Women's Armed Services Integration Act, permitting women to join the regular Army. In July of 1948, President Truman issued an executive order 9981 to end segregation in the military.

CW5 Huff served in several different military units throughout her Non-Commissioned/Warrant Officer (NCO/WO) career. She was assigned to the 204th Dental Detachment as a Dental Tech; 39th Brigade as a Personnel Admin Clerk; State Area Command (STARC) (-) AMA as a Personnel-Admin/NCO Instructor; 119th Personnel Service Company (119th PSC) as a Personnel Tech; and Joint Force Headquarters (JFHQ's) as a 420A Personnel Officer and Auditor.

Just like Ms. Cathay William, Pamela was also hired as a Federal Civil Service Technician in 1983, in North Little Rock and AR at Camp Joseph T. Robinson for the Arkansas Army National Guard as an Admin Clerk for the Combined Support Maintenance Shop (CSMS). She came in as a General Scheduled (GS) employee in the pay grade of GS-04. She was hired for this position during the time a discrimination suit (filed in 1980, decided in 1981) was in place. The Arkansas Army National Guard had been court directed to hire at least one black person for every two white persons hired until the level of black employees within the Arkansas Guard reached sixteen percent (16%), 653 F. 2d 1193 – Corenna Taylor v. General Jimmie "Red" Jones.

Pamela continues to fulfill her duties as a Federal Technician by increasing her knowledge within the Army National Guard and as a leader within the Military Organization. Her knowledge and training afforded her the opportunity to be hired at a higher level with increased responsibility. As she increased her knowledge, skills, and abilities (KSA's), Pamela became the first female African-American to be hired as a Federal Civil Service Technician at the GS pay grade of GS-13 with the Arkansas National Guard and the first African-American to be hired within the United States Property and Fiscal Office (USP&FO) Internal Review Division.

As an enlisted member during the 1970's, her unit (204th Dental Detachment) was activated for seven months and sent to Ft. Chaffee for the Cuban Relocation Operation. After this Operation, she was awarded the Humanitarian Service Medal. After several promotions as a non-commissioned officer, she made a major decision to become a Commissioned Warrant Officer in 1990. She attended and successfully graduated with honors from the Officer Candidate School at Fort McCoy Wisconsin.

As a WO1, she was assigned to the 119th Personnel Service Company (119th PSC); Upon completing her Warrant Officer Basic Course in 1991, she was mobilized with the unit and sent to Ft. Sill, Oklahoma. Her unit, the 119th PSC, replaced the Alpha Battery Headquarters. Her assignments included effectively overseeing the Deployment Center at Ft. Sill as the Personnel Records Chief (PRC), Mobilization Officer (Mob Off), and the Officer-in-Charge (OIC) of the Processing Center at Ft Sill, OK. While there, she served for nine months ensuring that over 4,000 soldiers, both active and reserve were adequately and successfully processed and ready to be deployed to IRAQ. After successfully completing her mission, CW5 Huff was recognized for her triple role as the PRC, MOB Off, and OIC of the Ft. Sill Processing Center, and as an outstanding leader. She was awarded the Army Commendation Medal for her contributions to the U.S. Army. She retired in May 2017 as the Supervisory Auditor for the Arkansas Army and Air National Guard.

# Who Cares...

## *Why is military history important?*

In the beginning is history foretold in the Old Testament: The Who, What, Where, When, Why, and How. Our youth must have a basic understanding of the issues confronting their state and country in order to choose their leaders wisely. In as much as, the leaders must have a much more sophisticated understanding to choose and to execute adequate policies. The knowledge and decisions that are made will affect the lives of soldiers and civilians – friendly, enemy, and neutral alike. The study of military history in America's colleges and universities today is seriously curtailed and distorted. We have far too little national attention paid to our military history to ignore or to downplay how this affects our future.

Our youth should know that since the establishment of the U.S. Military, African-Americans have answered the call to duty in service of the defense of the nation in all of its wars in spite of racial prejudice. During the American Revolution, blacks and whites served together in several units throughout the duration of the war. After the war, however, integration in the military would not be seen until after 1945. Blacks were often segregated into separate military units from their white counterparts. In many instances, these units were assigned menial tasks in support units and rarely saw combat. Those African-Americans who did see combat displayed great courage and bravery under fire, such as the famed 54th Massachusetts Volunteer Infantry in the Civil War, the 369th Infantry "Harlem Hellfighters" in World War I (highlighted in the exhibit), and the 761st Tank Battalion in World War II. In spite of racial discrimination and segregation, African-Americans continued to serve with distinction and gallantry.

When the United States entered World War I on the side of the Allies in order "to make the world safe for democracy," over 380,000 African-Americans answered the call to serve. Of this number, approximately 200,000 black soldiers were deployed overseas to the western front. More than half of those who served overseas were assigned to labor and stevedore units. About 42,000 men were assigned to combat units. These units included the all-black 92d and 93d Divisions. Though intended for front-line duty, Army leaders were reluctant to use blacks due to perceived inferiority and a lack of fighting prowess compared to white soldiers as well as the refusal of whites to serve alongside black units. As a result, four infantry regiments, including the 369th Infantry, were transferred to French forces, which welcomed African-American troops as equals due in part to France's experience with utilizing African colonial troops as well as its immediate need for more troops at the front.

The 369th Infantry, known as the "Harlem Hellfighters" for its courage and fighting prowess, is a prime example of the exemplary performance of black soldiers when given the opportunity. During the Meuse-Argonne offensive in late September 1918, the regiment, sustaining heavy losses, captured the crucial village of Séchault; at one point during the offensive, the 369th advanced faster than other French units in the same sector. As a result of its exemplary service, the 369th was awarded the French *Croix de Guerre*, France's highest military honor. By the end of the war, 171 soldiers of the regiment were awarded the Legion of Honor or the *Croix de Guerre.* The 369th's distinguished service in World War I helped to advance the quest for racial equality in America and eventual integration of the armed forces following World War II, with President Harry S. Truman's Executive Order 9981, thirty years later in 1948.

Benjamin O. Davis was the first black general in the U.S. Army and a major force in the desegregation of the American Armed Services. During a career that spanned fifty years—from the Spanish-American War as an enlisted soldier through World War II—Davis rose through the ranks despite rampant discrimination to become a respected leader and government adviser. He was promoted to brigadier general in 1940.

There was also the Tuskegee Airmen; they were the first black servicemen to serve as military aviators in the U.S. Armed Forces to fly with distinction during the World War II. Though subject to racial discrimination both at home and abroad, the 996 pilots and more than 15,000 ground personnel who served with the all-black units were credited with some 15,500 combat sorties and earned over 150 Distinguished Flying Crosses for their achievements. The highly publicized successes of the Tuskegee Airmen helped pave the way for the eventual integration of the U.S. Armed Forces under President Harry Truman in 1948.

Originally part of the U.S. 10th Cavalry Regiment, the Buffalo Soldiers became a separate group in September 1866. This occasion took place at Fort Leavenworth, Kansas. Native American tribes nicknamed the African-American soldiers of the 10th Cavalry, and the 24th and 25th Infantry, Regiments. The Buffalo Soldiers were active between 1866 and 1951. The United States Congress declared the Buffalo Soldiers as peacetime regiments consisting of African-Americans only and being part of the regular U.S. Army. Six regiments were authorized to be manned by black soldiers, but by 1869, there was a downsizing of all troops, and the black regiments were cut down to two infantry regiments and two cavalry regiments.

Buffalo Soldiers were instrumental in the American Civil War. They were mostly stationed at posts within the Great Plains as well as the southwestern regions of the nation. These soldiers fought bravely against the Indians, and a total of nineteen Medals of Honors were earned by them. Some of the battles of the Buffalo Soldiers and their predecessors included the fight at Cabin Creek, at Honey Springs in the summer of 1863/64, and the Red River War in 1875. The first black soldier to graduate from West Point, in 1877, was Henry O. Flipper. He became the commander of the 10th Cavalry Regiment at Fort Sill, which lay in Indian Territory.

Part of the duties of Buffalo Soldiers, aside from engaging in battle, was protecting the civilized Indian tribes on the reservations. They also were keepers of law and order in general, and they were active in building roads and military structures. The oldest Buffalo Soldier, Mark Matthews, died in September 2005. His body now rests in the Arlington National Cemetery. He was 111-years-old.

There are names you are unlikely to find in most history books such as: Susan Taylor King, Cathay Williams, MAJ Charity Adams, MAJ Marie Rogers, and LT. Phoebe Jeter, but military history of these and other black women span a sizable amount. African-American women have played a role in every war effort in the United States. Black women participated despite the evils of racial and gender discrimination. The endured physical discomfort and personal criticism, while many of their contributions were unrecognized and unrewarded. They placed themselves in danger's path – offering their abilities and strengths to preserve values and to ensure freedom.

Their heroism dates back to the Revolutionary War when inspired by the promise of freedom from slavery; some women served as spies, and others disguised themselves as men and fought side by side with them against the British. Harriet Tubman's heroics in the Civil War as a Union spy, volunteer nurse, and armed scout reportedly earned the former slave the nickname "General Tubman" from soldiers. Susan Taylor King, another former slave, joined the all-black First South Carolina Volunteers unit as a nurse and later started a school for children and soldiers.

## Biography

Pamela (Marshall) Huff was born in Little Rock, AR and graduated from Hall High School in 1975. Pamela received her bachelor's degree in organizational management from John Brown University and her Master of Arts degree in Human Resource Development from Webster University.

Pamela joined the Arkansas Army National Guard in September 1975 at the age of 17 and became a member of the 204th Dental Detachment Military Unit. Pamela started her career as a private (the lowest non-commission (enlisted) rank of an Army soldier). She continued as an enlisted soldier through the rank of Sergeant First Class (SFC/E-7).

SFC Marshall, at that time, made a major decision to become an Officer, not just an Officer, but a Commissioned Warrant Officer (CWO). As a CWO, she was trained and received specialized training in her field as a Personnel Officer throughout her military career field as a 420A. Throughout her career she continued to train and excel through the ranks, ending her military career as a Chief Warrant Officer Five (CW5). CW5 Huff became the first female and the first female African-American CW5 within the Arkansas Army National Guard. As of her retirement in June 2017 (41 years), she currently still maintains this status. During her tenure, she served in various assignments.

Joining the military would also provide Pamela with a lifetime of training/skills and opportunities. She was mobilized twice in 1980 for the Ft. Chaffee Cuban Relocation Operations, and again in 1990 during Desert Shield/Desert Storm.

She has risen to the top of her career field retiring in May 2017. She became the first African-American female to achieve the highest-ranking Warrant Officer (CW5) in the Arkansas Army National Guard (AR ARNG). Her tenacity and perseverance have paved the way for other minority women to achieve great stature in the military and the community. She was also the first African-American female instructor at the Non-Commissioned Officer (NCO) Military Academy for the AR ARNG. She has received many awards and decorations.

CW5 Pamela Huff held the status of a Human Resource Officer & Internal Supervisory Auditor for the National Guard until May 2017.

She is the wife of Mr. Sam Huff, Jr who is retired from the Marine/Navy. She is also the mother of Minister Rogike Britton. Pam & Sam are the proud grandparents of five grandchildren, three boys and two girls. She and her husband also have two fur babies, a Bichon, Kodiak and a King Charles Cavalier Spaniel, Roxie.

Their hobbies include traveling, home projects, gardening, and spending time with family, friends, and their fur babies.

Her favorite quote from The Bible is, "I Can Do All Things Through Christ Who Strengthens Me," **(Philippians 4:13 NKJV).**

*Accolades*

Upon Retiring in 2017:

- ∂ AR ARNG - 41 years;
- ∂ Federal Technician - 34 years;
- ∂ Bachelor of Science Degree in Organizational Management at John Brown University
- ∂ Master of Arts Degree in Human Resource Development at Webster University

Enlisted Military Career began in 1975 as follows:

- ∂ Private (PV1) 71A - 26 Sep 75
- ∂ Sergeant First Class (E-7) 71A – 20 Sep 90

Military Officer Career began in 1990 as follows:

- ∂ Warrant Officer One (WO1) 420A – 21 Sep 90
- ∂ Chief Warrant Officer 2 (CW2) 420A – 21 Sep 91
- ∂ Chief Warrant Officer 3 (CW3) 420A – 30 Jul 99
- ∂ Chief Warrant Officer 4 (CW4) 420A – 30 Jul 04
- ∂ Chief Warrant Officer 5 (CW5) 420A – 14 Aug 10

Medals/Ribbons and Awards:

- ∂ Legion of Merit
- ∂ Meritorious Service Medal
- ∂ Army Commendation Medal
- ∂ Army Achievement Medal
- ∂ Army Reserve Components Achievement (11)
- ∂ National Defense Service Medal (2)
- ∂ Humanitarian Service Medal
- ∂ Armed Forces Reserve Medal (4) with "M" Device
- ∂ Noncommissioned Officers Professional (3)
- ∂ Army Service Ribbon
- ∂ Arkansas Commendation Medal
- ∂ Arkansas Distinguished Service Medal
- ∂ Arkansas Service Ribbon
- ∂ Arkansas Federal Service Ribbon
- ∂ Several Certificates of Achievements/Letters of Commendations
- ∂ Veterans History Project

# Let's Stay Together

*Al Green (1971)*

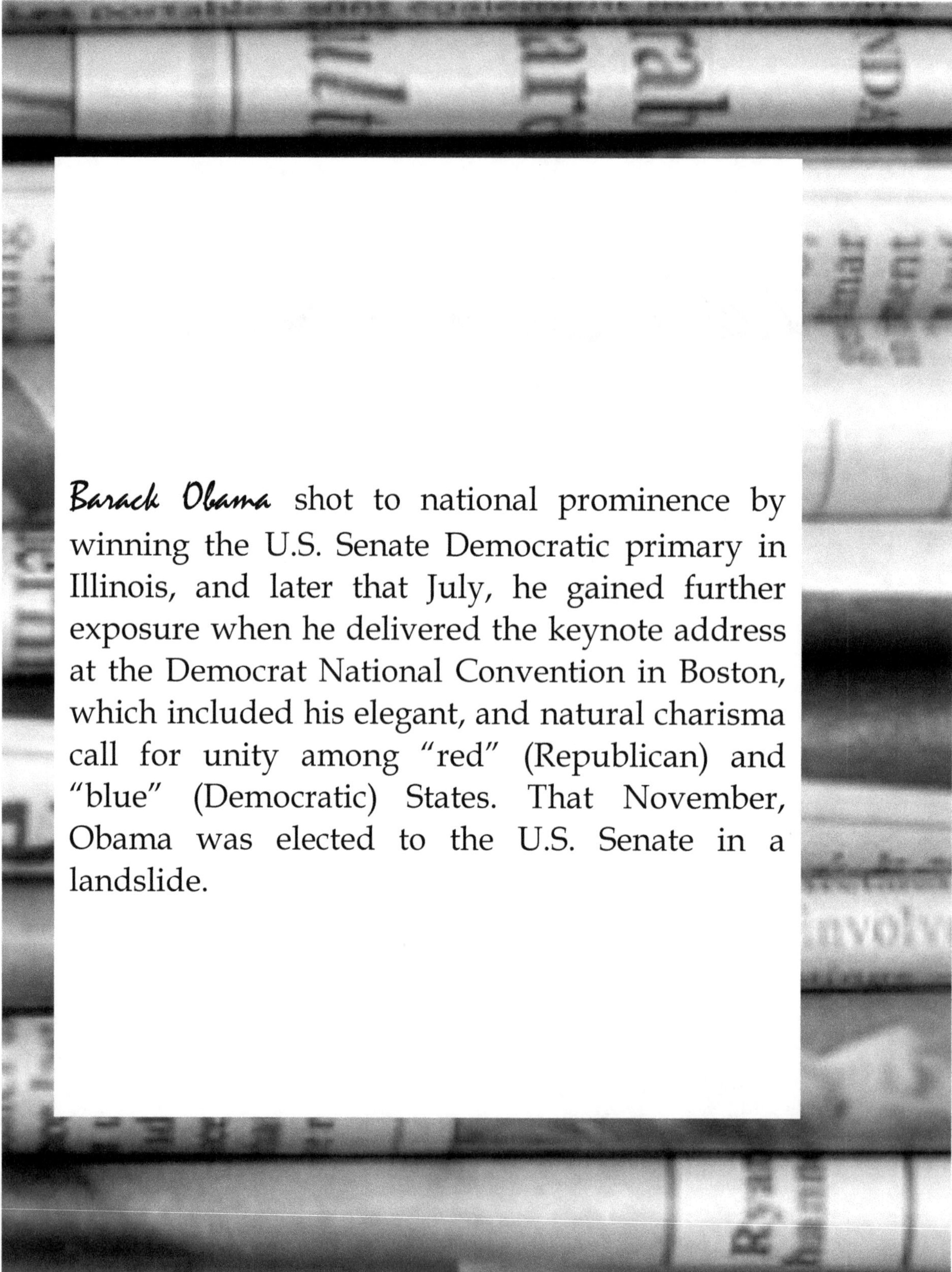

**Barack Obama** shot to national prominence by winning the U.S. Senate Democratic primary in Illinois, and later that July, he gained further exposure when he delivered the keynote address at the Democrat National Convention in Boston, which included his elegant, and natural charisma call for unity among "red" (Republican) and "blue" (Democratic) States. That November, Obama was elected to the U.S. Senate in a landslide.

# Chapter 5 Life in the White House

Janis Kearney

First and Only Presidential Diarist

## Similarities...

### A Lifetime of Dreaming from the Edge

I am often asked, "How did it happen that a poor sharecropper's daughter from southeast Arkansas was selected to serve as a personal diarist to a president?" It's been over 20 years since I served in that role, and I'm still asked that question several times each year. Believe it or not, I still don't have a simple answer to that question.

You see, while I don't believe any of us are born with entitlements to gifts in life, I do believe our life journeys lead us to the places we are meant to be. My journey from Varner Road to the White House was surely pre-ordained. Nothing that amazing could have happened without predestination. Even more, I'm convinced that none of this would have taken place without the foundation that began down on Varner Road, and with the unique guidance of TJ and Ethel Kearney, two amazing parents – poor, but wise cotton sharecroppers.

**A Miracle on 1600 Pennsylvania Avenue...**

I have written extensively about my time in the White House, first as a media affairs specialist and as a personal diarist to President William J. Clinton. I have likened it to an Alice in Wonderland experience – my leaving Varner Road in 1971 as green as they come; to attend college on the other side of the state; and 20 years later to be invited to walk into the most coveted house in the world to serve the president of the United States of America. Certainly, this was a prime example of good politics and a politician with their heart on right.

I pinched myself for eight years. I couldn't have dreamed that reality. I couldn't have imagined that the 42nd president of the United States would have invited me to the White House in 1993 and later select me to serve as his personal diarist.

But, that is what happened. That is the genesis of my belief in miracles and my conviction that anything is possible in this America if we open our hearts to possibilities.

My required role at the White House between 1995 and 2001, was to chronicle the daily events of the 42nd Presidency. How could anyone have known that this role fit my sensibility so perfectly or that it fed my love for writing, for storytelling, for researching and sharing history – and for presidential history?

I was paid to observe history taking place before my eyes. Little did the president know that I would have paid him to have such an opportunity. I was a born listener and observer, trained from childhood to listen and make myself invisible. I was a keen observer and could later recall the most mundane of conversations, actions, or interactions.

I became that fly on the wall of the White House. I was hardly able to succeed at invisibility, given that I was very often the only African-American woman in the room during the president's meetings—a 40-year-old African-American woman with braids.

For five years, I would continue in my role. The perks were endless, and the great leaders, A-list actors, and performers I met, left me humbled. Nothing, however, compared to having day to day access to a president of the United States, to my role as witness and chronicler of presidential history, and to watching and hearing it unfold before my eyes. Nothing could ever compare to seeing the intricacies of the U.S. Presidency that most Americans have only read about, and to know that the history books included just a tip of the excitement of what happens inside a U.S. Presidency.

But, there is always a journey that brings us to the point that we end up. There is a larger reason for us to be there, and I'll share that with you.

**The Train that Delivered me at 1600 Pennsylvania Ave…**

Let's begin at the beginning…down on Varner Road.

Because of American history and because of the Kearney family's personal experiences in southeast Arkansas, I grew up with a wary view of America's political system. The realization that I was now squarely in the middle of American politics brought my past and present full circle.

Everything I'd learned about politics, growing up in the southeast Arkansas Delta, had confirmed for me that politics did not work for a large majority of Americans, specifically those of us from poor and/or minority communities in the south. I learned about southern politics by listening intently to my father's conversations with other black men in the neighborhood. These conversations colored my view of politics and politicians.

Some of the experiences I witnessed firsthand – like my father's efforts over the years to purchase land and move his family beyond our roles as poor cotton sharecroppers. I was just a child, but I understood what was happening as my father's dreams were dashed over and over. Unquestionably, he was disheartened by a political system that seemed intent on keeping him where he was as obstructive to his efforts to move himself and his family forward.

American History confirms that our political system has not always worked for the poor and downtrodden. For most of the 20th Century, racial and social inequities were legal and accepted. Thousands of men and women fought and died to change these laws. Many continue to fight even today, to ensure the laws are activated, not simply on the books.

Thankfully, much has changed since my childhood on Varner Road. And, I am certain, now, that politics was never the culprit. There is nothing innately good or bad about American or even southern politics—but, how our political leaders wield their power.

Politics is part of our lives, intricately woven into every facet of our world. Every decision we make or fail to make is connected to our politics. And, guess what? Those of us born with the least in life, have the most to gain from good politics. It is even more important to participate in and invest in good politics.

It took me a while to realize this because the word "Politics," was rarely if ever used in the Kearney household. While my father, an amateur history buff adamant about getting his community out to vote, he didn't extend that enthusiasm to explaining all of this to his children. We never debated politics over family dinner. The Kearney children, like most in the community, were not encouraged –or allowed—to debate with parents or each other during family dinner. Even so, I'm pretty certain that many of my parents' bedroom discussions were about Arkansas' political environment and how it impacted our lives.

I was 12-years-old when I realized the role politics played in what was the Kearney family's most sacred of institutions, our schools. It was 1965, eight years after the world-renowned Integration of Central High School. Arkansas, like most southern states, resisted the integration law for as long as possible; so long, in fact, that I (and probably most of our parents) had given up the expectation that it would ever take place.

In 1965, integration caught up with us. Like most other small, rural school districts, the Gould School Board opted for something called, "Freedom of Choice," in hopes that this would soften the blow for white parents not happy to be sharing their school with black students.

Integration was not at the top of my list of concerns in the spring of 1965. I was most excited about matriculating from Fields Elementary to the junior high school next year. My friends and I spent an inordinate amount of our recess time imagining what it would be like to be in junior high school in the fall of 1965.

I was sorely disappointed by my parents' announcement later that summer about the Kearney children attending the "white school." Not only was I not excited about this traumatic change, but I worried for the rest of the summer about losing my place in my class hierarchy. Most importantly, I was saddened to be leaving many of my friends behind.

As was the case in the 1957 Integration at Central High, not all students at Fields Schools were transferred carte blanche to the white schools. The final decision regarding which families were invited to send their children to the "new" school, rested with the all-white Gould School Board, with recommendations from Fields School's black principal and teachers. That decision was based on the child's academic standing and the subjective decision on whether the child would be a good "fit" in this new environment.

Most of the Kearney children were transferred to the white schools. We left teachers that we loved and friendships we'd developed over the years. Thankfully, some of our friends were transferred to the new school with us. Other classmates we hadn't known well quickly became friends, thanks to our shared "outsider" status and daily proximity.

My parents believed education was second in importance, only to religion. Though they understood that "freedom of choice," was a piecemeal step toward full integration, they believed it was a step in the right direction. They wanted their children to receive the best education there was and saw this as a possibility for that. When my grades weren't satisfactory in my mother's eyes, she would look, shake her head, and say, "Girl, you just don't have an excuse not to learn, now."

No matter how educationally beneficial the transfer might have been, emotionally, it was unsettling for us children. And, for our parents, it was yet another opportunity for the white leaders to demonstrate control over our lives. Children in our communities were uprooted from what we knew, the friends we loved, and the teachers who cared about our future. In spite of its intentions the "Freedom of Choice," experiment would always represent a dark moment in my education experience.

There was at least one good thing to come out of the two-year experience. I found and began to use my voice. Though our parents had taught their children that we were "to be seen and not heard," that rule had to be quickly aborted when we moved into the new school environment. That rule worked between parents and children because there was an unspoken love and respect built into that relationship. In this new school environment, our silence was detrimental. Without our voices, we didn't exist.

Thus, it was during those two tumultuous years of the "Freedom of Choice," experiment that I broke my silence to voice my thoughts and even offer independent ideas. While my voice wasn't always appreciated or invited, it ensured that others recognized my existence. Even then, I was beginning to learn that much of the power of politics, is the power of having and using one's voice.

### Good Politics

So, my sense of politics was shaped during my 17 years on Varner Road, working on my father's cotton farm and interacting with black and whites in my community and schools. I learned as much from what my parents didn't say, as I did from what they said. What I saw and what my parents experienced convinced me that ours was a political system that worked best for those already in power, and rarely for families like mine.

I learned, in time, that while politicians did wield power, everyday Americans like my family had the potential to wield power as well. I realized, too, that there were good politicians who stepped into that arena with good intentions, who governed with the philosophy that every citizen counted, and who believed that every problem was all of our problems.

I first came upon this fresh, new proposition sitting in a political science class at the University of Arkansas at Fayetteville, with hundreds of other students. We were all spellbound by a beautiful, young professor by the name of Diane Blair. As she lectured on the importance of the political system, I found myself on the precipice of a political conversion. For the first time, I realized there were some redeeming values in politics that I could be a part of good politics and that good politics is when the laws and policies are put in place work for all.

This was a serious conversion. My family had survived an environment that represented much of what bad politics looked like from any practical vantage point. It was a time when too many political leaders ignored the plight of families like mine. An era when the `powers that be,' used that power to punish those who questioned the status quo and worked hard to ensure the status quo worked for some and isolated others.

But, gratefully, there was another side to this story. Political power can be shared. The poor and oppressed can be a part of the change they seek. And, yes, there is such a thing as good politics, which seeks to empower the masses.

Arkansas is a political dichotomy, unlike most southern states. For 40 years of the last 20th Century, we experienced an impressive reign of progressive – some would even call it liberal—politics. The state was blessed with great politicians who entered the arena for the right reasons – to serve all. While none of them were perfect human beings, they were astute politicians and most importantly...they had their hearts *on right*.

These were political leaders like William Jefferson Clinton, David Pryor, Dale Bumpers, and earlier leaders like Sid McMath and even Winthrop Paul Rockefeller. What politics has taught me over the years is that we don't need perfect men or women to be our politicians; we need politicians who come to it with the desire to serve all.

So, as I come full circle, it is good to reconcile the bad politics that were so evident in my early years on Varner Road, with the good politics that I now know is possible. I also know that it comes with hard and purposeful work – not only from the political leaders, but from the communities most impacted.

One of the most vivid examples of good politics in this new administration took place on November 4, 2008. I was back home on Varner Road. My journey that began in 1971, had brought me back here to spend time with my 103-year-old father. To say I enjoyed our time together would be an understatement. I treasured each moment I spent with my father, not so much because I was a good daughter, as it was my opportunity to learn from him. My father continued to grow wiser and continued to teach for as long as he lived. And, I never tired of learning.

On that historical day, I was there to watch the most historical presidential election either of us had ever experienced. Just two years ago, I'd interviewed Dad about his life, including his memories of the presidencies he'd witnessed. What a fascinating oratory. I never gave much thought of all the experiences that go into 100 years of living on this earth!

At that time, my father told me Franklin Roosevelt, John Kennedy, Lyndon Johnson, and William Jefferson Clinton were the greatest presidents of his lifetime. Tonight, there would be one more added to that list, even before he proved himself. The fact that he'd been elected was enough to convince Thomas James Kearney that there was something great about this man Barack Osama Obama.

I'd never stayed up all night to watch a presidential election before. That night, I did, and, so did my 103-year-old father. I opined more than once that night to the point that it looked as if Sen. Obama might lose. My dad gave me that half-smile, half-smirk, and simply shook his head. "This is our next president," he said, never relenting. I wondered how he could be so sure, especially after he told me what a hard decision it was for him in the primary. My family had been loyal Clinton campaigners for more than 30 years – and we were both excited that Hillary was getting into the presidential campaign.

The quandary came when Barack Obama threw his hat into the election arena too. My dad and I discussed this on every phone call and visit I made. While we weren't sure what his chances were or what he offered, it was an exciting quandary to have. Moreover, for the entire primary season, we were literally torn between these two good candidates.

After the primary, we were both sad to see Hillary lose; but her loss did make the way clear for us. From the point that Barack Obama made his acceptance speech at the DNC Convention that year, we were 100% behind his candidacy. And, the rest is history – Great history — Hard-fought history.

# Who Cares...

## *Why is presidential history important?*

In some ways, I have been a part of two of America's most unlikely presidencies of the 20th Century. The first, of course, was Arkansas' popular and longest-serving Governor William J. Clinton, the southerner without pedigree, and not born with a silver spoon in his mouth. Bill Clinton won the presidency with dogged hard work, sheer grit, pragmatism, and political acumen - against all odds.

I was blessed to have played a role in the Clinton Presidency from beginning to end. Beginning in 1992, at his campaign headquarters in Little Rock, Arkansas where I worked in the press office. After his election, I was part of the press transition staff, and in 1993, I joined the Clinton White House media affairs office. I served all eight years in the Clinton Administration, and five of those eight years as personal diarist to President Clinton, working as part of his post-presidential transition team through July 2001.

It was eight years later that Senator Barack Obama would be elected President Obama. And, while I was not a member of Sen. Obama's campaign in an official role, I did my small part during the general election – even campaigned for him in his last run for Illinois state senator.

But in a more ephemeral way, Barack Obama's elections and his presidency impacted my life just as much. He represented so much of all that my parents and so many black parents believed in and worked for for so many years. They taught us that we could ascend to whatever role we desired if we made our minds up to do the necessary work.

Barack Obama represented the dream that so many black parents had for their children, so many Black politicians had for their communities, so many black leaders throughout the years have had for America. Our forefathers fought and died for the day that Barack Osama Obama was sworn into the presidency.

On January 20, 2009, I traveled to Washington, DC to meet my husband for the presidential inauguration of America's 44th president. Having moved back to Arkansas from Chicago in 2007, it was more than a notion to fly into Washington DC at the height of winter for any reason.

But I gladly braved the freezing temperature for this occasion - to witness the inauguration of the first African-American president in U.S. History. I can't tell you how proud we were to be in Washington DC and to witness this celebration. There were families from all over the country and many visitors from around the world. It seemed the entire city was in celebration mode. Of course, that was not the case. We now know that not everyone was as happy or proud to see this kind of American history being made.

This realization hit home for me during my flight back to Arkansas after the inauguration. It was then that I realized the disconnect of how differently white Americans reacted to Barack Obama's election. I recall even now how eerily quiet the airports were. I was immediately reminded of the weeks and months following the

9-11 terrorist attacks when I traveled back and forth between Chicago and Boston. It was such a strange experience to be one of only a handful of passengers flying during that time. The two or three of us were free to sit in any part of the plane our hearts desired. I tried desperately not to focus long on "why" the planes were empty.

On January 21, 2009, the furtive glances of my fellow travelers, along with the quick head turns before our eyes could connect, told me more than I needed to know. As always, the airport televisions droned on; this time, at least, it seemed they were turned almost to mute, and no one wanted to show that they were paying attention. An airport with no laughter, no conversations, and no smiles after what was surely the most historic presidential election and inauguration in our lifetimes, was ominous. I feared what the next four years might bring.

Much of my fear proved prophetic. President Barack Obama fell into a presidency fraught with time bombs, and his success depended on how quickly and how well he detonated them – multiple middle east wars and conflicts, skyrocketing unemployment, housing stalls, toxic banking policies causing astronomical bankruptcies and loan defaults, failing automobile manufacturing, a failed healthcare system...and the list went on and on.

Top all of that off with a new president being saddled with a Congress who publicly announced that they would not work with him. Period. God must have been on Barack Obama's side. There is no other way he could have fought his way out of the box he found himself in, in 2009. While it took almost the entire first term to do it, slowly and surely America was shedding its economic shackles, and he was making bold moves toward pulling Americans out of the Middle Eastern conflicts.

No one would have convinced me, given his uphill battle during his first term, that Dad and I would again be celebrating President Obama's election in 2012. Again, he won singlehandedly, if not with quite as large margins as 2008.

It is this moment in American history that makes me so proud to be an American, in spite of our shortcomings. As Dad, now 106, sat with me watching the second inauguration of Barack Hussein Obama, we looked at each other and smiled. The pride in both of our faces was palpable.

Again, we were witnessing a miracle taking place. With all the forces pulling against him, Barack Obama was being catapulted into the White House once again. I was reminded of the president who was my boss, William J. Clinton; he had prevailed against all odds. The old folk down on Varner Road use to say, "God's not finished with you yet." That's how I felt about Barack Obama's second term. There was more work for him to do.

So many memories crowded my mind. How could I, who had always been taught to dream beyond my reality, and know that miracles do happen, not be moved by this miracle we were experiencing that day? We were, in fact, watching the outcome of good politics at its very best.

It was an especially emotional moment for my father as he witnessed something his reality could never have allowed him to believe when he was a child growing up in an era devoid of automobiles, before television, telephones, or internet. Yet, strangely, TJ and Ethel Kearney always made us believe that anything was possible, if we dreamed, then worked to make our dreams reality.

My pride in the Obama presidency went beyond my identifying with him because he happened to be African-American. It had more to do with America's ability to transcend race at this important moment in time. No matter that society and Americans have gone back and forth on their feelings about this president and no matter that there has been unprecedented disrespect shown him by fellow politicians, there is no turning back time. We moved beyond the invisible edict that said all American presidents must be white men. We can never return there.

I am completely convinced that neither my White House experiences, nor Barack Obama's presidency could have happened anywhere else except in these times, in these amazing United States of America. And, yet, what I also know is that nothing happens in a vacuum. I go back to the miracles in my own life that include a journey ending at the White House. Together and apart, these miracles changed my life and convinced me, yet again, that impossible dreams are only impossible to those who don't reach for them.

I remember, with amazing clarity, that cold, piercingly, bright day of January 20, 1993, when I walked into that White House. Eight years later, on another cold and grey January 20, I left 1600 Pennsylvania for the very last time and walked outside of those gates. I spent eight years of watching an amazing president and his advisors exemplify good politics to make life better for America – every facet of America, every corner of America, and every single human being who called themselves American.

**A Message to our Future Leaders**

I am convinced that this American story is not so much about me as it is about the power and possibility of dreams. It is a story that offers readers – especially young readers – trying to discern the distance between their everyday reality and the impossible dream that awaits them on the other side.

Just imagine what my answer would have been if my favorite teacher, Mrs. Jones, had sat down in front of me one day and said, "You, little Janis Kearney, daughter of the poor sharecroppers out on Varner Road, sister of 18 other siblings, will one day become a personal diarist to a president of the United States!"

"You will travel with the president and his aides to foreign lands, flying aboard the president's plane, Air Force One. You will meet many leaders of foreign countries and sit in meetings with the president and other world leaders as they discuss global issues impacting the world and strategize on how to resolve them."

Even for this child whose days revolved around dreams, the distance between my reality and the impossible dream my teacher asked me to imagine would have seemed insurmountable.

Miracles, the most important part of your journey will be the people who come into your life as mentors and guides. Sometimes, they come with a purpose in mind. Other times, they haven't the scantest knowledge of what gifts they bear. My life's journey represents the many gifts shared with me, the paths opened to me, and the lessons learned from wise friends and mentors along the way—those who taught me by example and others who helped shape me by sheer accident.

If I had to share five lessons that have been most critical to my journey and my growth, it would be these:

- ∂ **The God Issue**—No one was more surprised than I that in the midst of my journey, during my middle years, I finally came face to face with something that had been so much a part of my early life on Varner Road. Finally, I could embrace my spirituality, admit a love and need of God, and accept that He or She had been with me throughout my journey...and, in fact, was responsible for the good things that happened along my journey. As a child, I had been a questioner of God and why He allowed the world to be as it was. Admittedly, I don't pretend to have all the answers, even today. But I admit that I now believe God does, and He or She is in evident in all that we do and that belief sustains me.

- ∂ **The Parent Trap**—Anyone who has ever heard me talk about my journey, knows how much credence I give to good parenting. My greatest blessing beyond anything else was God's gift of TJ and Ethel Kearney in my life. Two undereducated, but supremely wise parents who without money, education, or a great deal of community support – successfully raised and shaped 17 productive citizens of the world through sheer hard work, love, and the belief that tomorrow would be brighter. Nothing is as important as good parenting.

- ∂ **The Pebble in the Water Phenomenon**—Simply put, everything we do, every act we take, and every person we bring into our lives impacts something larger than us – in a good or bad way. Our thoughts are powerful because they direct our actions. Our actions, no matter how small, are powerful because they impact our lives, our communities, and our world. Our small steps make deep impressions.

- ∂ **Politics is Life**—This was the title of a column I wrote for a while out of Chicago. In a nutshell, it means that everything in our lives, every problem, every issue, and every complaint has some political ramification or resolution. Good politics is about us everyday people taking responsibility for our destinies, rather than sitting on our hands and waiting for our leaders to ply us with all the answers. Young people must do as they did in this last election and take ownership of their lives and their futures. There is no better way than to get involved in politics, as early as possible. We're never too young or old to embrace politics and use it to make our lives and our world a better place.

- ∂ **The "I" Effect**—This means much the same as `we are the change we seek.' But, before we can embrace this truism, we must accept the fact that there is power within each of us. I was blessed to have been taught early on that I was worthy--even when few people outside our family acknowledged our worth. It takes just one person to change the world... remember Mandela, Gandhi, Roosevelt, Lincoln, King, Obama, and Clinton? You can change the status quo; you can make life better. You can assure that tomorrow works for everyone if you embrace the power of "I" – the power of one.

Biography

Janis F. Kearney is an Arkansas native, and one of 19 children born to cotton sharecroppers in the small southeast Arkansas town of Gould, Arkansas. While neither of her parents graduated from high school, Janis' mother attained her GED shortly at the same school that Janis attended and graduated from in 1971.

Janis credits her parents for any bit of success she has experienced in life. In spite of TJ and Ethel Kearney's limited education, they instilled in their children the importance and power of education, faith, and hard work in each of them. That important foundation paid off – eighteen of their nineteen children were college graduates.

Janis attended Fields Elementary School, the all-black, segregated elementary school in Gould. She graduated from the newly integrated Gould High School in 1971. She attended the University of Arkansas at Fayetteville in fall 1971. At just 17-years-old, Janis says she had never traveled alone outside her hometown and was never so scared in her life.

Janis married and had her first child in 1973, while still a student at the university. She was at the end of her sophomore year when she became a married student and mother. She was (she recalls) ten days overdue and still attending classes when her son, Darryl made his debut.

Against all odds and scant encouragement from some, Janis continued her studies while caring for her son, never once interrupting her classes. After completing her undergraduate degree with a B.A. in Journalism in 1976; Janis applied to and was accepted into the university's Master of Public Administration program in 1977.

Janis and her husband moved to Little Rock after his graduation from the university in 1977. She worked for the State of Arkansas for nine years as a program manager, then as a director of information for Arkansas' Migrant Education program. In 1987, she purchased the *Arkansas State Press Newspaper* from her mentor and civil rights legend, Daisy Bates - who led the renowned 1957 Civil Rights Integration of the Little Rock Central High School. Janis served as publisher through 1992, when she took a sabbatical to work in the Clinton/Gore Campaign.

Janis joined the Clinton White House Media Affairs office in 1993. In March 1993, she was appointed assistant administrator and director of the Office of Public Communications at the U.S. Small Business Administration. In 1995, she was appointed as the first-ever personal diarist to a president and served in that role from 1995 until the end of the Clinton Administration in 2001. In this role, she chronicled the Clinton

Presidency and collected and archived presidential documents to be transferred, first, to the National Archives and later, to the Clinton Presidential Library.

After the Clinton Administration ended in 2001, Janis and her husband moved to Chicago. They resided there for the next six years. Between the years of 2001-2007, Janis became a fellow in the W.E.B. Du Bois Institute for African-Americans at Harvard University. It was during this time that she began research on her Clinton presidential biography, ***Conversations: William Jefferson Clinton...from Hope to Harlem.***

**In 2002, Janis was appointed as a Chancellor's Lecturer at Chicago City Colleges, and as a Roads Scholar by the Illinois Humanities Council. In 2005, she was** selected as a Humanities Fellow at DePaul University in Chicago, where she lectured and did programming for the college. In 2007, Kearney returned to her home state of Arkansas to take an appointment as a Humanities Scholar and Professor at Arkansas State University in Jonesboro - where she taught memoir writing and presidential history.

Janis is married to Bob J. Nash, former director of the White House Personnel Office under President William J. Clinton. Their blended family includes three children: Darryl Lunon II, Creshelle Nash, and Eric Nash, and three grandchildren.

## Accolades

- Public lecturer and educator
- Guest lecturer around the country including Canada and the UK
- Workshop creator (*Read.Write.Share* Writer's Weekend, *Writing our Lives* Memoir Writing workshop in Little Rock, and the *Read.Write.Share* Writer's Workshop in Fort Smith, Arkansas.)
- Founder of Writing Our World Publishing (formerly WOW! Press)
- Author
    - *Cotton Field of Dreams*; *Something to Write Home About: Memories of a Presidential Diarist; Daisy: Between a Rock and a Hard Place*, and her most recent book, *Sundays with TJ: 100 Years of Memories on Varner Road.*
- Board Member
    - The AR Pioneer Chapter of Pen Women, of which she served as president between 2013-2014, the Executive Board of LifeQuest of Arkansas, the Little Rock Metro Chapter of the National Association of University Women, and the International Women's Forum of Arkansas.
- Founder and chair of the Celebrate! Maya Project of Arkansas
- National and local recognitions and honors: inducted into the National History Makers archives of outstanding African-American leaders, selection as a founding recipient of the Silas Hunt Legacy Award from the University of Arkansas, Fayetteville, received the University of Arkansas Outstanding Alumni Award, and the University of Arkansas Journalism Lemke Award in 2009
- In 2016, recognized by the City of Little Rock for outstanding contributions in the area of Literary Arts
- In 2016, Janis was inducted into the prestigious Arkansas Writers Hall of Fame.

# Look to You

*Whitney Houston (2009)*

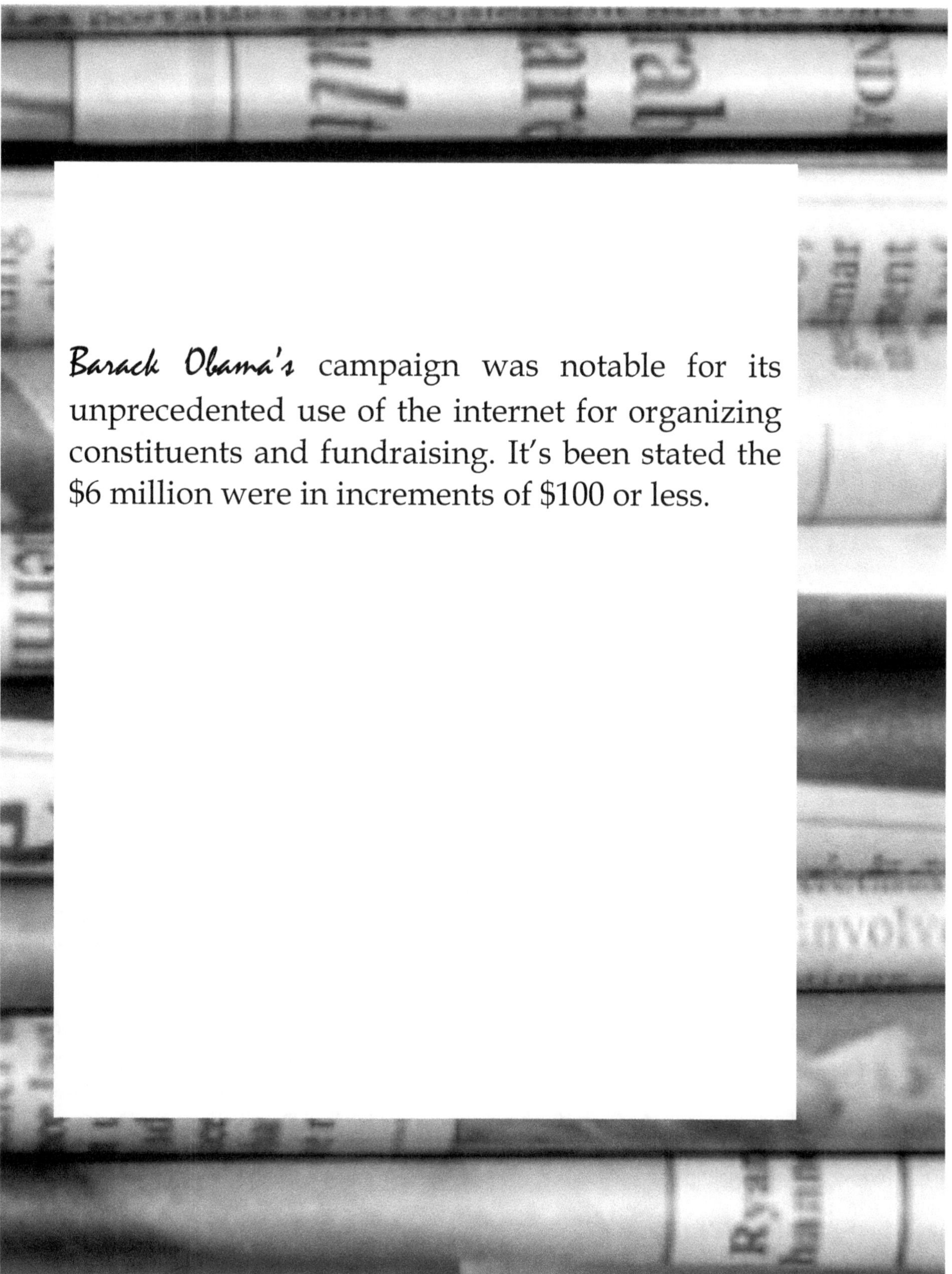

*Barack Obama's* campaign was notable for its unprecedented use of the internet for organizing constituents and fundraising. It's been stated the $6 million were in increments of $100 or less.

# Chapter 6 Education

## *Thelma Mothershed-Wair*

One of Nine, to First Integrate Little Rock Central High School in 1957

## Similarities ...

### *A Strategy for Life*

I was born November 29, 1940, to Arlevia and Hosanna Moore Mothershed in Bloomburg, Texas. I was the third of six children born to this union. My siblings are Lois, Grace, Gilbert, Michael, and Karen.

Mother moved with the three oldest to Scott, Arkansas in about 1942 while our father was serving in World War II. He was a 2nd Lieutenant with the 2nd Platoon Company B Training Battalion. We lived with my mother's brother, Milton, his wife, Mabel, and her sister, Mary. They lived on the Moore family farm. Gilbert was born there in 1943. Michael was born in Little Rock, Arkansas in 1952 and Karen in 1960.

There was a one-room school for area black students. I was too young to attend. The teacher was my great aunt, Pearl Armstrong.

We moved to North Little Rock, Arkansas - Military Heights Area in 1943. I attended Hillside Elementary School. I was unable to walk to school because of a congenital heart defect known as Tetralogy of Fallot. This caused me to be short of breath and to tire easily. Lois and Grace pulled me to school in a little red wagon until I became physically unable to attend classes. After a short time, a teacher provided by the school district came to our home.

The family moved to Little Rock, Arkansas about 1950. I was still physically unable to attend regular classes and was assigned to a special education classroom, so I would not have to change classes. My condition stabilized to a point that in seventh grade I attended classes at Paul Laurence Dunbar Junior High and Horace Mann Senior High Schools.

In 1957, the schools in Little Rock were preparing to integrate. I was entering the eleventh grade. There were a lot of meetings and much discussion at the schools and with Mrs. Daisy Bates as to how to best achieve this goal. A number of students signed up to go to Central but dropped off the list for various reasons, mostly economic. Some parents had been threatened that their jobs were in jeopardy. Jefferson Thomas's father lost his job at International Harvester. My father lost a part-time job. He worked for the Veterans Administration full time. He continued in that position until he retired. My parents and I discussed the possibility of job loss. It was decided that I would attend Central High School. The students and their parents who decided to attend Central High School met with Mrs. Bates many times to discuss strategy for arrival and departure from the school.

The nine of us were unable to attend the first day because of the large angry mob of local white residents. Elizabeth Eckford was caught up in the mob because she traveled alone that morning to Central. The rest of us had met at Mrs. Bates' home and traveled in a group.

Orville Faubus, governor at the time, ordered the National Guard to the school to prevent any black students from entering the building. To counter this, President Dwight Eisenhower ordered the 101st Army Division from Ft. Campbell, Kentucky to escort and to protect us in the school. Each of us had an assigned serviceman who would escort us to class and stand outside until class was over. The nine students were Earnest Green, Melba Patillo, Carlotta Walls, Jefferson Thomas, Terrance Roberts, Minnie Jean Brown, Elizabeth Eckford, Gloria Ray, and myself.

I got through the year relatively unscathed. Someone threw rocks at my parent's car and broke a window. There were many late-night calls to my home with name calling and threats. Throughout the ordeal, Mrs. Bates and our parents kept us focused on our education and our right to attend Central High School.

The following summer Governor Faubus ordered all schools in Pulaski County to be closed for the 1958-1959 school year. Some students were forced to lose a year of schooling because they had no family or connections outside of Pulaski County. Private schools were opened to accommodate the white students. My brother, Gilbert, went to Texas to live with our mother's sister, Carrie Fudgen, and her family.

I took correspondence courses from Philander Smith College in Little Rock, Arkansas and Hadley Tech in St Louis. I was hosted in St. Louis by Mr. and Mrs. Shelby Freeman. I received my diploma from Central High School in 1959 by US mail.

# Who Cares...

## *Why is educational history important?*

Attending Central High School during the time of integration was hard. At times it was more than scary, it was potentially life-threatening. All we wanted was the same educational opportunities as white children. It was hard for us to wrap our minds around the fact that there were so many people who didn't want that for us.

All history is important, but I believe educational history is extremely important. Young people need to know that there was a time when it was against the law to even know how to read and that you could be severely whipped if you were caught. Older people need to remember and never forget.

We don't ever want our educational freedoms to be taken from us again because it is education from which most everything else is based. I can't think of one thing we do that doesn't require you to know how to read.

You have probably heard the joke (that isn't funny) that if you want to hide anything from black people, put it in a book. That joke (again, not funny) speaks to the reputation we have of no longer placing value on our education. People fought and died for our educational rights, and I personally don't ever want us to forget how important the fight was.

I still care.

Don't you?

## Biography

Thelma Mothershed-Wair was accepted for an undergraduate study at Southern Illinois University in Carbondale, Illinois. She needed one more credit to qualify as a freshman; this was completed at University High School. Her classmate at SIU was Minnie Jean Brown.

In 1964, She graduated with a Bachelor of Science in Home Economics Education. She returned to Arkansas that year to seek employment in the school system. Unfortunately, she was not able to find employment easily. So, she attended Capital City Business College to expand her skills while waiting for interviews.

In the summer of 1964, a fellow classmate and graduate of SIU visited Little Rock and asked her to marry him. He was what she wanted – a man with an education like her father. They were married December 26, 1965 and returned to his hometown, East St. Louis, IL to make their home. Fred, her husband, taught science at Clark Jr. High School. She got a position teaching clothing and textiles at Rock Junior High.

Her supervisor, James Earl Little, wrote a program called Career Planning for Elementary Students. This was approved by the State of Illinois. The program called for a person with a teaching background and a degree in counselor education. Mr. Little asked her to take the position called Elementary Career Education Counselor. She accepted the position, taught home economics for 10 years, and counseled for 18 years.

In 1996, the State Education Department realized that many educators were seeking employment but had few openings. They devised a plan called "5&5". Five years could be added to your age or years of service. She was credited with 33 years of service and retired that year.

After her retirement, she didn't settle down. Instead, she began to work part-time at the Red Cross teaching life skills to homeless women.

She returned to Arkansas in 2003 because of her diagnosis of Multiple Sclerosis. The stiffening of her muscles caused a serious change in what she was capable of doing; she needed some assistance with activities and daily living. Thelma's sisters assisted her until she needed more help. Currently, she has a home health aide on a daily basis.

Thelma's husband, Fred, died in 2004 after a long struggle with dementia.

The couple's son, Scott, lives in Plainfield, IL and is employed in the technology industry. Thelma and Fred were blessed with a loving daughter-in-law, Valerie. Scott and Valerie have two sons, Brennan Dallas Wair, who graduated in 2017 from Marquette University, and Gabriel Scott Wait, who is a freshman at the University of Illinois, majoring in Criminal Justice (Gabriel also has a passion for baseball and is very good at the sport).

Thelma continues to live in Little Rock with her family.

"I am no longer ambulatory and therefore require assistance. My Multiple Sclerosis progresses slowly," she asserts. "Even with this, Life is good."

## Accolades

- ∂ Honorary Doctorate in Humane Letters, 2016
- ∂ NAACP recognition
- ∂ The Spingarn Medal
- ∂ Congressional Gold Medal, President William Clinton
- ∂ Many awards and plaques from schools and civic organizations
- ∂ Greek Organizations Recognition: Alpha Kappa Alpha, Alpha Phi Alpha, Delta Sigma Theta, Zeta Phi Beta, and Kappa Alpha Psi. Alpha Kappa Alpha

# I Can Only Imagine

*MercyMe (1999)*

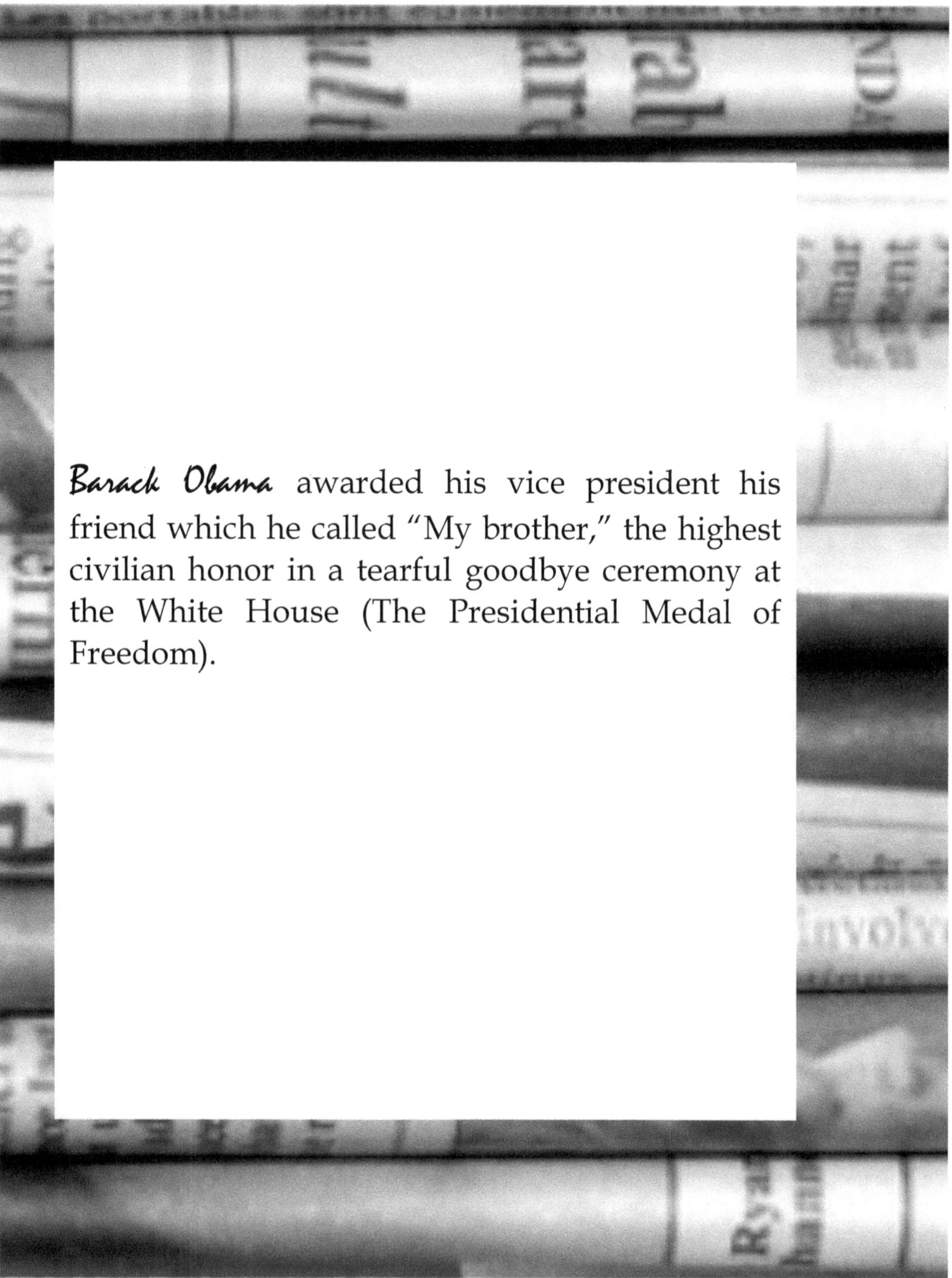

*Barack Obama* awarded his vice president his friend which he called “My brother,” the highest civilian honor in a tearful goodbye ceremony at the White House (The Presidential Medal of Freedom).

# Chapter 7 Politics

## Lottie Shackelford

First Female Mayor of the City of Little Rock

## Similarities ...

### A Change Has Come

The significance of being the "first" isn't always about being the best, and it isn't always about achieving before anyone else. In my circumstance, the importance of being the "first" came from a deeper understanding that we have no time to wait for anyone but ourselves. As I reflect on my legacy as the first woman mayor of Little Rock, Arkansas, I begin to find the simple connections between it and President Obama's legacy as the first African-American president of the United States. These simple connections come from a shared belief.

President Barack Obama said, "Change will not come if we wait for some other person or some other time. We are the ones we've been waiting for. We are the change that we seek."

There is never too small of a difference or a change to be made, and if no one begins to advocate for it, then the change will never happen. My career as an advocate began as a member of the PTA, President Obama's career as a politician began as a church-based community organizer. Both roles and organizations could be considered minuscule when contemplating the issues that needed to be impacted; however, my community needed change and who else but me? That attitude is the similarity that I clearly see in reflecting on my journey and the legacy of our former president as one of the voices in our communities. As a member of the PTA, I vividly remember going to City Hall constantly championing for various causes. In the same way, President Obama was instrumental in creating vital programs in his community. We both became the change we wanted to see, and becoming this change allowed us both, without our knowledge, to begin laying the framework of an even greater legacy that would continue to affect so many.

As your work continues to grow, often, so does your impact. I grew from the PTA to the Little Rock Board of Directors to mayor just as President Obama grew from that community organizer, to state senator, then US senator, and eventually to president. Our work grew, and when your work grows, you must grow with it. I entered the 'real world' of politicking and all of the experiences that come with it. I learned how to continue to be the voice of change even in environments that were unfamiliar or even at times hostile. This is where the significance of being the 'first' once again appears in a way that has nothing to do with being the best. As the first female mayor, I had to learn how to ensure my voice was heard in the way I needed it to be. I had to continue being the change I wished to see with no outline for how it was done; much in the same way, President Obama learned what it meant to govern with the caveat of being the first black president of the United States. There were no other women I could seek counsel from who knew exactly how I felt during that time, just as there were no other men who knew exactly what it meant to be a black man in the Oval office. Being the first is not only being the change you need to see, but it is also becoming a blueprint that needs to be created.

I have officially retired from politics and seeing as President Obama has successfully completed two terms at the highest office in the land, the last parallel that I can confidently draw between our former president and myself is that the work and the *change*, never stops. We never stop. I live and operate in a space where I am keenly aware that I rest on the shoulders of the many people who were also qualified for the many opportunities that have been afforded me. I never stop my work because it is my job to help as many people as I can before I am done.

It reminds me of the foundation, *My Brother's Keeper*, which President Obama left as a part of his legacy, "That's what 'My Brother's Keeper' is all about, helping more of our young people stay on track, providing the support. They need to think more broadly about their future, building on what works when it works, in those critical life-changing moments."

I said earlier that being the first was about more than being the best. The most important connection, the most important take-a-way, is that while President Obama and I both share the legacy of being 'first.' The work that we continue to do will ensure that neither of us will be the 'only.'

# Who Cares ...

## *Why is political history important?*

Our youth should know their history; everyone should know their history. Knowing your history is essential to knowing who you are and where you are. Maya Angelou once said, "The more you know of your history, the more liberated you are." The act of knowing is so much more than the memorization of facts and information. To know something requires that you understand it; the why and the how behind the facts and the context gives you a true understanding. When our young people consider the importance of history, the past, and its impact on the present and the future, it becomes evident that it is not enough to acknowledge that something has happened. They must ask questions, seek answers, and make the connections needed to fully understand why certain events happened the way they did, or why certain events have helped to shape today's thinking – the minuses and the pluses. Maybe it's wondering whose shoulders you are now standing on or whose footprints you are walking in and how your actions can influence those who follow.

This then begs the question of, what's the point? Why should I care about knowing my history in this very demanding and thorough manner? My earlier reference to Maya Angelou is one that begins to touch on the rationale behind history's influence and impact. There is a feeling of liberation and freedom that you experience when you have that knowledge of – I know why! While history is often rough and difficult to embrace, the empowerment and sense of pride you feel from that knowledge is so rewarding. You begin to really feel that you, too, are IMPORTANT.

If you are aware of why circumstances are as they are, you can better problem solve with solutions that will have your desired effect. Knowing your history also translates into taking the time to explore where we have been, what got us there, and what were the implications of our being there. Knowing your history gives you the opportunity to improve your circumstances.

History is truly the telling of his-story and her-story, so it's very important that young people know if what they are hearing is the truth or an untruth. Knowing one's history enables one to grow and learn from the past while trying to determine a path for the future. History is a great tool, and every young person should want to have that tool in their toolbox for reflection and projection. It's also a great comforter because when you know how and why something happened, your confidence is boosted.

Knowing your history gives you the power of insight in a way that would otherwise be impossible. The liberation of which Maya spoke comes from that power. We cannot control what happened in this world nor much of what happens now, but by knowing the history, we learn a timeless lesson – life is filled with both tragedy and triumph; the more we learn, the better our humanity and survival.

## Biography

*Photo 1 PHOTOGRAPH BY ASHLEE NOBEL*

Lottie Shackelford began her career as an advocate when she became a member of the PTA. "We were constantly going down to City Hall championing one cause or another," she said smiling. "We called it 'Playing Captain, May I?'"

Her role evolved but didn't begin there. Shackelford's mother, who worked as a home extension agent, called her a joiner because she was active in so many organizations and extracurricular activities as a youth. Shackelford fondly remembers family discussions.

"During that era, you didn't think in terms of career choices; the emphasis was on being prepared. Her parents instilled in their children the need to get an education. Education, particularly in the African-American community, was the overall equalizer. It was discussions about education, helping others, life lessons, and realizing our potential that my parents shared around the dinner table."

Shackelford's father was a chef on a railroad and later a commercial truck driver, who wanted his children to excel and to take advantage of every opportunity. "He used to say, 'I want you to come home brain-tired, not body-tired.'" So, it was understood that she and her siblings would attend college.

While Shackelford attended classes at Philander Smith College, she did not immediately obtain her degree. She got married and had three children; her father became ill, and she helped her mother care for him, delaying her pursuit of higher education. "But I promised myself, I'd go back," she said, "and when my oldest child was a senior in high school, I knew I couldn't let my children finish college before me." She went that day and registered for classes. She earned a Bachelors in Business Administration from Philander while juggling her many responsibilities and pursuing her interest in the political arena.

In 1974, Shackelford unsuccessfully ran for the Little Rock Board of Directors. "I didn't win, but I learned a lot. I remained interested and continued to be active in the community. I also enrolled in the Arkansas Institute of Politics at Hendrix College," she said.

In 1978, she was appointed to the Little Rock Board of Directors; she was later elected and re-elected to the board, whose members served at large, three times.

"As a board member, one of the biggest issues we addressed was cable TV. The process was one of my first experiences with the 'real world.' There was a lot of money involved, and as a representative for the city, it was my job to extract as many benefits as possible for its citizens. We really had to seek out information, use resources, and come together as a group to ensure success. It's important to be sure that when you cast a vote, you can sleep at night, knowing you did your best," Shackelford said.

Her dedication to Little Rock and its residents paid off. In 1987, Shackelford became the capital city's first elected female mayor. This distinction earned national attention, Shackelford feels, partially due to 1957's integration crisis. "Many times, I was called to do things that previous mayors had not ... presentations and speaking engagements ... [my years in office] were a very rewarding experience."

During her tenure, Shackelford presented papers on local government, economic and electoral issues, and served on the National League of Cities. Her ability to advocate, to motivate, to organize, and to garner support was well known.

In 1992, Shackelford's areas of expertise were again recognized; she served as the deputy campaign manager for the Clinton/Gore presidential campaign, a role, she said that encompassed much more than the general public realizes.

"While my role was to help build upon relationships I'd built in the past, I also helped solicit support on a national level and helped local/state people access the federal government through local offices," she said. She was later appointed to the office of co-director of intergovernmental affairs for the Clinton Transition Team.

She became another "first" in 1993 when she was appointed to the Overseas Private Investment Corporation (OPIC). She was the first African-American to serve in this capacity. When she departed in 2003, her "valuable counsel and guidance" to the OPIC and its objectives were well noted by her colleagues.

"The ten years I served on OPIC were a real opportunity. Our mission was to encourage businesses based in the United States, to invest in developing countries, and to help minimize the risks of those investments. I traveled to Europe, Asia, and countries in South Africa. It was one of the most fascinating times of my life," she said.

She reflects on the victories and disappointments in her stellar career. One of the biggest disappointments was losing the Little Rock mayoral race in 1974. "It was major. I was not accustomed to losing," she said, laughing. "That loss helped me realize the importance of helping others who are seeking election. Running for public office is a good lesson in humility — one that I've carried to this day."

One of her greatest challenges has been personal, the loss of family members. "While I've served [politically], I've lost my father, brother, sisters, and my mother. Each day the Lord has given me is a victory. Each measure of success society has given me has been a reminder that I have work to do to earn my place here on earth."

Shackelford has no problem disclosing her age. "I'm thankful and appreciative of every year," and though she has officially retired, she is still very busy. She took her granddaughter, one of six grandchildren, to Washington, D.C., to attend a Christmas party at the White House. She's a member of Links, Inc., and of

Delta Sigma Theta Sorority in which she has served as a member of the National Social Action Committee. The sorority has recognized Shackelford's many accomplishments with the Delta Sigma Theta Sorority Trailblazer and Mary Church Terrell Awards.

"I still dabble in politics ... I like to help others," Shackelford said. "I rest on the shoulders of the many people who were also qualified for the many opportunities that have been afforded me."

## Accolades

- Political Traveler
  - Her travels also involved politic forums in other countries including Russia, West Germany, and Taiwan. "I also participated in a lecture tour for women to encourage them to pursue political careers."
- Democratic Delegate
  - In 1980, she served a term as a delegate, a role she skillfully performed for an additional six Democratic National Conventions.
- Vice Chair of the Democratic National Committee
  - In 1989, she was elected vice chair of the Democratic National Committee. She was the first African-American woman to be elected to a national party office and was re-elected every four years until 2009.
- Global USA, Inc Lobbyist
- Board of Directors
  - Medicis Pharmaceutical Cooperation, Phoenix
  - Civic Organizations member
    - Urban League
    - National Association for the Advancement of Colored People

# Aint No Stopping Us Now

*McFadden and Whitehead (1979)*

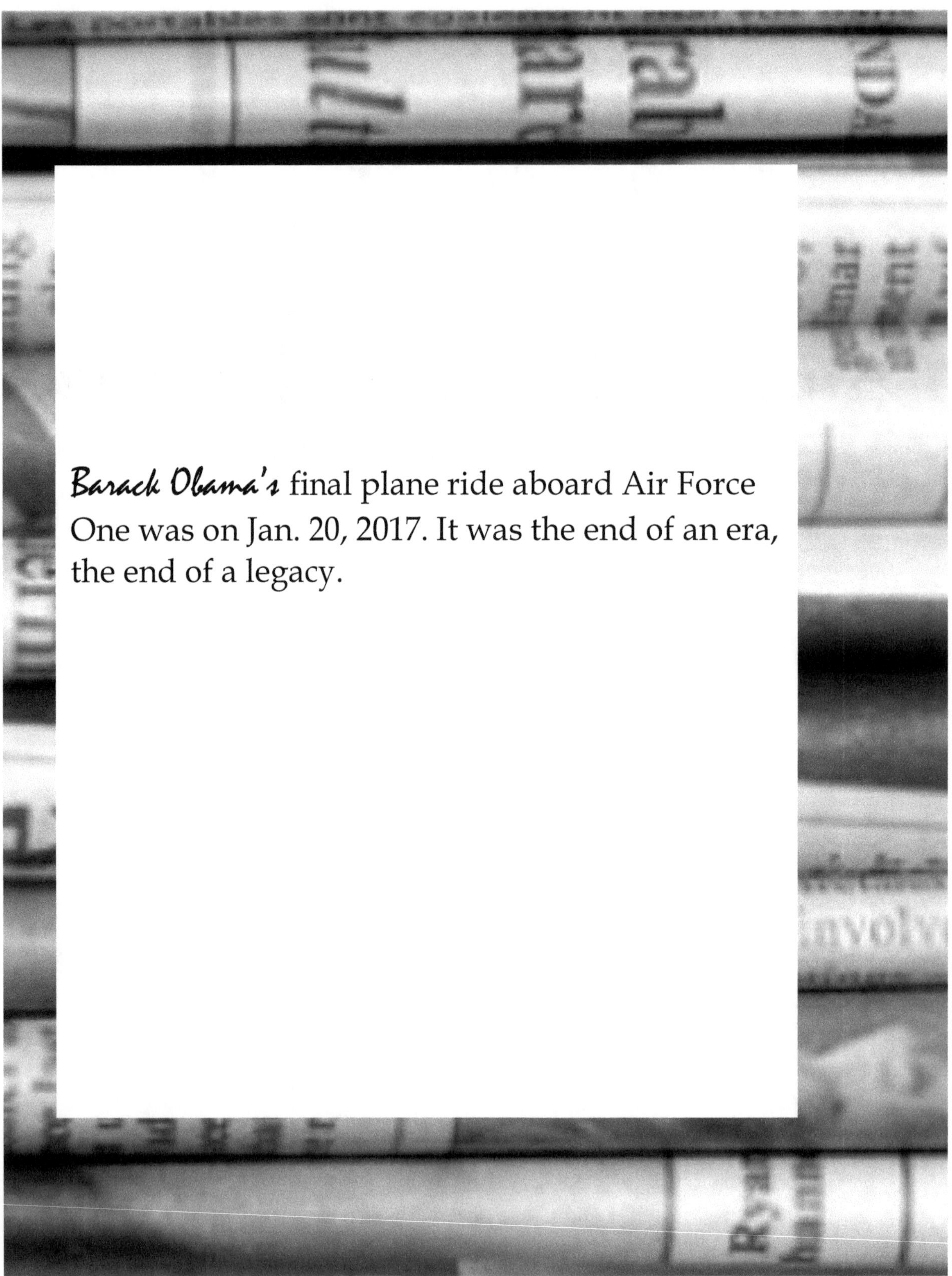

*Barack Obama's* final plane ride aboard Air Force One was on Jan. 20, 2017. It was the end of an era, the end of a legacy.

# Chapter 8 Legalities

## Judge Joyce Elise Williams Warren

First African-American Juvenile Judge in Arkansas

## Similarities …

### A Host of Firsts

When Barack Obama was elected president of the United States, he became its first Black Commander-in-Chief. At the time of his election, I had already experienced a handful of "firsts."

I was an accidental pioneer. After attending Gibbs Elementary School in Little Rock, my first "first" came when, at the age of 11, I became one of the first ten black students to integrate Westside Junior High School in 1961. When that opportunity arose, my mother and grandmother thought I should seize it. Years later, my grandmother told me that someone had said they thought it would be too dangerous for me to participate in the school desegregation effort. My great-grandmother responded, "Joyce will be fine." She was right!

I remember the first day of school. I rode with some friends. We were driven by the father of one of the two classmates who lived next door to each other. Once we were inside the school, I remember pacing up and down the hall, too scared to go into my homeroom. I mean, I was *terrified*! But then, my homeroom teacher, Donald Bratton, came out to greet me. "Come on in," he said. He turned out to be my Latin teacher-and one of the nicest teachers I had.

The mistreatment came quickly. We were called the N-word, spat on, kicked, and otherwise tormented. Two of my black male classmates, Kenneth Jones and Alvin Terry, fought some white boys all the time. They'd then be suspended and sent home. I wondered, "How in the world did they stay in school?"

One day, a white boy tried to trip me as we were going to an assembly. This was not like me at all – I took my fist and hit him in his back as he went past me. I thought, "Oh my God," just knowing that I would get into trouble. But he didn't do anything, and I didn't get in any trouble.

Through it all, I kept in mind that I was as good as anybody else and that education was too important to let racism discourage me from obtaining my education.

I remember breaking my leg in the seventh grade when I slipped on some ice on the sidewalk in January of that year. My mother and grandmother didn't want me in school on crutches because they feared somebody would knock me down the steps. Fortunately, I had a homebound teacher the rest of that semester.

From Westside, I headed to Little Rock Central High School, which had made world history in 1957 when it was desegregated by the Little Rock Nine.

I arrived there in 1964 and graduated in 1967.

While in high school, I wanted to be a dentist. I don't like needles; I don't like blood – but I wanted to be a dentist. Isn't that strange? But that's what I aspired to be. After high school, I spent a year and a half at Rockford College in Rockford, Illinois with my goal in mind. I remember taking organic chemistry. I had three weeks to decide whether to keep the class or to drop it. The textbook was ominously thick, and I didn't understand a thing in the book.

I said, "Nope, not good," and I dropped the class.

At that point, I had already met my future husband, James Medrick "Butch" Warren. He was virtually the boy next door. Our grandmothers lived a few houses from each other on the same street when we were small children, and we played together on the sidewalks of 33rd Street in the south end of Little Rock. We were friends throughout our childhood, becoming the best of friends in high school. He asked me out on a date to the movies when we were at Central, but we didn't start dating as a couple until August 1968, the end of my summer while I was home from Rockford College. Soon, I returned to Illinois; meanwhile, James headed to Arkansas Tech University in Russellville, Arkansas. At the end of that fall semester, he called me and said "I'm going home and will attend Little Rock University. I decided I wanted to come home too. We both came home, enrolled at Little Rock University, and took sociology and other classes together. I majored in sociology and anthropology, graduating in 1971, from what had then become the University of Arkansas at Little Rock (UALR).

By this time, I had decided I was going to be a social worker. That's what you do with a Sociology degree. But James asked, "Why don't you take the law school admissions test in Memphis?" My grandmother thought it was a great idea.

I said "OK." I had no problem going to law school, but I had no desire to practice law. I didn't want to go into the courtroom; I just thought it would be terrifying.

I started law school in August of 1971.

James and I married in 1972. James graduated from UALR in 1972 and started law school in the fall of that year. After our first two sons were born, however, James decided to go to work, in management, for the telephone company to support our family. I continued my studies, attending law school at night and graduating in five years.

James, who had been my encourager, became my career cheerleader. It was he who informed me that I was the first black female to graduate from what is now the University of Arkansas at Little Rock Bowen School of Law. I had no clue that this was another "first." All I had in my mind at the time was being a good wife, mom, and law student--hoping to get a law degree.

After I graduated from law school in 1976, James encouraged me to apply for a job as a law clerk. I did so and got a job with Arkansas Supreme Court Associate Justice Darrell Hickman. I didn't realize that I had become the first black law clerk for the Arkansas Supreme Court.

From there, I went on to serve as an Arkansas Assistant Attorney General. My boss was the young Attorney General Bill Clinton, who would later become the country's 42nd president. When he was elected Arkansas' governor in 1978, I served as one of his administrative assistants and a liaison to the state Health Department and several state boards and commissions.

Governor Clinton then sent me to the state Health Department, where I served as a legal counsel from November 1979 to February 1981. But that job was eliminated when the state legislature decided that all state-agency lawyers needed to be part of the attorney general's office. I then decided to practice law from my home.

I subsequently got a job as a staff attorney with Central Arkansas Legal Services.

After James learned the then current Pulaski County juvenile judge was leaving, he told me I needed to apply for that position. I went, "What?" And I pretty much fought him every step of the way, thinking I couldn't do it. But my husband assured me that I was the perfect candidate. As always, I heeded his advice and applied.

Soon afterward, James and I were getting ready to leave for vacation in San Francisco. We were literally walking out of the door when the telephone rang. I answered, and it was someone from the office of Don Venhaus, Pulaski County Judge at the time. The caller told me, "We want to interview you for the juvenile judgeship. Can you come Monday?" We cut our trip short, so I could be back in time. We arrived in Little Rock at 2 p.m. Monday; the interview was at 4 p.m.

I was the last interviewee. I got the job!

Although President Obama was relatively young – 47 – when he was voted into the Oval Office in 2008, I was only 33 when, in January 1983, I became the juvenile judge for Pulaski County, Arkansas. Again, I had no clue that I had achieved another pair of "firsts." I was not only the first black female juvenile judge in the state, I was the first black female judge in Arkansas - period!

In 1987, the Arkansas Supreme Court declared it was unconstitutional for the juvenile court system to be under county jurisdiction. Governor Clinton appointed me to the Arkansas Juvenile Justice Commission to make recommendations about how the new juvenile court system would be structured under the state jurisdiction and how many judges would be needed. This was about an 18-month process.

After a few months on the Commission, it dawned on me that the new, state-level judgeship would entail the same duties I had performed in my judgeship for the county, so I decided to apply for one of the positions. I called Clinton and told him I wanted to be appointed. He appointed me to one of the 17 juvenile judgeships created by the state. On August 1, 1979, I became a Circuit-Chancery Judge, Seventh Division, for the Sixth Judicial District, which encompasses Pulaski and Perry Counties. Those judgeships were appointed because they were part of a brand-new system for juvenile court.

The Juvenile Justice Commission had recommended three judges for Pulaski and Perry counties, but the state legislature had created only one – the position I filled.

In October of 1989, the lawmakers voted to create another spot, an elected position. They sent the bill to Governor Clinton to sign into law. Had they not created that second spot, my judicial role in juvenile court would have ended at least for that time. To my knowledge, Arkansas is the only place in the entire world where you can't run for the same position for which you've previously been appointed. My term as an appointed state juvenile judge was supposed to end in December 1990, so I decided to act quickly. Governor Clinton and I were at a program at the former Camelot Inn Hotel in downtown Little Rock. It was a Friday evening. I was onstage when Governor Clinton joined me onstage. I whispered in his ear, mentioning my knowledge of the piece of legislation creating the new judgeship. I asked Clinton if he was going to sign the bill into law. He said, "Yes."

Justice Hickman, the state Supreme Court Justice for whom I had clerked, had once told me that if I ever decided to run for office, I needed to get my name out there first. On Sunday – two days after Clinton confirmed to me that he would sign the bill and before he actually signed the bill – I announced that I was running for that judgeship. I was elected--without any opponent!

Without realizing it, I became the first black person elected to a trial court judgeship at the state level. Thank God, I have never had an opponent the many times I have run for re-election.

Currently, my position is 10th Division Circuit Judge in the Sixth Judicial District, which still includes Pulaski and Perry Counties. As of April 2017, I've been on the bench about 33 years, nearly 28 of those years for the state.

Other "firsts" came.

I was the first black female appointee and the first black chairperson of the Arkansas Board of Law Examiners, to which the state Supreme Court had appointed me. I served a pair of three-year terms, plus an additional year. I was also the first black female chairperson of the Arkansas Judicial Discipline and Disability Commission. In October 2010, I became the first black president of the Arkansas Judicial Council, which consists of all the judges of the circuit court and Court of Appeals, justices of the Arkansas Supreme Court, retired judges and justices, and director of the Administrative Office of the Courts. I must say, once again, I had no clue I was blazing these trails. It was always my husband who made me aware of these "firsts." James would contact the appropriate sources to verify that my "firsts" were indeed, "firsts."

For someone who wanted to be a dentist and was terrified by the thought of being in a courtroom, I have found this to be my passion. I cannot think of anything else I'd rather do, and I'm truly blessed to do it. I am blessed to be a public servant. When I first told people I was going to law school, some would say, "You're too timid. You can't be a lawyer." I *was* timid--I did not have the confidence to step beyond my comfort zone. James gave me the confidence and support to do what I needed to accomplish my goals. He was surely sent to me by God.

As a judge, I have jurisdiction over children from birth to 21 and when children are under court jurisdiction. I have jurisdiction of their parents, guardians, and custodians. I decide cases involving delinquency, truancy, families in need of services, abuse and neglect, termination of parental rights, adoption, and guardianship. I also hear paternity cases. As part of my job responsibilities, I must hold people accountable for their actions.

I start by telling people, "We are all human. We all make mistakes, and we hope every day that we're trying to be better people, step by step." Let's say I'm presiding over a dependency and neglect case. I'll tell the parents something like this:

"Mom and Dad, you've made some bad mistakes. Mom, you've used drugs while you were pregnant with your child, and now your child's in state's custody--but we have a plan. Dad, you used drugs too. The plan is for you to get your child back, but you're going to have to do this, this, and this. You've only got a certain amount of time to do it."

And we look at it from the kid's eyes. I'm believing you can do it. Why? Because I believe people are capable of change. If we don't think people are capable of change, what are we doing, especially in the helping profession? If you just write people off and say they can never change, that's just a disservice. So, I tell those parents, "You *can* do it – but you've got to be *willing* to do it, and you've got to *want* to do it."

When I must terminate someone's parental rights, I am sympathetic and respectful. I tell the parent I couldn't imagine being in their spot. When parents are obeying court orders and improving as parents, I also let them know when they do a good job. I also let them know the child's best interest, the need for permanency, and the necessity of a fit parent.

Now, there's always something that, thinking back, I wish I'd done differently. When I was a county juvenile judge, I remember a teen mom who came to court for a custody case. Her mother was with her. While the teen mom was talking, her mother tried to interject. I said, "Hold on. You're not really a part of this case. You are her mother, and I appreciate that, but this is her case, so you can't be talking for her. She's talking now." The teen mom's mother started to protest. I said, "I'm not trying to be funny, but *she's* the one who had sex with the baby's father. She saw something in him, and they got together, so you're not in this."

The teen mom's mother said, "You don't understand. He *raped* her."

I thought, "Oh my God. She got pregnant as the result of a rape." I said, "I am so sorry." I determined that I would never put my foot in my mouth like that again.

Then, I made a vow to never assume anything, whether in or out of the courtroom.

Surprisingly, I didn't experience much racial discrimination on the career trail I blazed, although, I sometimes *did* have to prove myself as both a black person and a woman. I recall one instance when I was an assistant attorney general and I had to go to federal court in Texarkana for a habeas corpus case. There I was sitting in the courtroom, nervous as I could be, waiting for the hearing to start. When the judge came in, he looked around and asked, "Where is the assistant attorney general?" I responded, respectfully, "Here I am, your honor." Then, there are those times when you're the sitting judge in the courtroom, and you have white folks coming in, and it is very obvious that they don't like black folks. You can just tell by their demeanor and attitude. I'm thinking, "Here I am, sitting up here. I'm going to be honest, and you are just going to have to deal with me. I'm going to treat you fairly and justly."

But the biggest doubts about my ability came from me. I remember being worried during law school that I was going to flunk this or that test. But my supportive husband was always there to encourage me. He had confidence in me. I remember him once giving me a motivational gift – a special medicine bottle that he had a pharmacist friend make up for me that was marked "Preparation C" for Confidence.

By the way, I still have that precious bottle.

# Who Cares ...

## *Why the law is important to history?*

The teachers in my family took care of the whole child. So, I try to maintain a holistic approach in my courtroom. Communication is essential, especially in juvenile court. When a juvenile alleged to be a delinquent appears before me with an attorney and admits to the charge(s), I explain the entire process before I accept the admission. I tell the juvenile what the law authorizes the court to order. If I accept the juvenile's admission, then, I ask the juvenile why he or she broke the law.

Let me recreate a typical conversation:

Start by asking, "Why did you break into the lady's house?"

"I don't know," says the juvenile.

"It's been six months and you don't know why? Have you thought about it at all?"

"No."

"Tell me why. Think about it now. If you don't have a reason, tell me you don't know why –then I'll thank you for telling the truth. But surely you've thought about it."

"Well ... my friend told me to do it."

"How old are you?"

"Sixteen."

"How old was your friend?"

"Fifteen."

"So, you've got a friend who's 15; you're 16. You've got a mom and a dad who's trying to tell you what to do, but you didn't listen to them. You listened to your friend who is younger than you are! Does that make sense?"

That's when the juvenile says, "I just guess I was trying to fit in," or "I'm bored."

To the latter I'll usually reply, "If you're bored, here's what you need to do. Go to the library and read a book. Write. Do some puzzles. Watch TV. Play basketball. Do some homework. Do some chores."

As parents and adults, it's our responsibility to take care of children. It's a societal responsibility. Children need to be taught. Children are to be molded. That's what I love about the juvenile division of circuit court. This is our chance to do the most we can do, as early as we can do it, to keep wayward children from continuing down the wrong path. I think it's important for people to know that raising a child is a collective effort. I often remark, in court, that being a juvenile division judge is like being a parent; you try to figure out what works, and if it doesn't work, you regroup and try something else.

I love what I do! I like to talk to the kids. I tell them, "I'm as nice as I can be, and I'm just as patient as I can be. But if you keep leaving home without permission and staying out all night long, and your mother comes in and fills out that affidavit for a pickup order for you, I'm going to grant her request." I don't like to lock kids up, but sometimes I must do so to protect the kid or somebody else. When a child is carrying a gun and shooting up in the air or at someone or breaking into someone's car or house, lockup may be necessary.

I will tell a young person, "You're 16. You're of average intelligence. Now, your prefrontal cortex has not developed well, and I understand that. But you still know right from wrong. So, when your mother said don't leave the house after 8 o'clock, and you sneaked out at 3 in the morning, you *knew* that was wrong. You put yourself at risk of harm."

Then, I tell parents this, "Sometimes it's easier for me to say no than it is for you, and *somebody* has to say no sometimes."

I'm empathetic with those who come into the courtroom over which I preside. I share their concerns. I laugh with them. I cry at adoptions, and sometimes, I've cried at termination hearings. Most people know that I genuinely care about them. I say, "Now, I love you as a person – period – and I'm going to do what I can legally to make sure you get all the things that you need." If I make a mistake, I'll be the first one to say so. Then, I apologize.

The bottom line is, I love what I do, although it wears me out, physically, mentally, and emotionally. The most exhausting cases are the dependency-neglect cases. Some involve babies who have broken bones or babies born with drugs in their systems. It just breaks my heart just as it breaks my heart when I see kids continuing to do wrong. Even worse, I've had kids who have been killed.

I'll come to court and someone will ask, "Did you see in the paper last week?"

I'll say, "No, I didn't."

"Well, we have to close out his case because he's dead at 15." It's just terrible!

Even though children are the responsibility of all adults, we adults must have our act together too. I once spoke at a Christian Alliance for Orphans (CAFD) Conference in Nashville, Tennessee. There were about 2,500 people at the conference, and they came from different parts of the world. I had five minutes to speak. Over the years, I had taken the proverb "It takes a village to raise a child, but it takes a competent village-not a village of idiots. We are not a village of idiots." Everybody's got a part to play like a puzzle. I have to do my part, the kids have to do their part, the parents have to do their part, schools have to do their part, agencies have to do their part, and other entities in the community have to do their part.

Just as President Obama caused many black children, especially boys, to realize they could grow up and become president, I have caused many black children, especially girls, to realize they could grow up and become a judge. I like to go to schools and organizations to talk to and about kids.

In the courtroom I ask kids, "What do you want to do when you grow up? Do you want to finish school?"

I tell them, "Education is important. You're in the eighth grade now, and you've missed several weeks of school. You want to be a lawyer. So, if you're going to graduate from high school, and go on to law school, do you know you've got to get out of the eighth grade?"

The child then says, "I need to go to school."

I respond, "O.K., that's fine. You need to do your homework."

The child may say, "I want to be a dentist--or maybe I want to be an artist."

I say, "Well, why can't you be both?"

"You can be a dentist, and you can do art on the side, or you can be an artist while you go to dental school. Nothing says you can't do more than one thing, but you must have some education to do it." If a child wants to be a basketball player, I will tell them "That's cool."

But I then ask, "Don't you think it's important to go to school? When they put that contract in front of you, shouldn't you know how to consult a lawyer?"

I tell children that they need to be intelligent about life and its various situations. You want to be able to read, write, and do some math so you can have intelligent conversations with people and get through life. You may need to have a bank account. You're going to have to read signs. You're going to have to read medications, have a driver's license, etc. So, it's important to have an education.

But, you need a life education too. You can't just say you *want* to be so-and-so; you have to work for it.

I tell kids they can do anything in the world except live forever. There are two things males can't do – live forever and give birth.

But beyond that, I tell young people, "You can do it. You just have to be willing to put in the hard work. If you have a dream, go for it – just do the best you can. As my husband, James, says, "You're going to be living anyway, aren't you? So, you may as well be doing something constructive. Just because you have a path doesn't mean it's going to be a straight path. Sometimes, people are forced to interrupt their studies or work a job they dislike. If you have a goal, keep it in mind. But you have to believe in yourself, and you can't let people say you can't do something. Think of all the successful people who wouldn't be where they are today if they listened to naysayers."

I encourage young people to think beyond their limitations and to remember it's never too late to do so. I tell them not to let people control them or define who they are. I tell them not to worry about what people say. If they have a vision or a dream, they should go for it!

I tell them, "If I can do it, anybody can!"

Another thing I tell kids is they don't have to *like* the rules, but they must *obey* them. I remind them that adults must follow rules too. I explain that, even as a judge who issues orders, I, too, have to obey rules, and I don't like some of the rules either. I remind kids that all of us are products of our environment.

I'll tell a teenager, for instance, that he needs to stop saying somebody "made him do" something. I'll say, "You're 17, and life is about choices."

My sixth-grade teacher, Clarence Horn, Sr., who was also a deacon at my church, Mt. Zion Missionary Baptist Church, lectured his students about being observant and responsible. He would say, "Every tub has to sit on its own bottom." In other words, you're responsible for your own actions. I use Mr. Horn's saying quite liberally and quite often.

I also stress the ability to overcome. I've had kids in court who have been raped by their parents and who have been otherwise abused and traumatized, but yet have still made good decisions. I have had kids in court who have had the best in life but made bad decisions. Everybody's different, but it comes to a point where you must take responsibility for your own actions to be a responsible, productive adult.

It is hoped that, with appropriate services, accountability, structure, and direction, I, as a judge, can help young people reach their full potential for greatness.

Just like President Obama, James and I believe in family. James and I have been married 45 years. We have three adult sons: Jonathan, Jamie and Justin. We instilled in them the same respect for education, equality, justice, self and others, high aims, and hard work that were instilled in us by both our families. We spent time with them, helped them with their homework, and went to school events like parent-teacher conferences and after-school activities. We exposed them to education, art, music, and travel. My husband coached them in basketball and baseball and guided each of them through their Cub Scout and Boy Scout years which culminated in each of them reaching the highest rank in Scouting -- Eagle! We invested time, love, hard work, prayers, tears, laughter, and well thought out discipline into our sons. As humans, we are not perfect – especially when it comes to parenting, which is the hardest job of all. But we did our best. Just as President Obama's job put his children in the limelight, my job as a juvenile division judge put my children in the limelight. I have learned this very real and very tough lesson; it is the parent's responsibility to give a child the foundation the child needs. Then, it is up to the child to take that foundation and build on what he wants.

Children need to know that education is important - education that comes from the classroom as well as from life. Children need to be well-rounded – intellectually, emotionally, physically, and socially. It is up to every adult to advocate for the needs of every child; for that child deserves the best we can give.

**Why Youth Should Know Their History: Past, Present, and Future**

I think all history is important, whether it's the history of your family, the history of your race/ethnicity, the history of your country, or the history of your world. Every person has a responsibility to do something that's going to improve the lives of others. If the younger generation doesn't know what happened to the previous generation, that younger generation may not take seriously the opportunities laid out for them.

One thing I like to tell people is that it is our responsibility, as Americans, is to help shape history by voting. In particular, it's important for black Americans to vote. I don't care how tired you are, how much it wears on your nerves to put up with the endless political commercials, the fighting among candidates, and the standing in line at the voting precinct. Remember, people died for the right to vote! They shed blood, sweat, and tears. They spent sleepless nights hoping and dreaming for this right. Some people never got to vote, although it was on their minds and hearts. So, I think we do a disservice to our country and to our heritage if we don't take the time to vote.

It's the same thing with education. Sadly, black people have a long way to catch up, as far as education is concerned. We are still dealing with inequalities in education. Just as with voting, people fought, died, cried, bled, and dreamed to be able to read and write. In the courtroom, I tell kids of all races, "You get to go to school. You get a free education, and you don't even take advantage of it as you should. You're capable of doing more than you're doing. I promise you – once you are grown, you're going to look back and you'll think, 'O.K., I didn't pay as much attention to my education as I should have; I should have done better.' We all go back and reflect on things and think, 'I could have taken this a little more seriously.' You need to do the best you can, and do not take your opportunities for granted. If you do not take full advantage of them, you will regret it."

What's more, we need to make a point of taking care of each other. I often remark that we, as humans, are not meant to be alone. We are people who need connection and interaction. If you're alone on an island, you may enjoy the solitude, but if you develop appendicitis, I doubt you can cut yourself open and take your appendix out. We need each other, period. Everybody has a part to play in this society in which we must live, but we need to be responsible about it. That's where knowing our history and our heritage comes in.

Knowing other people's history is important too. How are we going to get along with somebody when we don't know anything about them? Look at the Native Americans and how they were treated. We all suffer from historical trauma – black people, Native Americans, Jews, Asians, Hispanics, and white people. We are all connected, and we can't escape history.

As philosopher George Santayana put it, "Those who cannot remember the past are condemned to repeat it."

History repeats itself, whether we want it to or not. It's up to us to do what we can to mitigate the repetition of *bad* history. In order to do that, we need to know where we came from and where others came from. We need to recognize our differences, respect our differences, and embrace our differences. Most importantly, we need to keep in mind that we are more alike than unalike. Not only should we know what *we* went through, but history also gives us a mandate to find out what *others* went through, try to *understand* what they went through, and try to make things better for *all*.

We black people, in particular, have a responsibility to know where we came from, what we're doing now, what we need to do, and the good and the bad about it all. Many of us don't want to talk about slavery, but how can we not? It's part of our historic fabric. In addition, we have a responsibility to go beyond the history we are given in school. We must dig down and find those untold stories. Look at the book and Oscar-nominated movie, "*Hidden Figures,*" about the black female scientists who worked for the National Aeronautics and Space Administration.

We didn't have a clue *about "Hidden Figures!"* And how many of us, as black children, knew about black cowboys? There is so much we missed because we were colored right out of the history books!

There is much to learn from our history- good and bad. The bad that happened to us is something we can't change; it's also something about which we should not be ashamed, but we don't want to keep perpetuating it. We have a responsibility to make things better, to lift ourselves up, to try to do the best we can, and to take as many people as possible with us. We must acknowledge the fact that we are all in this together, and we have to learn how to get along. Until all of us -all races- sit down and air out our differences without killing each other, we'll never get anywhere.

My message to youth: Learn your history – all of it. Don't be satisfied with what you're told. Go beyond the schoolbooks to find out your complete history. Then take it, learn from it, and do what you can do to make the world a better place.

## Biography

Judge Joyce Warren was born October 25, 1949, in Pine Bluff, Arkansas, to Albert Lewis Williams, Jr. and Marian Eloise Longley Williams. They were both attending historically Black Arkansas Agricultural, Mechanical and Normal College, now known as the University of Arkansas at Pine Bluff.

As a baby, she went to Little Rock, Arkansas, to live with her maternal grandmother, Ezella Robinson Blount. Her parents divorced when she was 3, and her younger sister, Janice, was not yet 1. They were raised by their mother. Their grandmother was also a major positive influence in Joyce's life.

Joyce comes from a family of educators. Both of her parents went on to be public school teachers. Her grandmother and two maternal aunts were also teachers. All three had master's degrees they earned at Hampton University in Hampton, Virginia. It was the first time three sisters had earned master's degrees at the same time. Joyce's mother obtained her master's degree and studied for a doctorate at the University of Arkansas at Fayetteville but discontinued her studies because she realized she did not want to be in administration. She wanted to stay in the classroom, where she felt she could make the most of her education in early childhood development.

Despite the meager salaries of teachers, especially black teachers, Joyce and her sibling had a wonderful childhood. She says that she saw, up close and personal, how much time and effort their mother and grandmother spent preparing lesson plans, calling their students' parents with any concerns, and delivering food and clothes to students and families in need. They ministered to the *whole* child. This holistic approach to teaching was such a necessary tool – one that has, unfortunately, eroded over time.

Education was important in the family. There was never any question of whether Janice and Joyce would attend college; the only question was *which* college they would attend. In black families, education was and still is, considered essential to success – financially and socially.

Their mother, grandmother, and aunts took great pains to ensure that Janice and Joyce were exposed to everything that would enable them to function successfully in the world. As Joyce was frequently reminded by her Aunt Mildred, who taught home economics at Paul Laurence Dunbar Junior High School in Little Rock, socialization begins at home. The two children were taught good manners, proper English, good penmanship, to look people in the eye when speaking or being spoken to, and to show respect for their elders and persons in positions of authority. They had a village – family, teachers, ministers, Sunday School teachers, and other role models-awesome role models who came in and out of our lives.

Joyce's mother and grandmother always told her that she could be whatever she wanted to be and that she should have lofty goals. Working hard to reach those goals, Joyce was a child who obeyed rules and never wanted to break them.

Joyce was always taught that, while she was no better than anyone else, she was certainly as *good* as anyone else, irrespective of color. Both she and Janice also knew they had to tow the line because, again, she was the child, grandchild, and great-niece of teachers – teachers who were held in high esteem in the black community and even among some white teachers and administrators.

Convinced that God is the reason for her success, Joyce always prays and strives to do her best and to learn from her mistakes. Every day, she asks God for knowledge, wisdom, understanding, and patience. Each day she strives to utilize those attributes, especially patience!

"It helps that I love people," proclaims Warren.

Her overall philosophy is Proverbs 3:5-6: "Trust in the Lord with all thine heart; and lean not unto thine own understanding. In all thy ways acknowledge him, and he shall direct thy paths."

## Accolades

- ∂ Featured in a cover story in the October 15, 1989, edition of *Arkansas Woman*, a publication of the *Arkansas Democrat* newspaper (now the *Arkansas Democrat-Gazette*)
- ∂ Cover story in the *Arkansas Democrat's* April 7, 1991 High Profile section
- ∂ Named Juvenile Judge of the Year, in October 2000, by the Arkansas Coalition for Juvenile Justice.
- ∂ Chosen as one of the top 100 women in Arkansas by *Arkansas Business* magazine (late 1990s)
- ∂ Listed in three editions of *Outstanding Young Women in America*.
- ∂ Named the 2012 National CASA (Court Appointed Special Advocates) 'Judge of the Year'
- ∂ Author of *A Booklet for Parents, Guardians, and Custodians in Child Abuse and Neglect Cases*, (2003) which has been widely distributed in Arkansas and other states and has been translated into Spanish.
- ∂ Featured in the 2008 CNN television special *Black in America – The Black Man*, seen by more than 20 million people.
- ∂ February 2011, Philander Smith College in Little Rock presented me with a Living Legends Award.
- ∂ February 2012, I was chosen as one of the 10 Most Influential Black Arkansans by the *Arkansas Democrat-Gazette.*
- ∂ August 2015, Governor Asa Hutchinson appointed me to the Youth Justice Reform Board.

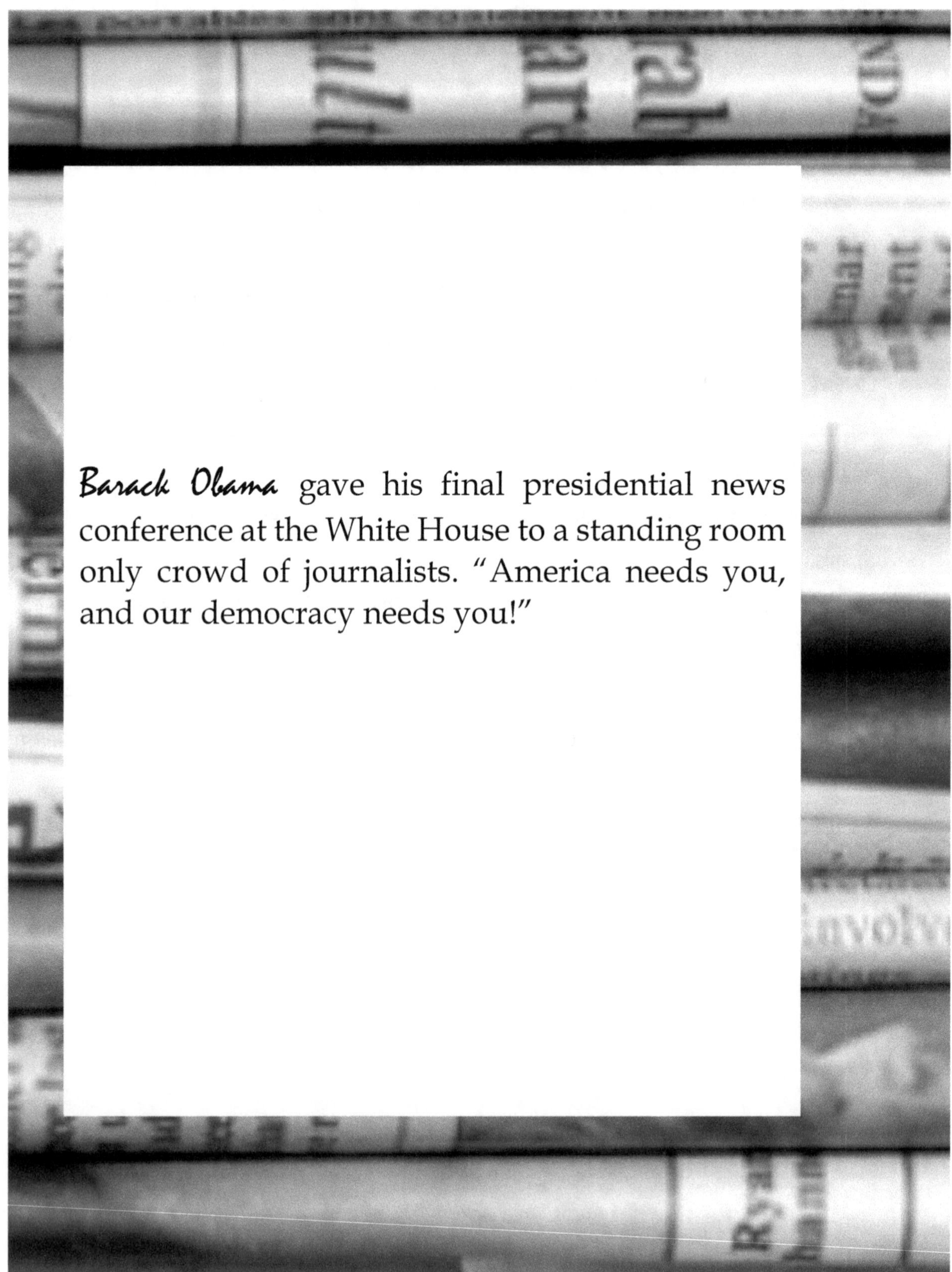

*Barack Obama* gave his final presidential news conference at the White House to a standing room only crowd of journalists. "America needs you, and our democracy needs you!"

# Conclusion

## *Phyllis Hodges*

It's **His**tory. It's **My** story. It's **Our** story.

## Similarities…

### *A Life in Comparison*

The Obama presidency was phenomenal. When it comes to history, no-one will ever forget that on November 4, 2008, we, The United States of America elected our first African-American president, President Barack Obama. It felt as though we belonged; we were somebody… we had arrived.

We had ownership; must I go on…

It was an experience that only a black person could explain. We laughed, cried, danced, and shouted; we were all numb, in a state of shock.

This was real; it was history.

We, the people, had been given hope. We saw someone who looked like us, someone who is intelligent, someone who represents all of us as: a husband, father, son, leader, friend, and a businessman.

I've lived it. I've seen it. I've been a part of it!

I must say as a youth growing up in school, I never read much about it. It wasn't there. "Black History," what was that? Sadness, Fear, Depression, and Death. The only people whom were talked about were Harriet Tubman, Rosa Parks, George Washington Carver, Martin Luther King, maybe Jackie Robinson, and a few others. But even so, the conversations were all so sad; there was nothing that would really lift you up and no one whom you really desired to become because of the many challenges that you would hear about.

There was also no one in those stories who looked like me or shared the same experiences. This is why I feel this book is so important. I want people, our youth, to see themselves in the people who have blazed a trail for them. I want them to know that their lives are no different and that if they can do it, so can you!

I decided to chronicle my life and compare it to the life of Barack Obama. I wanted to see what he was doing with his life during the key times in my life.

What I learned was that he and I had many of the same experiences: education, careers, marriages, and children.

This just proves that each of us have the potential for greatness!

**His timeline. My timeline. Our timeline:**

- 1958
    - Phyllis Marshall was born.
- 1961
    - Barack Obama was born.
- 1970-76
    - Phyllis attended public schools: K-12 grade, Rightsell Elementary School, Paul Laurence Dunbar Junior High School, and graduated from Hall High School
- 1980s-2001
    - Barack Obama graduated from Punahou High School in 1979. He graduated with a bachelor's degree from Columbia in 1983. He entered Harvard Law School in 1988 and graduated with JD in 1991.
- 1974-85
    - Phyllis married husband Byron, and their children, Candince and Bryan, were born.
- 1992
    - Barack married Michelle.
- 1992-95
    - Phyllis received over ten certifications from local and international fitness institutes.
- 1996
    - Barack was elected to Illinois State Senate.
- 1997-2004
    - Phyllis receive degrees and license from universities and seminaries:
        - Agape College
        - Full Counsel School of World Missions and Evangelism
        - Full Counsel Gospel Ministry License
        - Missionary Baptist Seminary
- 1998
    - Barack and Michelle's daughter, Malia, was born.

- ∂ 1999
    - Phyllis was appointed to the Governor's Council on Physical Fitness and Sports.
- ∂ 2000
    - Oct. 15, 2000 was the ribbon cutting and grand opening of the *Carousel Fit 4 Life Wellness Center* as well as the writing of my first book, "A Divine Connection."
- ∂ 2001
    - Barack and Michelle's daughter, Sasha, was born.
- ∂ 2004
    - Barack was elected to the U.S. Senate; he delivers the keynote speech at the Democratic Convention.
- ∂ 2007
    - On February 10th, 2007, Barrack announces his candidacy for president.
- ∂ 2008
    - Barack Obama elected the first African-American president.

# Who Cares ...

## *Why is ALL history important?*

My dad, James Marshall Senior, was a role model for me, along with so many others. He was that good looking, strong, black man who always had money. He was a businessman and an entrepreneur. He knew how to hustle. He owned a BBQ business in which he created his own special BBQ sauce. He created a Christmas tree business; he would spray these trees bright colors and sell them to families.

He was also a bootlegger. *Yes, I said bootlegger.*

Back in the day, it was illegal to sell alcohol on Sundays, but Dad was determined to provide for his family. The first Blue law was from 1837-1982. My father chose to do whatever it took to bring money into the family. Although my dad sold booze, he prided himself on not taking a drink. He also was an investor; he would invest in properties and other people's business.

Dad didn't have any formal business training. He was a self-taught businessman who attended Paul Laurence Dunbar High School. There weren't many role models back then to learn from or to shadow. Dad lived a long life, but, unfortunately, he died in 2007 at the age of 86 and didn't live to see our first African-American president.

The history of my father is my legacy. I watched him, and while I didn't know it then, I was learning how to be an entrepreneur from him. I learned the value of hard work, sacrifice, and not only investing in properties but also investing in people.

History, all history, is important because it can help shape the lives of others. We can all learn from Barack Obama's legacy of hope, inspiration, and change.

Biography

Phyllis Hodges, CFT, LHM has more than 30 years of experience as a fitness and clergy educational trainer. Phyllis had the opportunity to open the *Jim Dailey Fitness Center*, (formally known as the War Memorial Fitness Center) in 1992. She implemented health programs and developed programs at various city facilities in Little Rock (i.e. Paul Laurence Dunbar Community Center, East LR Center, Southwest Community Center, and the Adult Leisure Center).

In addition to these services, she was the director of the first Girls Health & Fitness Summer Camp (Camp iRock) sponsored by the Arkansas Minority Health Commission. This venture brought in yearly celebrities, including Actress Raven Simone and the 1996 Olympic Gold Medal Gymnast Dominique Dawes.

In 2014, Phyllis and her granddaughters were featured in the family section of the *Arkansas Democrat-Gazette*.

On February 11, 2016, Byron and Phyllis were featured on KARK Arkansas Today Show for their 43rd anniversary.

On February 14, 2016, Phyllis and her husband were featured in the *Arkansas Democrat-Gazette* celebrating a unique beginning.

In 2017 Phyllis served as a guest writer on health and fitness for *Arkansas Talks* newspaper.

She is the Fitness Specialist for Good Shepherd Senior Center, Parkstone Place Retirement Center, Fox Ridge Retirement Center, The Manor Assisted Living Community, and Robinson Nursing and Rehabilitation Center.

Phyllis attended Missionary Baptist Seminary, Agape College (formally Agape School of World Evangelism), and Full Counsel School of Ministry. As a minister, Phyllis is committed to serving. As a certified licensed professional trainer and clergy, she owns the only faith-based health and wellness center in the state of Arkansas, the Carousel Fit-4-Life Wellness Center. Her vision is shaping up the world spiritually, mentally, physically and financially.

## Accolades

- Certification in International Fitness
- National License Personal Training
- Certified Fitness Arthritis Instructor
- Certified Exercise Safety
- Certified National Dance
- Certified International Sports Science
- Certified Instructor "Get Healthy Stay Balanced (Nutrition)"
- Marathon runner since 2008
- Author of "A Divine Connection" (working on a Wellness DVD)
- Community Involvement:
- Board of Directors and Advisors consists of medical doctors, business professionals, and community leaders. Her involvement and connection with various boards and commissions (past and present) include: Little Rock Racial Culture Diversity Commission, the Governor's Council on Physical Fitness, Baptist Health Medical Center Advisory Board, and Main Street Argenta Advisory Board.
- Starting in October 2001, until now, each October 15th is proclaimed Phyllis Hodges Carousel Day by the Governor of Arkansas.
- As of 2001, proclamations from local mayors (North Little Rock, Little Rock, Jacksonville, Sherwood, Wrightsville, and Conway) were presented to Phyllis via the Carousel.
- 2003 Full Counsel School of Ministry Esteemed Presidential Award
- 2015 received a Capitol Citation from Arkansas' Secretary of State Mark Martin.
- 2017 received the Woman of Excellence Award for Health/Social Service, presented by Sister Friends United, Inc.
- 2017 received an Ambassador of Beauty Award as a finalist of Shades of Beauty Expo.
- 2017 featured on cover of ML Magazine with two other health professionals and provided with a centerfold article on *page 17* to highlight being in business for 17 years

# An Experience of a Lifetime

# An Epic Assignment

**Jade Crosby**
7th Grader/eStem Charter School

---

A Letter from the First Lady Mrs. Michelle Obama

Hi, I'm Jade Crosby. I'm writing this letter regarding my experience of receiving a letter from Mrs. Michelle Obama. The reason I wrote my letter to First Lady Mrs. Michelle Obama is because my 7th grade English class had an assignment where we had to write a letter to someone who inspired us or made a huge impact on the world. I knew right then that I wanted to write to Mrs. Michelle Obama, but I didn't know what to write to her. After school, I went home and told my sister, Ca'Ron, about the assignment. I told her that I wanted to write to First Lady Mrs. Michelle Obama, but I didn't have a topic.

Ca'Ron gave me some ideas, and the one that stood out most dealt with helping kids learn how to eat in moderation and have healthy lifestyles. Then, Ca'Ron asked, "What's your favorite dessert?" I replied, "Ice cream." At that moment, I decided to write about how ice cream could be healthy if you ate it in moderation. I stayed up all night writing this letter to make sure it was perfect. My teacher revised it the next day. On that Friday, we turned in our final drafts and put them in envelopes. Next, we looked up the addresses to the place where we would send the letters (Pennsylvania Avenue), wrote it on the envelopes, added stamps, and sent them off. My teacher, Mr. Matlock, was sending them off that evening.

A month or two later, I got called to the office. I was nervous and scared; I thought I was in trouble. As I was walking into the office, I saw a lady holding this large manila envelope. She handed it to me and smiled. I looked at it, and the first thing I saw were these big bold black letters that read: THE WHITE HOUSE and TO Jade Crosby.

Even though they spelled my last name wrong, I was so happy to get a response. I decided I would wait to open it until I called my grandmother on my lunch break. Still, I told my friends, and they were so proud of me and even considered writing a letter themselves. I used my cousin Olivia's phone to call my grandma. She was so excited; she told me to open the package to see what was in it.

I opened it, and there was another white envelope inside with an official letter from the first lady on official White House stationery with an official White House seal. The package included several pictures of the dogs, the first lady, and the president. The letter I received (paraphrased) thanked me for writing and agreed that ice cream was indeed healthy when you eat it in moderation.

My grandma said, "You're going to be on the news!" The next week my teacher and I were being interviewed by the news station, Channel 4. It was on FOX 16 news too.

I was so shy, but I was happy to tell other kids that they can achieve anything if they put their minds to it as I had done. *The Arkansas Democrat-Gazette* shared my story about being the *first and only* 7th grader at eStem Charter School to receive a letter from the White House.

# A Blessing

**Joshua Strong**
UAPB Marching Band

---

President Obama's First Inaugural Event

My story starts a few months prior to President Barack Obama's inauguration parade. My high school band director, Mrs. Cathy Williams, called the University of Arkansas at Pine Bluff (UAPB) Band, the Marching Musical Machine of the Mid-South (M4), Director, Mr. John R. Graham, Jr. to schedule for him to audition a few of the seniors in band with me and also to have him work with us for our concert contest. Mr. Graham couldn't make it, so Mr. Harold Fooster came and worked with the band holding auditions for the seven of us who chose to audition for M4.

After the audition, Mr. Fooster told me he could tell I was nervous, but I did really well. He also said I would receive a full-tuition scholarship offer from the band and told me I should watch the mail for my scholarship letter. As that day went on, my friends and I were all happy to be offered scholarships to UAPB. Time went by; I had yet to receive a letter from the band, and I began to worry. I started to ask the other seniors who auditioned if they had received anything, and they all said no. I decided to call after school was out. When school was out, I called the band office and spoke with Ms. Shelia Early. She was so nice and professional over the phone. She assured me that my letter was on the way and that I should be getting it in the mail soon. I felt reassured that I would enter UAPB in the fall of 2009 with a band scholarship.

A few more weeks passed, and we started discussing Barack Obama's presidential inauguration in Mrs. Minnis' English class. We were watching the inauguration on the TV. We saw M4 march down Pennsylvania Avenue playing "Ain't No Stopping Us Now," and it was at that moment that Mrs. Minnis decided to give us a paper to write. She wanted us to write a profound essay on the significance of the song and to discuss why we thought UAPB decided to play that song in front of President Obama and his family. Like much of the class, I left dreading the assignment because we as a class had "senioritis." Needless to say, I went home to start the assignment, but before I did, I checked the mail, and to my surprise, there was a letter addressed to me from the UAPB Band Department.

The letter that I received included the full tuition scholarship that Mr. Fooster promised me. The following months quickly came and passed. I reported for band camp and the start of my collegiate career. During band camp, I met some wonderful people who have helped me along the way and who have also challenged me to do better than I ever expected. Time flew by during my college years, and soon, I was in line at graduation. My advisor, Dr. Jessie J. Walker, walked up to me and told me that I had been accepted into the graduate school at the University of Arkansas at Pine Bluff and that I would receive a full scholarship.

As you can imagine that was the highlight of the day, besides getting my diploma, because I did not have a job lined up or anything after graduation. The following week, I came up to the university to make my schedule for graduate school and was then offered an internship with the Pine Bluff Arsenal which I gladly accepted.

For the next year, my day consisted of classes, the internship, and band. During class, I learned more about my chosen field of study such as the different types of programming languages and different methods of using those languages other than the ones listed in the book. While at my internship I had the opportunity to use what I learned in a real-life environment.

When all of my classwork and internship obligations where done, I started helping the band. I wanted to help the band because that was my way of giving back to Dear Mother (UAPB). Time flew by while I was in the master's program, and soon, it was time for me to graduate again. I started looking for jobs and applied to several.

Graduation day came and went, and I still had yet to receive a call from anyone. One day while I was applying for another job, one of my friends from preschool asked me to help her with her graduate school project, and I agreed. We met with Mr. Robinson who was her client for the project. During the meeting Mr. Robinson asked me about my skills and knowledge of the subject and told me to come back later, so I did. It was then that he offered me a job as a webmaster for the Division of Enrollment Management at UAPB, and I gladly accepted. I started the following day.

A few weeks went by; I was leaving for lunch, and my advisor saw me. He asked me, "Have you ever considered teaching?"

I said, "No, I haven't, but I wouldn't mind teaching."

He told me to think it over and to let him know in the upcoming weeks. I gave the thought some time as he suggested and also spoke with my mom, aunt, cousins (who are all teachers) and my dad before I made my decision to accept the teaching position at UAPB.

Deciding to teach was one of the best decisions I have ever made. Now, I get to recruit students to the university, to maintain the website for the Division of Enrollment Management and to teach the children who have been recruited here. My time at UAPB has been nothing but a blessing from the moment I auditioned to the moment I saw them marching down Pennsylvania Avenue and I walked across the stage to receive my degrees.

# A Humbling Experience

**Rishard Carr**
Central High School Marching Band

---

President Obama's Second Inaugural Event

The school band at the historic Central High School in Little Rock Arkansas was selected to go to Washington D.C. and to play in the inauguration of the first black president, Barack Obama in 2013! It was awesome because we were a part of history being made! It was one of the greatest opportunities that I, Rishard Ramone Carr, had ever encountered.

I was 16-years-old at Central when I found out we had been selected as one of the bands to perform at the inauguration. It blew my mind! I played in the band from the 9th grade to 12th grade. I wanted to play the drums at Horace Mann Magnet School my junior year, but everyone was signed up to play that instrument. Playing drums makes you look cool. Everybody loves the drummer!

At that time, my band director, Mr. Johnson encouraged me to try another instrument. I chose the baritone and continued playing in the band at Central. Music plays an important part in my life. I come from a family of musically inclined people. My grandfather, James Edward Watson Sr., sang on the corners with his friends back in the days like the Five Heartbeats and now sings in the church choir. My grandmother, Vera Mae Watson, sang in the choir at Union A.M.E. Church; my mother, Lynda Cooper, and Aunt Gail Dandredge, grew up singing in the choir at Union and now at New Creation where my Aunt Gail is first lady. My sister, Candice Cooper, is an upcoming R&B artist, and my brother, Matthew Watson, played in the band at Horace Mann and Central and made beats for songs.

I was bound to be involved in music some way or another. It's part of our story! My chest was poked out proudly to represent this historical school. Little Rock Central High School - the high school that was so famously integrated by federal officials in 1957, is now racially mixed through the efforts of The Little Rock

Nine. NBC's Lester Holt reported on the band as we practiced each day during class time and after school. We had a lot of fundraisers and events lined up to help with the cost of travel and lodge in Washington D.C.

Our community, city, state, and parents supported us wholeheartedly! For at Little Rock Central High, we marched to the beat of a different drum! Seeing so many fellow Americans come out to celebrate and extend their congratulations towards President Obama, gave me a broader sense of hope. Someone who looks like me, a black man, serving in the highest job in the United States of America, encouraged me even more to pursue my dreams and make them a reality!

Thank you, Dr. Martin Luther King and others who risked their lives standing for justice and marching, so we could be free! Many blacks paved the way for me and for those under me. I still can remember the actual moment when I saw the president. It was cold in Little Rock, Arkansas when we boarded many charter buses to make the trip but brutally cold in Washington D.C. My hands were numb with hardly any feeling to them even with gloves and hand warmers. It didn't matter because we pressed on and proudly played on.

I wasn't directly close to President Obama, but I was close enough to catch a glimpse of him smiling and waving back at the whole band. A warm form of peace from within rushed all over me and in my veins. Not even the chill could keep me from being out there embracing this historical moment. We were in complete awe of seeing the president of the United States. We stopped playing, and our band director hollered out to us, "Keep playing!"

It was a very humbling experience that I will always cherish and tell my children.

# UAPB Commencement

## Eartha Dobbins

My Granddaughter's Graduation

---

### UAPB Commencement

*(Photo Courtesy of the University Museum and Cultural Center on the campus of the University of Arkansas at Pine Bluff)*

Christen, the second child born to our oldest daughter and her husband, was preparing for her graduation. Invitations were mailed, and she was using social media. It seemed that only a few years ago, she was in my closet putting on my heels and hats. I reflected on her first year of life and the serious illness that came upon her. At five-months-old, Christen was abruptly diagnosed with a hole in her diaphragm. The medical staff did not offer any positive outcome. This baby endured two major surgeries within three weeks. Family and friends prayed, and God answered. This amazing child continued to develop as a normal youth despite living with a rapid growth syndrome that can affect vital organs, especially the heart.

My husband shares in my reflection, "Chris was our personal 'Whitney Houston' songbird." We knew that she enjoyed hearing music; a little smile would surface on her face as her mom or I would sing, 'Yes, Jesus Loves Me.'

Christen became a star volleyball player for North Little Rock West Campus. It may seem as though I am "bragging" on my granddaughter, but I am not; Chris was a good academic student with a stellar personality. Her health remained a factor, yet it never impeded her goals.

She came by to let us know that her hard work had paid off and that graduation would be May 10, 2010! We were ecstatic!!! After we finally settled down, she announced that First Lady Michelle Obama may be the commencement speaker. I knew that Mrs. Obama was sought after all over the country for speaking engagements, as well as her husband, the 44th president of the United States of America.

Christen enjoyed keeping us in suspense; she never knew that I was doing some research on my own. It was certain that Mrs. Obama would be the 2010 spring commencement speaker, and grandparents were assigned to a special seating. My daughter told me to dress casually and to relax; she might as well had been talking to the wind. Mrs. Obama represented so much to me. She was royalty with grace and dignity. She was the Proverbs 31 woman. Many women my age, as a child, never saw or played with a black doll. So, it was more than I ever hoped for - to have *the* Michelle Obama doll in my home.

We arrived early at the Pine Bluff Convention Center. My family knew that we were witnessing history. I thought about Mrs. Obama standing with her husband while Senator Obama announced to the world that he would seek the office of president of the United States of America. Her demeanor was quiet, poised, and confident.

My thoughts were interrupted by a few people passing by saying hello and congratulations. Attorney John Walker waved to us, and we gave him a "thumbs" up.

Finally, the pomp and circumstance ended. Mrs. Obama was introduced by Chancellor Lawrence Davis, a champion for progress. She really didn't need an introduction; her name was enough. I, along with the audience, stood to receive her, and with that award-winning smile, she received us. She began her message with assurance. The message was for the graduates, but we were included. She reminded us that "...obstacles would come, therefore learn to 'face up' to the problem, learn from mistakes and never give up. Great strides have been made in medicine and many other fields, so challenge yourself to do your best, even when some think it is too late."

I was dancing in my seat - so were many around me.

It was a great day to see and hear a great lady!!!!

# Fun Facts

# Did You Know?

President Barack Obama served two terms as the Democratic President.

His first term campaign focused on the twin themes of *Change* and *Hope* in uncertain times.

Obama's running mates were Hillary Clinton and John McCain.

Mr. Obama awaited the first term election results at his Chicago home after a marathon 21-month campaign.

After only serving four years in the Senate, Barack sought election as one of the youngest and lesser experienced presidential candidates in national political affairs.

Jim Carley managed Obama's 2004 United States Senate campaign.

In his first term as senator, Barack Obama gave the keynote address at the 2004 Democratic National Convention in Boston. He committed most of the 2,300-word speech to memory.

Obama began writing his speech on the same day that Mary Beth Cahill (John Kerry's campaign manager) called to offer him the keynote spot.

President Obama's vision, "There is a United States of America ... not a black America, not a white America, not a Latino America, nor an Asian America."

Positions held by Barack Obama included United States senator of Illinois, president-elect, and president of the United States of America.

Thousands of blue signs that read simply "United" were stocked piled inside the Pepsi Center for distribution to convention delegates at whatever moment Obama's high command deemed appropriate.

Twenty million households tuned into the broadcast and cable news network Tuesday night, when Clinton headlined, according to the Nielsen ratings. Seventeen million watched Monday (Michelle Obama), 18.5 million Thursday (Biden); all those numbers beat the best numbers posted by John Kerry's convention in 2004.

President Obama joked by saying he was running for president to keep 10-year-old Malia and 7-year-old Sasha under lock and key. "The real reason is secret service protection for my two daughters as they enter into their teenage years. Whenever a young man comes by for a date, we're going to have one of these mean-looking guys with glasses that don't crack a smile. They're armed and dangerous."

# The Untold History

There were eight women who ran for the White House (Minorities being women, Asian-American, and African-American before women had the privilege to vote).

**Victoria Woodhull 1872**

Women's rights leader, Victoria Woodhull, became the first female candidate for president nearly 50 years before women gained the right to vote.

**Belva Ann Lockwood 1884**

Equal Rights Party's tickets

**Margaret Chase Smith 1964**

Republican Party

**Shirley Chisholm 1972**

First African-American to be elected to Congress in 1969 made history again. First African-American woman of a major party to run for a presidential nomination.

**Patsy Matsu Takemoto Mink 1972**

First Asian-American woman to seek the Democratic presidential nomination. President Obama posthumously awarded Mink the Presidential Medal of Freedom in 2014.

**Linda Jenness 1972**

Jenness was only 31. She didn't meet the constitutional age requirement to serve. Her name was only on the ballot in 25 States.

**Lenora Fulani 1988**

Ran as a 3rd party candidate on the New Alliance Party ticket.

**Carol Mosley Braun 1992**

First and only African-American female senator in U.S. History. She threw her hat into the presidential ring in 2004.

# Additional Facts

On February 10, 2007, in Springfield, Illinois, Obama officially announced his candidacy for president.

A victory in the Iowa Caucuses in January 2008 made him a challenger to Senator Hillary Clinton of New York, who he outlasted in a primary campaign to claim the Democratic Nomination in early June 2008.

Barack Obama delivered a speech in Chicago's Grant Park. He acknowledged the historic nature of his victory (which came 143 years after the end of the American Civil War and the abolition of slavery).

Obama's inauguration was on January 20, 2009.

Obama defeated Republican Mitt Romney on November 6, 2012, to win a second term in the White House.

# More Facts

Provided by the Associated Press

## *Obama's Economic Proposal ...*

I recall lots of people, especially seniors, talking about receiving a $300 stimulus check in the mail. I also had friends on unemployment during that time. It was challenging for them to find employment, so while receiving their unemployment checks when the time expired, there was a clause, so they could receive an extension on the unemployment benefits.

- ∂ Swift passage by Congress of a new physical stimulus bill either before or soon after he takes office in January
- ∂ Immediate extension of unemployment benefits for those who cannot find work
- ∂ A rescue plan for the middle class that invest in intermediate efforts to create jobs and to provide relief to struggling families
- ∂ Efforts to address the spending impact of the financial crisis on other sectors of the economy including small businesses and state and municipal governments
- ∂ Aid for the struggling auto industry and related businesses such as auto suppliers which face severe hardships
- ∂ Reviewing of the implementation of the 700 billion financial rescue plans to insure it is achieving its central goal of stabilizing financial markets while protecting tax payers, helping home owners, and not unduly rewarding the management of the financial firms receiving government assistance
- ∂ A set of energy, healthcare, education, and tax relief policies designed to grow the middle class and revive the economy

As small business owners, we were affected greatly. It was as though it was a ripple effect. My clients were struggling to pay for their services and that led to my business struggling to keep up. Thank God, He provided, and we are about to celebrate 18 years.

# Still More Facts

Provided by the Associated Press

## Obama's Economic Advisers

Members of President-Elect Barack Obama's transition economic advisory board, as provided by Obama's office:

∂ **David Bonior**, Former Democratic Congressmen from Michigan
∂ **Warren Buffet**, Chairman and Chief Executive Officer of Berkshire Hathaway
∂ **Roel Campos**, Former Commissioner of the Securities and Exchange Commission
∂ **William Daily**, Former Commerce Secretary
∂ **William Donaldson**, Former Chairman of Sec
∂ **Roger Ferguson**, Former Vice Chairman of the Federal Reserve Board of Governors
∂ **Jennifer Granholm**, Michigan Governor
∂ **Anne Mulcahy**, Chairman and CEO Xerox Corp
∂ **Richard Pearson**, Chairman of the Board for Time Warner Inc.
∂ **Penny Pritzker**, Chairman and Founder of Classic Residence by Hyatt
∂ **Robert Reich**, Former Labor Secretary
∂ **Robert Rubin**, Former Treasury Secretary
∂ **Eric Schmidt**, Chairman and CEO of Google
∂ **Lawrence Summers**, Former Treasury Secretary
∂ **Laura Tyson**, Former Head of the Council of Economic Advisories under President Clinton
∂ **Antonio Villaraigosa**, Los Angeles Mayor
∂ **Paul Volcker**, Former Federal Reserve Chairman

# Test Your Knowledge

1. Who conceded to the election of the first black president?
2. What was Obama's platform?
3. How many electoral votes did Obama earn during the first term win?
4. Who was Obama happy to vote with?
5. How many electoral votes are needed to win the presidential election?
6. What position did Obama hold prior to becoming president of the United States?
7. Where is Obama's homestead located?
8. What was one of Obama's favorite lines during one of his 2016 rallies?
9. In most of the crowds surrounding Obama in 2004, what chant could be heard?

**Choose from the options below:**

Yes, we can

Change

Senator John McCain

Western Village of Kogelo, Kenya

365

Senator of Illinois

His daughters

You don't need to boo; you just need to vote!

270

# Test Your Knowledge: Answers

1. Who conceded to the election of the first African-American president? (Senator John McCain)
2. What was Obama's platform? (Change)
3. How many electoral votes did Obama earn during the first term win? (365)
4. Who was Obama happy to vote with? (His daughters)
5. How many electoral votes are needed to win the presidential election? (270)
6. What position did Obama hold prior to becoming president of the United States? (Senator of Illinois)
7. Where is Obama's homestead located? (Western Village of Kogelo, Kenya)
8. What was one of Obama's favorite lines during one of his 2016 rallies? (You don't need to boo; you just need to vote!)
9. In most of the crowds surrounding Obama in 2004, what chant could be heard? (Yes, we can)

# African-American Colleges

**Alabama:**
Alabama A&M
Alabama State University
Bishop State Community College
Concordia College Alabama
Gadsden State Community College
J.F. Drake State Technical College
Lawson State Community College
Miles College
Oakwood University
Selma University
Shelton State Community College
Stillman College
Talladega College
Trenholm State Community College
Tuskegee University

**Arkansas:**
Arkansas Baptist College
Philander Smith College
Shorter College
University of Arkansas at Pine Bluff

**California:**
Charles R. Drew University of Medicine and Science

**Delaware:**
Delaware State University

**District of Columbia:**
Howard University
University of the District of Columbia

**Florida:**
Bethune Cookman University
Edward Waters College
Florida A&M University
Florida Memorial University

**Georgia:**
Albany State University
Clark Atlanta University
Fort Valley State University

Interdenominational Theological Center
Morehouse College
Morehouse School of Medicine
Morris Brown College
Paine College
Savannah State University
Spelman College

**Kentucky:**
Kentucky State University
Simmons College of Kentucky

**Louisiana:**
Dillard University
Grambling State University
Southern University and A&M College
Southern University at New Orleans
Southern University at Shreveport
Xavier University of Louisiana

**Maryland:**
Bowie State University
Coppin State University
Morgan State University
University of Maryland Eastern Shore

**Mississippi:**
Alcorn State University
Coahoma Community College
Hinds Community College
Jackson State University
Mississippi Valley State University
Rust College
Tougaloo College

**Missouri:**
Harris-Stowe State University
Lincoln University – Missouri

**New York:**
CUNY – The Medgar Evers College

**North Carolina:**
Barber-Scotia College
Bennett College
Elizabeth City State University

Fayetteville State University
Johnson C. Smith University
Livingstone College
North Carolina A&T State University
North Carolina Central University
Saint Augustine's University
Shaw University
Winston-Salem State University

**Ohio:**
Central State University
Wilberforce University

**Oklahoma:**
Langston University

**Pennsylvania:**
Cheyney University of Pennsylvania
Lincoln University – Pennsylvania

**South Carolina:**
Allen University
Benedict College
Claflin University
Clinton College
Denmark Technical College
Morris College
South Carolina State University
Voorhees College

**Tennessee:**
American Baptist College
Fisk University
Knoxville College
Lane College
Lemoyne-Owen College
Meharry Medical College
Tennessee State University

**Texas:**
Huston-Tillotson University
Jarvis Christian College
Paul Quinn College
Prairie View A&M University
Southwestern Christian College
St. Philips College
Texas College

Texas Southern University
Wiley College

**Virgin Islands:**
University of the Virgin Islands

**Virginia:**
Hampton University
Norfolk State University
Virginia State University
Virginia Union University

**West Virginia:**
Bluefield State College
West Virginia State University

# Presidential Letters

# From Obama to Trump

## FULL LETTER

Dear Mr. President -

Congratulations on a remarkable run. Millions have placed their hopes in you, and all of us, regardless of party, should hope for expanded prosperity and security during your tenure.

This is a unique office, without a clear blueprint for success, so I don't know that any advice from me will be particularly helpful. Still, let me offer a few reflections from the past 8 years.

First, we've both been blessed, in different ways, with great good fortune. Not everyone is so lucky. It's up to us to do everything we can (to) build more ladders of success for every child and family that's willing to work hard.

Second, American leadership in this world really is indispensable. It's up to us, through action and example, to sustain the international order that's expanded steadily since the end of the Cold War, and upon which our own wealth and safety depend.

Third, we are just temporary occupants of this office. That makes us guardians of those democratic institutions and traditions -- like rule of law, separation of powers, equal protection and civil liberties -- that our forebears fought and bled for. Regardless of the push and pull of daily politics, it's up to us to leave those instruments of our democracy at least as strong as we found them.

And finally, take time, in the rush of events and responsibilities, for friends and family. They'll get you through the inevitable rough patches.

Michelle and I wish you and Melania the very best as you embark on this great adventure and know that we stand ready to help in any ways which we can.

Good luck and Godspeed,

BO

http://www.cnn.com/2017/09/03/politics/obama-trump-letter-inauguration-day/index.html

# From George W. Bush to Barack Obama

## JANUARY 20, 2009

Dear Barack,

Congratulations on becoming our President. You have just begun a fantastic chapter in your life.

Very few have had the honor of knowing the responsibility you now feel. Very few know the excitement of the moment and the challenges you will face.

There will be trying moments. The critics will rage. Your "friends" will disappoint you. But, you will have an Almighty God to comfort you, a family who loves you, and a country that is pulling for you, including me. No matter what comes, you will be inspired by the character and compassion of the people you now lead.

God bless you.

Sincerely,

GW

http://abcnews.go.com/Politics/abc-george-bushs-inauguration-day-letter-barack-obama/story?id=44896610

Jan 20, 2009

THE WHITE HOUSE
WASHINGTON

Dear Barack,

Congratulations on becoming our President. You have just begun a fantastic chapter in your life.

Very few have had the honor of knowing the responsibility you now feel. Very few know the excitement of the moment and the challenges you will face.

There will be trying moments. The critics will rage. Your "friends" will disappoint you. But, you will have an Almighty God to comfort you, a family who loves you, and a country that is pulling for you, including me. No matter what comes, you will be inspired by the character and compassion of the people you now lead.

God Bless you. Sincerely, GW

# "The Black National Anthem"

**James Weldon Johnson**

**Song title:** Lift Ev'ry Voice and Sing
**Also known as:** The Black National or Negro Anthem

Lift ev'ry voice and sing,
Till earth and heaven ring.
Ring with the harmonies of Liberty;
Let our rejoicing rise,
High as the list'ning skies,
Let it resound loud as the rolling sea.
Sing a song full of the faith that the dark past has taught us,
Sing a song full of the hope that the present has brought us;
Facing the rising sun of our new day begun,
Let us march on till victory is won.

Stony the road we trod,
Bitter the chast'ning rod,
Felt in the days when hope unborn had died;
Yet with a steady beat.

Have not our weary feet,
Come to the place for which our fathers sighed?
We have come over a way that with tears has been watered,
We have come, treading our path through the blood of the slaughtered,
Out from the gloomy past,
Till now we stand at last
Where the white gleam of our bright star is cast.

God of our weary years,
God of our silent tears,
Thou who has brought us thus far on the way;
Thou who has by Thy might,
Led us into the light,
Keep us forever in the path, we pray.
Lest our feet stray from the places, our God, where we met Thee,
Lest our hearts, drunk with the wine of the world, we forget Thee,
Shadowed beneath thy hand,
May we forever stand,
True to our God,
True to our native land.

# Photo Gallery

*Photo 2 Salem March and autographed picture of First Lady Michelle Obama, a gift given to Jade.*

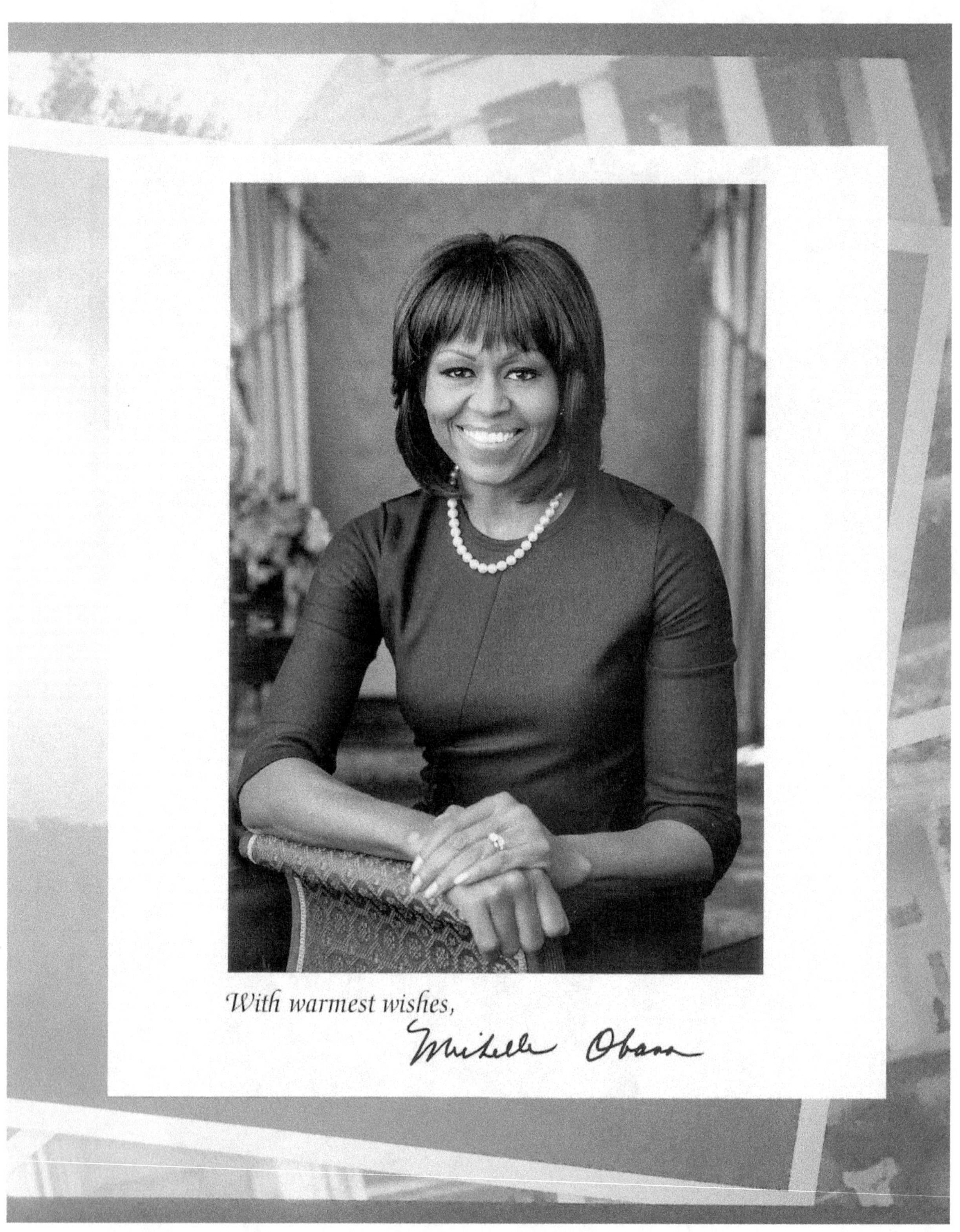
With warmest wishes,
Michelle Obama

*Photo 3 Autographed picture of First Lady Michelle Obama, a gift to Jade.*

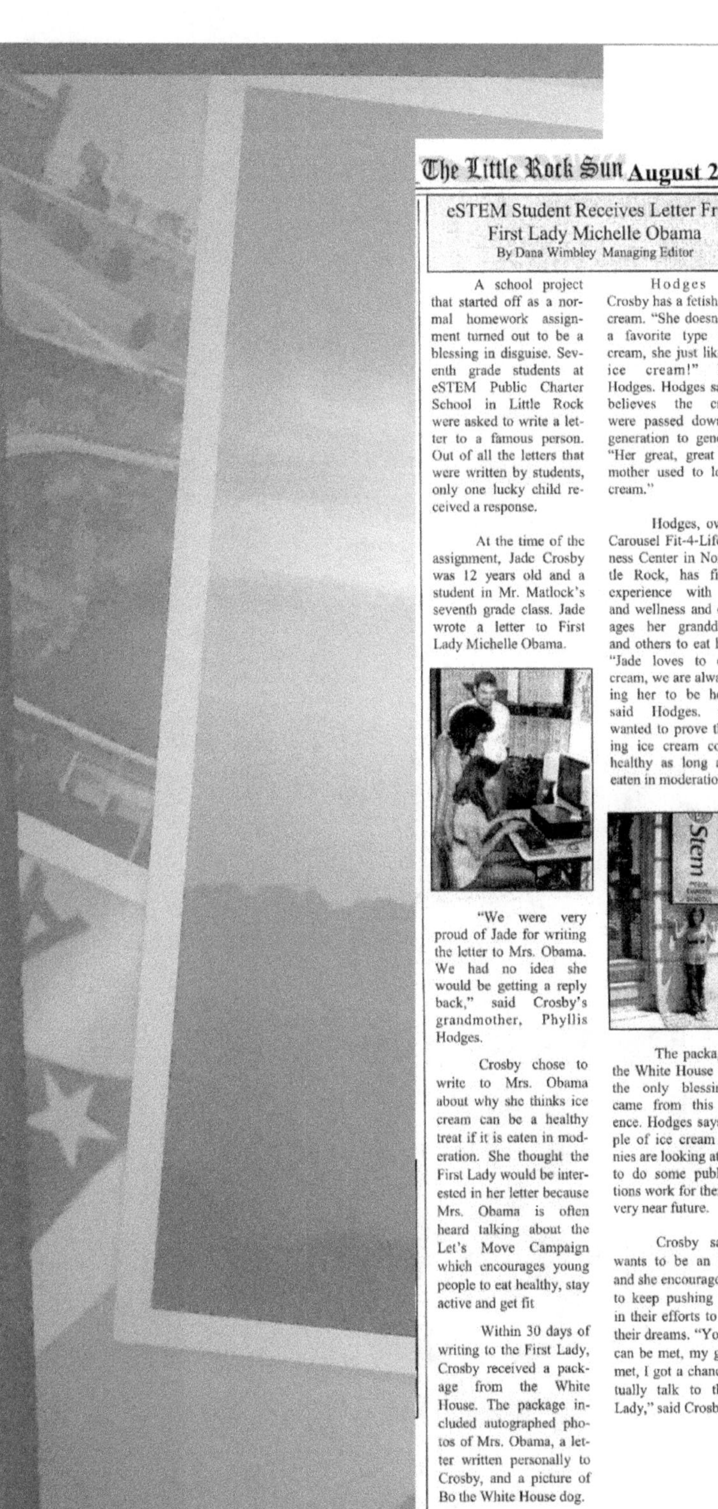

The Little Rock Sun August 2, 2013

## eSTEM Student Receives Letter From First Lady Michelle Obama

By Dana Wimbley Managing Editor

A school project that started off as a normal homework assignment turned out to be a blessing in disguise. Seventh grade students at eSTEM Public Charter School in Little Rock were asked to write a letter to a famous person. Out of all the letters that were written by students, only one lucky child received a response.

At the time of the assignment, Jade Crosby was 12 years old and a student in Mr. Matlock's seventh grade class. Jade wrote a letter to First Lady Michelle Obama.

"We were very proud of Jade for writing the letter to Mrs. Obama. We had no idea she would be getting a reply back," said Crosby's grandmother, Phyllis Hodges.

Crosby chose to write to Mrs. Obama about why she thinks ice cream can be a healthy treat if it is eaten in moderation. She thought the First Lady would be interested in her letter because Mrs. Obama is often heard talking about the Let's Move Campaign which encourages young people to eat healthy, stay active and get fit

Within 30 days of writing to the First Lady, Crosby received a package from the White House. The package included autographed photos of Mrs. Obama, a letter written personally to Crosby, and a picture of Bo the White House dog.

Hodges says Crosby has a fetish for ice cream. "She doesn't have a favorite type of ice cream, she just likes cold ice cream!" laughs Hodges. Hodges says she believes the cravings were passed down from generation to generation. "Her great, great grandmother used to love ice cream."

Hodges, owner of Carousel Fit-4-Life Wellness Center in North Little Rock, has firsthand experience with health and wellness and encourages her granddaughter and others to eat healthy. "Jade loves to eat ice cream, we are always telling her to be healthy." said Hodges. Crosby wanted to prove that eating ice cream could be healthy as long as it is eaten in moderation.

The package from the White House was not the only blessing that came from this experience. Hodges says a couple of ice cream companies are looking at Crosby to do some public relations work for them in the very near future.

Crosby says she wants to be an attorney and she encourages others to keep pushing forward in their efforts to achieve their dreams. "Your goals can be met, my goal was met, I got a chance to actually talk to the First Lady," said Crosby.

*Photo 4 Little Rock Sun Newspaper: Jade received letter and autographed photo from First Lady Michelle Obama.*

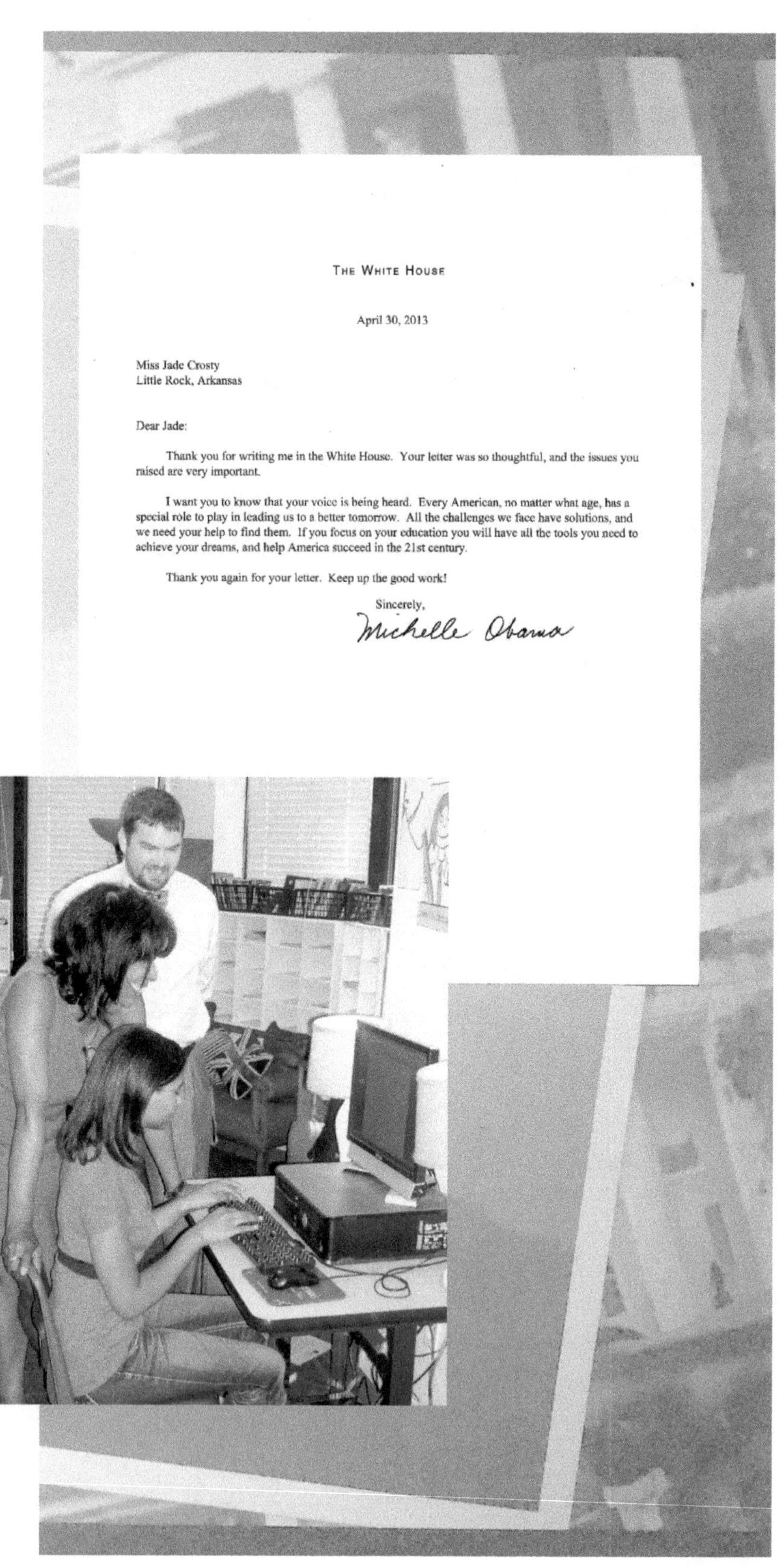

THE WHITE HOUSE

April 30, 2013

Miss Jade Crosty
Little Rock, Arkansas

Dear Jade:

Thank you for writing me in the White House. Your letter was so thoughtful, and the issues you raised are very important.

I want you to know that your voice is being heard. Every American, no matter what age, has a special role to play in leading us to a better tomorrow. All the challenges we face have solutions, and we need your help to find them. If you focus on your education you will have all the tools you need to achieve your dreams, and help America succeed in the 21st century.

Thank you again for your letter. Keep up the good work!

Sincerely,

Michelle Obama

*Photo 5 A personalized letter to Jade from First Lady Michelle Obama (Pictured: Mr. Matlock (English teacher), Grandmother Phyllis and Jade).*

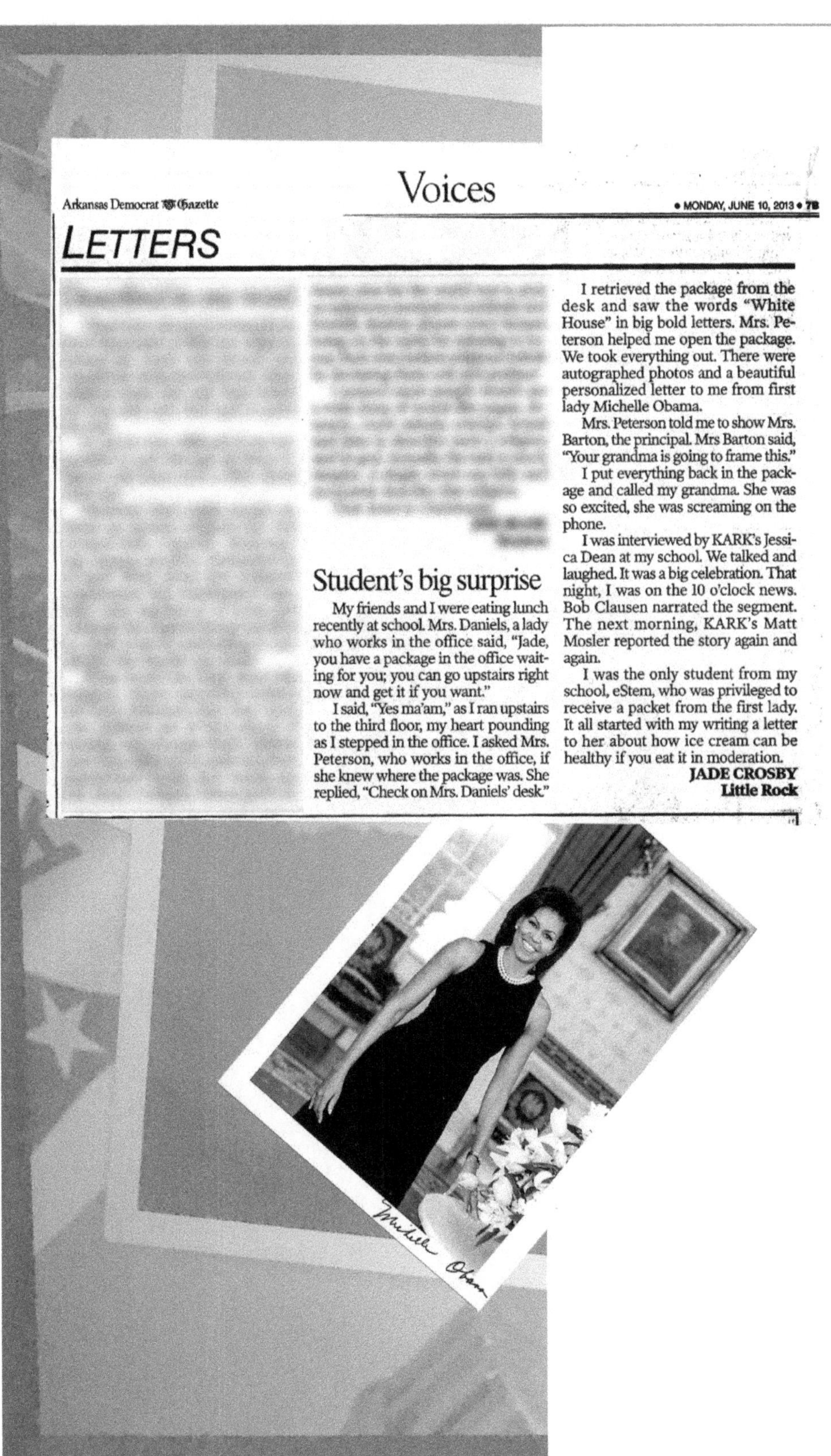

Arkansas Democrat-Gazette

Voices

• MONDAY, JUNE 10, 2013 • 7B

## LETTERS

### Student's big surprise

My friends and I were eating lunch recently at school. Mrs. Daniels, a lady who works in the office said, "Jade, you have a package in the office waiting for you; you can go upstairs right now and get it if you want."

I said, "Yes ma'am," as I ran upstairs to the third floor, my heart pounding as I stepped in the office. I asked Mrs. Peterson, who works in the office, if she knew where the package was. She replied, "Check on Mrs. Daniels' desk."

I retrieved the package from the desk and saw the words "White House" in big bold letters. Mrs. Peterson helped me open the package. We took everything out. There were autographed photos and a beautiful personalized letter to me from first lady Michelle Obama.

Mrs. Peterson told me to show Mrs. Barton, the principal. Mrs Barton said, "Your grandma is going to frame this."

I put everything back in the package and called my grandma. She was so excited, she was screaming on the phone.

I was interviewed by KARK's Jessica Dean at my school. We talked and laughed. It was a big celebration. That night, I was on the 10 o'clock news. Bob Clausen narrated the segment. The next morning, KARK's Matt Mosler reported the story again and again.

I was the only student from my school, eStem, who was privileged to receive a packet from the first lady. It all started with my writing a letter to her about how ice cream can be healthy if you eat it in moderation.

**JADE CROSBY**
**Little Rock**



*Photo 6 Arkansas Democrat-Gazette: Story on Jade's surprise (signed autograph photo of First Lady Michelle Obama).*

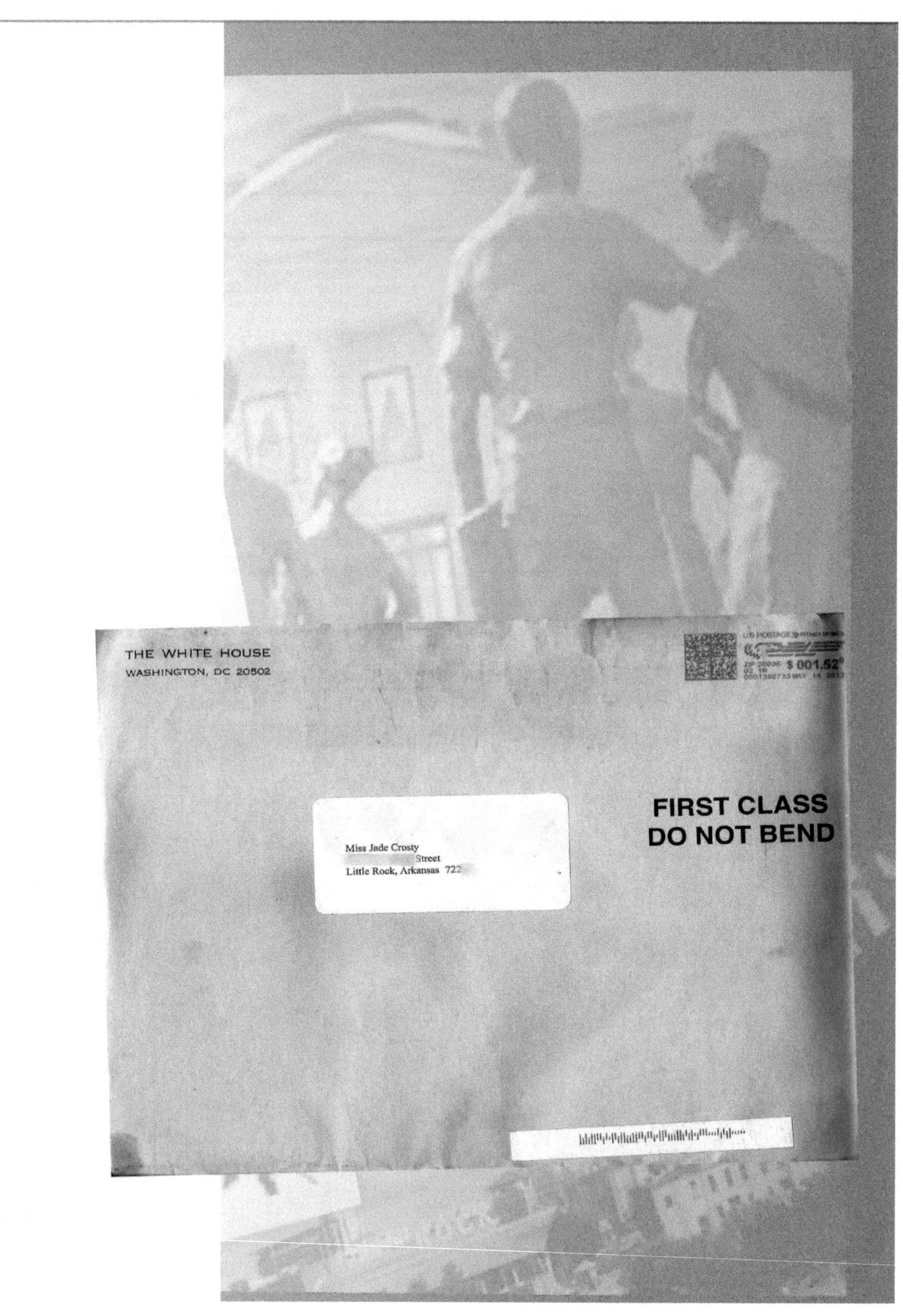


*Photo 7 White House envelope addressed to Jade.*

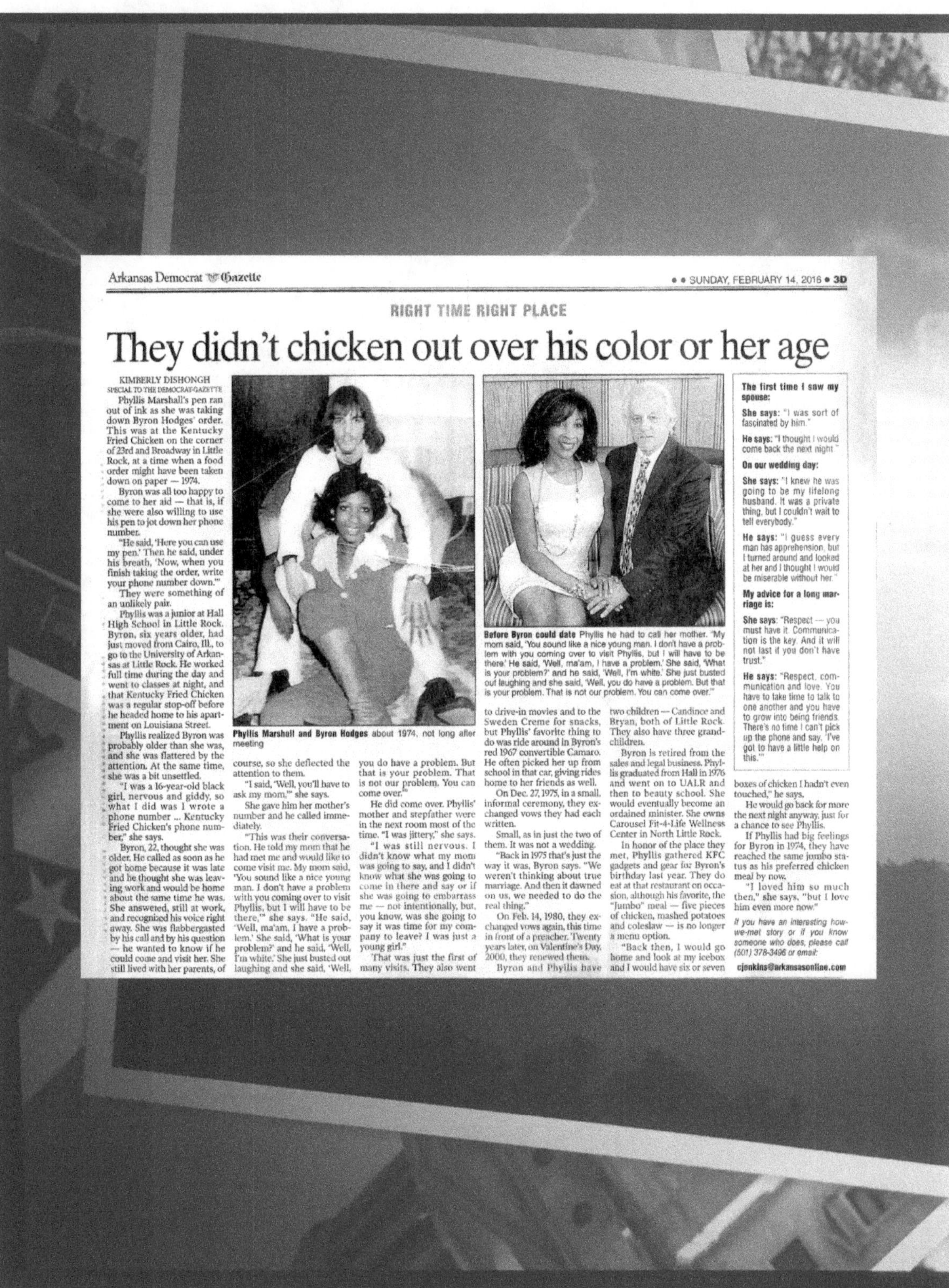

Arkansas Democrat-Gazette • • SUNDAY, FEBRUARY 14, 2016 • 3D

RIGHT TIME RIGHT PLACE

# They didn't chicken out over his color or her age

KIMBERLY DISHONGH
SPECIAL TO THE DEMOCRAT-GAZETTE

Phyllis Marshall's pen ran out of ink as she was taking down Byron Hodges' order. This was at the Kentucky Fried Chicken on the corner of 23rd and Broadway in Little Rock, at a time when a food order might have been taken down on paper — 1974.

Byron was all too happy to come to her aid — that is, if she were also willing to use his pen to jot down her phone number.

"He said, 'Here you can use my pen.' Then he said, under his breath, 'Now, when you finish taking the order, write your phone number down.'"

They were something of an unlikely pair.

Phyllis was a junior at Hall High School in Little Rock. Byron, six years older, had just moved from Cairo, Ill., to go to the University of Arkansas at Little Rock. He worked full time during the day and went to classes at night, and that Kentucky Fried Chicken was a regular stop-off before he headed home to his apartment on Louisiana Street.

Phyllis realized Byron was probably older than she was, and she was flattered by the attention. At the same time, she was a bit unsettled.

"I was a 16-year-old black girl, nervous and giddy, so what I did was I wrote a phone number ... Kentucky Fried Chicken's phone number," she says.

Byron, 22, thought she was older. He called as soon as he got home because it was late and he thought she was leaving work and would be home about the same time he was. She answered, still at work, and recognized his voice right away. She was flabbergasted by his call and by his question — he wanted to know if he could come and visit her. She still lived with her parents, of course, so she deflected the attention to them.

"I said, 'Well, you'll have to ask my mom,'" she says.

She gave him her mother's number and he called immediately.

"This was their conversation. He told my mom that he had met me and would like to come visit me. My mom said, 'You sound like a nice young man. I don't have a problem with you coming over to visit Phyllis, but I will have to be there,'" she says. "He said, 'Well, ma'am, I have a problem.' She said, 'What is your problem?' and he said, 'Well, I'm white.' She just busted out laughing and she said, 'Well, you do have a problem. But that is your problem. That is not our problem. You can come over.'"

He did come over. Phyllis' mother and stepfather were in the next room most of the time. "I was jittery," she says.

"I was still nervous. I didn't know what my mom was going to say, and I didn't know what she was going to come in there and say or if she was going to embarrass me — not intentionally, but, you know, was she going to say it was time for my company to leave? I was just a young girl."

That was just the first of many visits. They also went to drive-in movies and to the Sweden Creme for snacks, but Phyllis' favorite thing to do was ride around in Byron's red 1967 convertible Camaro. He often picked her up from school in that car, giving rides home to her friends as well.

On Dec. 27, 1975, in a small, informal ceremony, they exchanged vows they had each written.

Small, as in just the two of them. It was not a wedding.

"Back in 1975 that's just the way it was, Byron says. "We weren't thinking about true marriage. And then it dawned on us, we needed to do the real thing."

On Feb. 14, 1980, they exchanged vows again, this time in front of a preacher. Twenty years later, on Valentine's Day, 2000, they renewed them.

Byron and Phyllis have two children — Candince and Bryan, both of Little Rock. They also have three grandchildren.

Byron is retired from the sales and legal business. Phyllis graduated from Hall in 1976 and went on to UALR and then to beauty school. She would eventually become an ordained minister. She owns Carousel Fit-4-Life Wellness Center in North Little Rock.

In honor of the place they met, Phyllis gathered KFC gadgets and gear for Byron's birthday last year. They do eat at that restaurant on occasion, although his favorite, the "Jumbo" meal — five pieces of chicken, mashed potatoes and coleslaw — is no longer a menu option.

"Back then, I would go home and look at my icebox and I would have six or seven boxes of chicken I hadn't even touched," he says.

He would go back for more the next night anyway, just for a chance to see Phyllis.

If Phyllis had big feelings for Byron in 1974, they have reached the same jumbo status as his preferred chicken meal by now.

"I loved him so much then," she says, "but I love him even more now."

*If you have an interesting how-we-met story or if you know someone who does, please call (501) 378-3496 or email:*

**cjenkins@arkansasonline.com**

**Phyllis Marshall and Byron Hodges** about 1974, not long after meeting

**Before Byron could date** Phyllis he had to call her mother. "My mom said, 'You sound like a nice young man. I don't have a problem with you coming over to visit Phyllis, but I will have to be there.' He said, 'Well, ma'am, I have a problem.' She said, 'What is your problem?' and he said, 'Well, I'm white.' She just busted out laughing and she said, 'Well, you do have a problem. But that is your problem. That is not our problem. You can come over.'"

**The first time I saw my spouse:**

**She says:** "I was sort of fascinated by him."

**He says:** "I thought I would come back the next night."

**On our wedding day:**

**She says:** "I knew he was going to be my lifelong husband. It was a private thing, but I couldn't wait to tell everybody."

**He says:** "I guess every man has apprehension, but I turned around and looked at her and I thought I would be miserable without her."

**My advice for a long marriage is:**

**She says:** "Respect — you must have it. Communication is the key. And it will not last if you don't have trust."

**He says:** "Respect, communication and love. You have to take time to talk to one another and you have to grow into being friends. There's no time I can't pick up the phone and say, 'I've got to have a little help on this.'"

*Photo 8 Arkansas Democrat-Gazette: Profile article on Phyllis and Byron Hodges' childhood love life (Written by Kimberly Dishongh).*

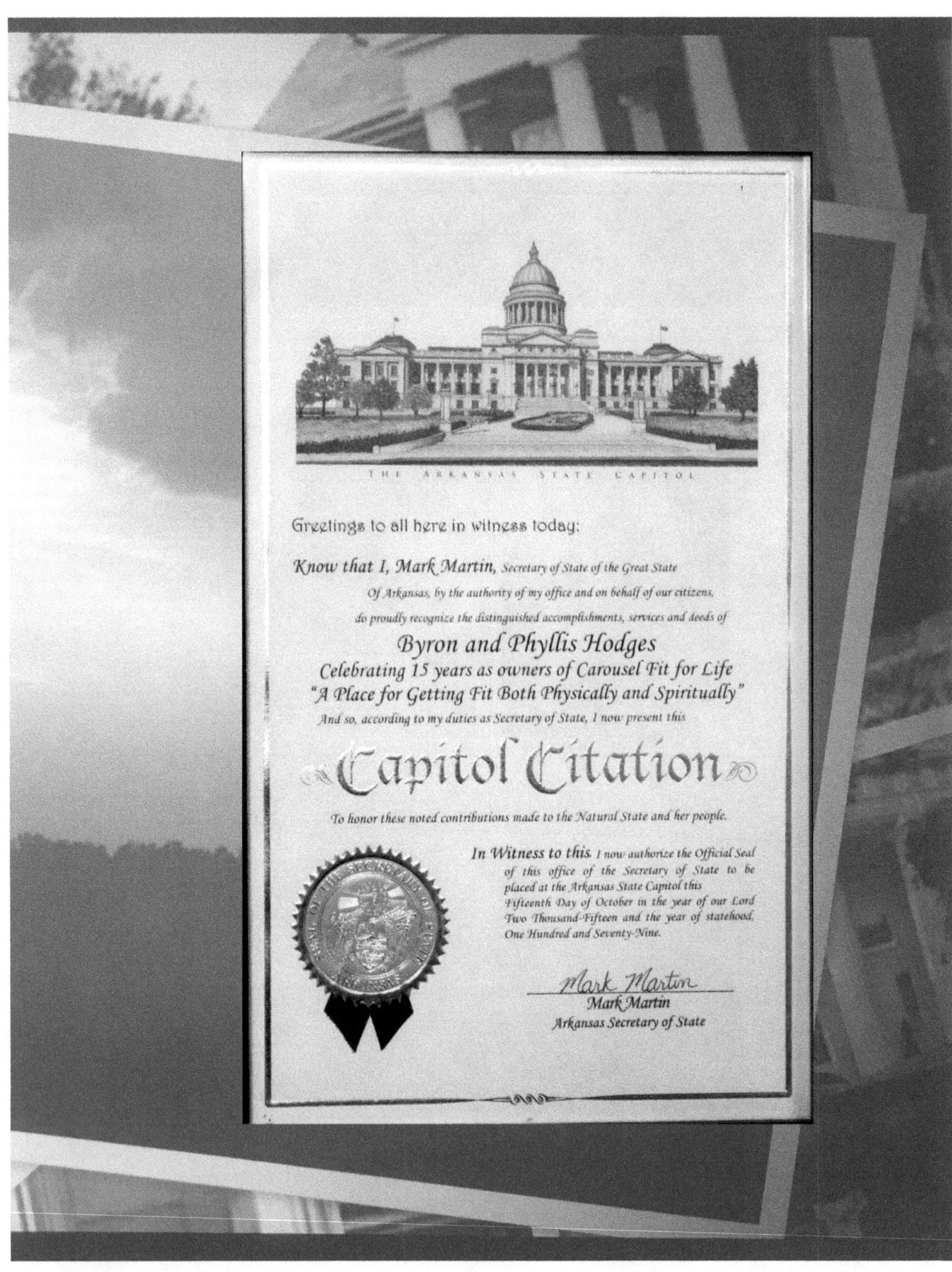

THE ARKANSAS STATE CAPITOL

Greetings to all here in witness today:

*Know that I, Mark Martin, Secretary of State of the Great State Of Arkansas, by the authority of my office and on behalf of our citizens, do proudly recognize the distinguished accomplishments, services and deeds of*

*Byron and Phyllis Hodges*

*Celebrating 15 years as owners of Carousel Fit for Life*

*"A Place for Getting Fit Both Physically and Spiritually"*

*And so, according to my duties as Secretary of State, I now present this*

Capitol Citation

*To honor these noted contributions made to the Natural State and her people.*

*In Witness to this I now authorize the Official Seal of this office of the Secretary of State to be placed at the Arkansas State Capitol this Fifteenth Day of October in the year of our Lord Two Thousand-Fifteen and the year of statehood, One Hundred and Seventy-Nine.*

Mark Martin

*Mark Martin*

*Arkansas Secretary of State*

*Photo 9 Capitol Citation from Arkansas Secretary of State, Mark Martin.*

STATE ARKANSAS PRESS

Volume XXVII, No. 16 Thursday, April 16, 1992

War Memorial Fitness Center, the new face at the Park

*Photo 10 (top) Arkansas State Press Newspaper: History Makers: First African-American and First Iranian Director and Assistant Director, War Memorial Fitness Center (renamed Jim Dailey Acquatics Fitness Center).*

*(bottom) Services offered at the Carousel Fit 4 Life Wellness Center.*

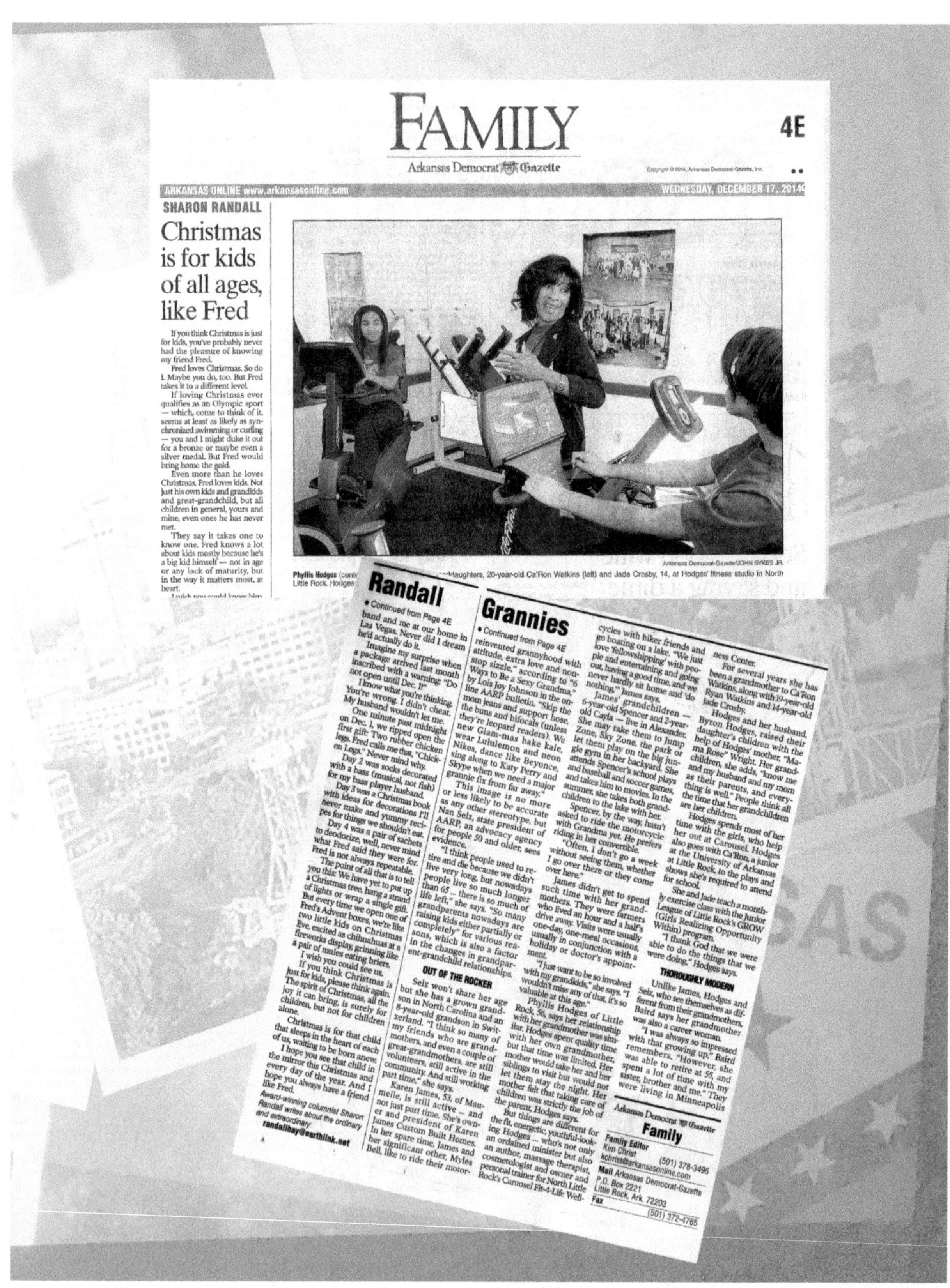

# FAMILY

4E

Arkansas Democrat-Gazette

ARKANSAS ONLINE www.arkansasonline.com WEDNESDAY, DECEMBER 17, 2014

SHARON RANDALL

## Christmas is for kids of all ages, like Fred

If you think Christmas is just for kids, you've probably never had the pleasure of knowing my friend Fred.

Fred loves Christmas. So do I. Maybe you do, too. But Fred takes it to a different level.

If loving Christmas ever qualifies as an Olympic sport — which, come to think of it, seems at least as likely as synchronized swimming or curling — you and I might duke it out for a bronze or maybe even a silver medal. But Fred would bring home the gold.

Even more than he loves Christmas, Fred loves kids. Not just his own kids and grandkids and great-grandchild, but all children in general, yours and mine, even ones he has never met.

They say it takes one to know one. Fred knows a lot about kids mostly because he's a big kid himself — not in age or any lack of maturity, but in the way it matters most, at heart.

[illegible]

Arkansas Democrat-Gazette/JOHN SYKES JR.

Phyllis Hodges (cent… …ddaughters, 20-year-old Ca'Ron Watkins (left) and Jade Crosby, 14, at Hodges' fitness studio in North Little Rock. Hodges…

## Randall

• Continued from Page 4E

band and me at our home in Las Vegas. Never did I dream he'd actually do it.

Imagine my surprise when a package arrived last month inscribed with a warning: "Do not open until Dec. 1!"

I know what you're thinking. You're wrong. I didn't cheat. My husband wouldn't let me.

One minute past midnight on Dec. 1, we ripped open the first gift: Two rubber chicken legs. Fred calls me that, "Chicken Legs." Never mind why.

Day 2 was socks decorated with a bass (musical, not fish) for my bass player husband.

Day 3 was a Christmas book with ideas for decorations I'll never make and yummy recipes for things we shouldn't eat.

Day 4 was a pair of sachets to deodorize, well, never mind what Fred said they were for. Fred is not always repeatable.

The point of all that is to tell you this: We have yet to put up a Christmas tree, hang a strand of lights or wrap a single gift. But every time we open one of Fred's Advent boxes, we're like two little kids on Christmas Eve, excited as chihuahuas at a fireworks display, grinning like a pair of mules eating briers.

I wish you could see us.

If you think Christmas is just for kids, please think again. The spirit of Christmas, all the joy it can bring, is surely for children, but not for children alone.

Christmas is for that child that sleeps in the heart of each of us, waiting to be born anew.

I hope you see that child in the mirror this Christmas and every day of the year. And I hope you always have a friend like Fred.

*Award-winning columnist Sharon Randall writes about the ordinary and extraordinary.*

**randallbay@earthlink.net**

## Grannies

• Continued from Page 4E

reinvented grannyhood with attitude, extra love and non-stop sizzle," according to "6 Ways to Be a Sexy Grandma," by Lois Joy Johnson in the online AARP bulletin. "Skip the mom jeans and support hose, the buns and bifocals (unless they're leopard readers). We new Glam-mas bake kale, wear Lululemon and neon Nikes, dance like Beyonce, sing along to Katy Perry and Skype when we need a major grannie fix from far away."

This image is no more or less likely to be accurate as any other stereotype, but Nan Selz, state president of AARP, an advocacy agency for people 50 and older, sees evidence.

"I think people used to retire and die because we didn't live very long, but nowadays people live so much longer than 65 ... there is so much of life left," she says. "So many grandparents nowadays are raising kids either partially or completely" for various reasons, which is also a factor in the changes in grandparent-grandchild relationships.

### OUT OF THE ROCKER

Selz won't share her age but she has a grown grandson in North Carolina and an 8-year-old grandson in Switzerland. "I think so many of my friends who are grandmothers, and even a couple of great-grandmothers, are still volunteers, still active in the community. And still working part time," she says.

Karen James, 53, of Maumelle, is still active ... and not just part time. She's owner and president of Karen James Custom Built Homes. In her spare time, James and her significant other, Myles Bell, like to ride their motorcycles with biker friends and go boating on a lake. "We just love 'fellowshipping' with people and entertaining and going out, having a good time, and we never hardly sit home and 'do nothing,'" James says.

James' grandchildren — 6-year-old Spencer and 2-year-old Cayla — live in Alexander. She may take them to Jump Zone, Sky Zone, the park or let them play on the big jungle gym in her backyard. She attends Spencer's school plays and baseball and soccer games, and takes him to movies. In the summer, she takes both grandchildren to the lake with her.

Spencer, by the way, hasn't asked to ride the motorcycle with Grandma yet. He prefers riding in her convertible.

"Often, I don't go a week without seeing them, whether I go over there or they come over here."

James didn't get to spend such time with her grandmothers. They were farmers who lived an hour and a half's drive away. Visits were usually one-day, one-meal occasions, usually in conjunction with a holiday or doctor's appointment.

"I just want to be so involved with my grandkids," she says. "I wouldn't miss any of that, it's so valuable at this age."

Phyllis Hodges of Little Rock, 56, says her relationship with her grandmother was similar. Hodges spent quality time with her own grandmother, but that time was limited. Her mother would take her and her siblings to visit but would not let them stay the night. Her mother felt that taking care of children was strictly the job of the parent, Hodges says.

But things are different for the fit, energetic, youthful-looking Hodges ... who's not only an ordained minister but also an author, massage therapist, cosmetologist and owner and personal trainer for North Little Rock's Carousel Fit-4-Life Wellness Center.

For several years she has been a grandmother to Ca'Ron Watkins, along with 19-year-old Ryan Watkins and 14-year-old Jade Crosby.

Hodges and her husband, Byron Hodges, raised their daughter's children with the help of Hodges' mother, "Mama Rose" Wright. Her grandchildren, she adds, "know me and my husband and my mom as their parents, and everything is well." People think all the time that her grandchildren are her children.

Hodges spends most of her time with the girls, who help her out at Carousel. Hodges also goes with Ca'Ron, a junior at the University of Arkansas at Little Rock, to the plays and shows she's required to attend for school.

She and Jade teach a monthly exercise class with the Junior League of Little Rock's GROW (Girls Realizing Opportunity Within) program.

"I thank God that we were able to do the things that we were doing," Hodges says.

### THOROUGHLY MODERN

Unlike James, Hodges and Selz, who see themselves as different from their grandmothers, Baird says her grandmother was also a career woman.

"I was always so impressed with that growing up," Baird remembers. "However, she was able to retire at 55, and spent a lot of time with my sister, brother and me." They were living in Minneapolis

Arkansas Democrat-Gazette
**Family**
**Family Editor**
Kim Christ
kchrist@arkansasonline.com (501) 378-3495
**Mail** Arkansas Democrat-Gazette
P.O. Box 2221
Little Rock, Ark. 72203
**Fax** (501) 372-4765

*Photo 11 Arkansas Democrat-Gazette Newspaper: Article featuring Phyllis and her two granddaughters, Ca'Ron and Jade working out at the family owned business, The Carousel Fit 4 Life Wellness Center.*

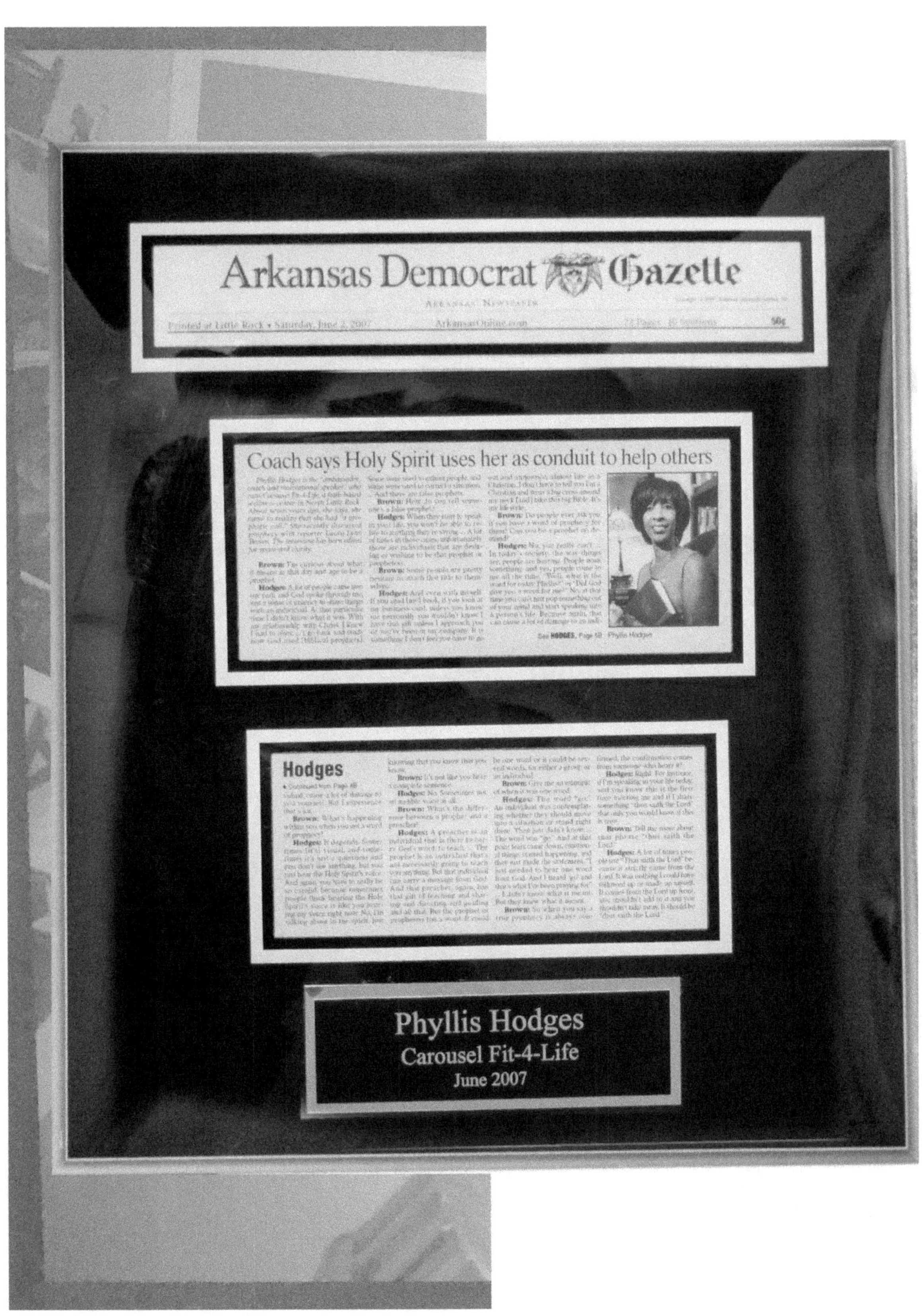

Arkansas Democrat Gazette

Printed at Little Rock • Saturday, June 2, 2007

Coach says Holy Spirit uses her as conduit to help others

Hodges

Phyllis Hodges

Carousel Fit-4-Life

June 2007

*Photo 12 Arkansas Democrat-Gazette 2007 special tribute to Phyllis Hodges*

*Photo 13 The unveiling of the book cover, "8 Years of Unforgettable History" held at Hawgz Blue Café, North Little Rock, Arkansas.*

*Photo 14 Governor Mike Huckabee presents the first business proclamation to Byron, Phyllis, and the advisory team.*

*Photo 15 Governor Mike Huckabee presents Phyllis, Byron, and the advisory team a business proclamation.*

*Photo 16 (top) Grandson Ryan holds the business proclamation that was presented by Governor Mike Huckabee to the Carousel Fit 4 Life Wellness Center.*
*(bottom) Granddaughter Jade is assisting Governor Mike Huckabee with the business proclamation, presented to the youth board and advisors.*

*Photo 17 The Carousel Fit 4 Life advisory team is presented with the business proclamation by Governor Mike BeeBe*

*Photo 18 Carousel Fit 4 Life Wellness Center advisors standing on the Arkansas State Capitol steps with Governor Mike Beebe during another successful year of business (Byron is holding the business proclamation).*

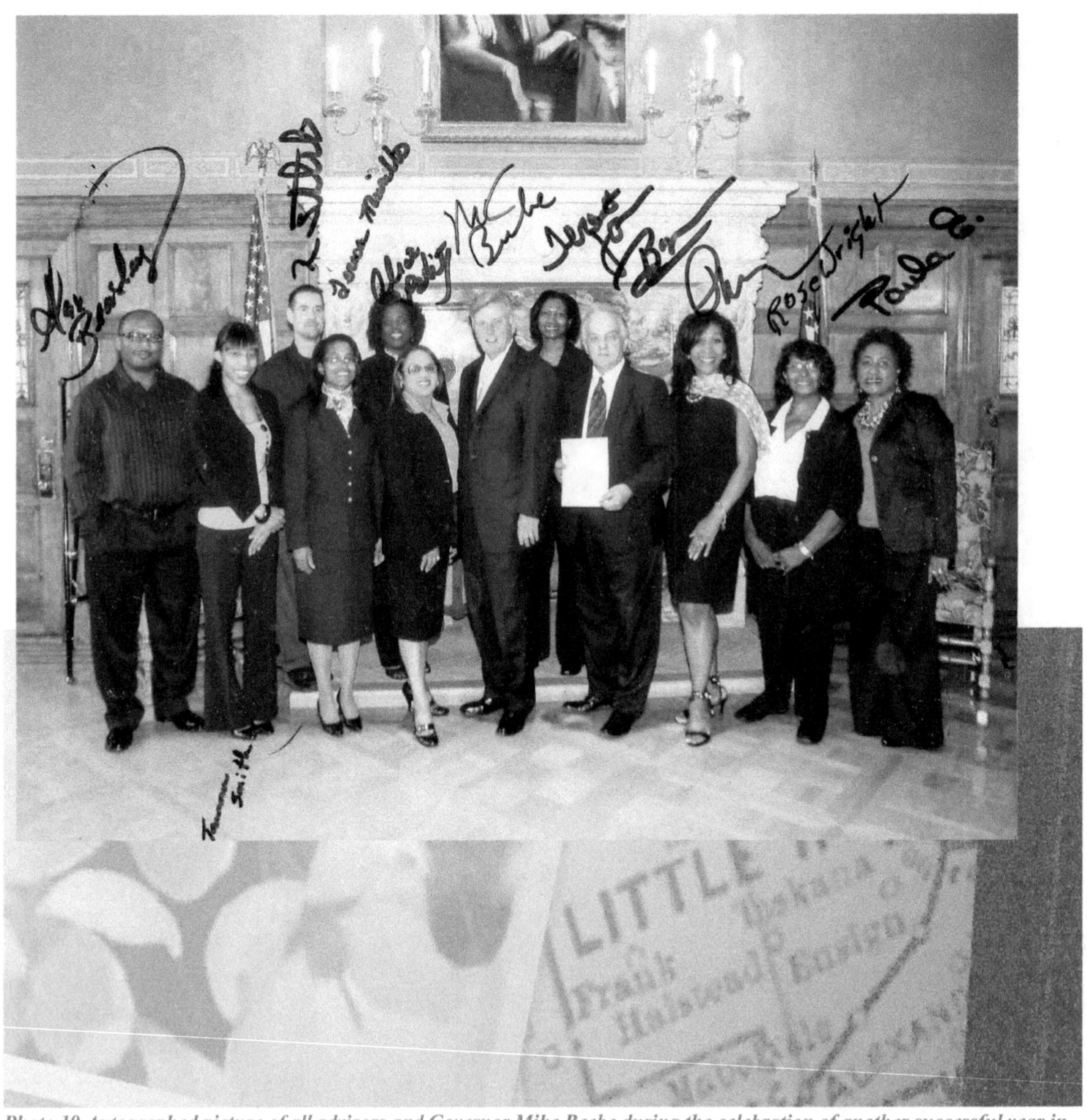

*Photo 19 Autographed picture of all advisors and Governor Mike Beebe during the celebration of another successful year in business (Byron is holding the business proclamation).*

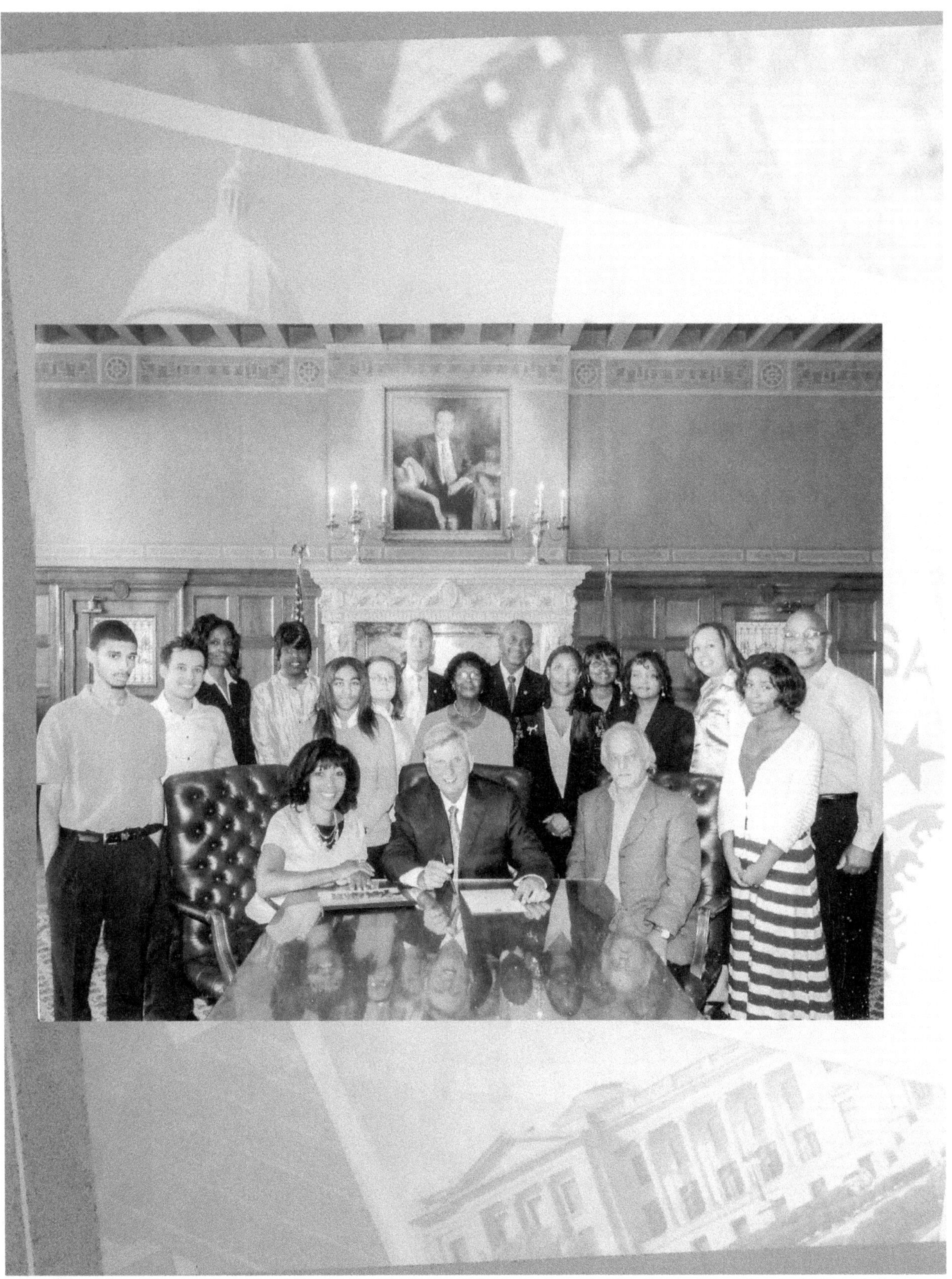

*Photo 20 At the table with Governor Mike Beebe, Phyllis, and Byron surrounded by the youth board and advisors during a special proclamation moment.*

*Photo 21 Phyllis holding the Carousel proclamation with Governor Mike Beebe, Byron, and the advisors while standing on the senators' steps inside the Arkansas State Capitol.*

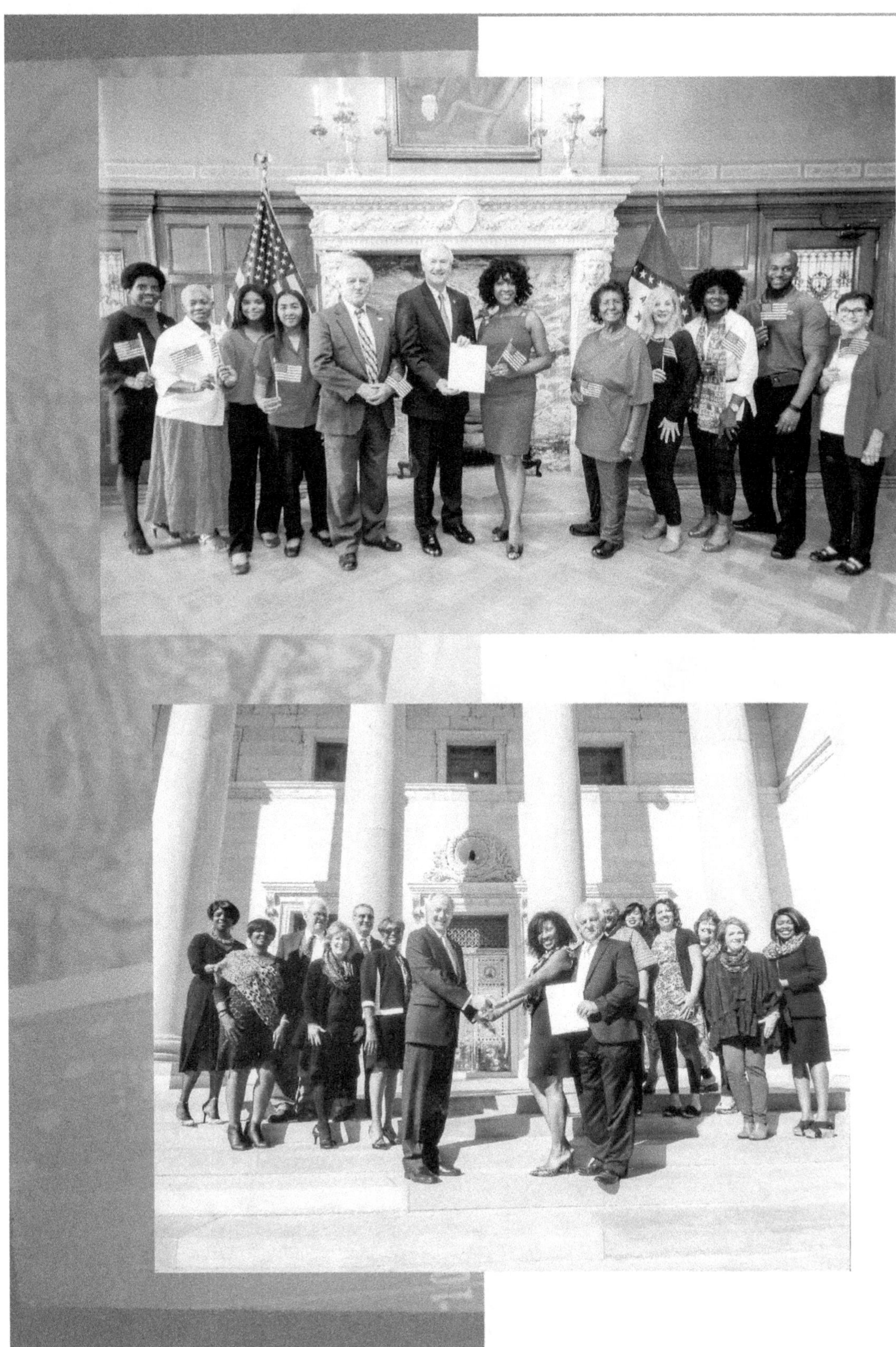

*Photo 22 (top) Election year: Governor Asa Hutchinson presents Phyllis and the Carousel team with a business proclamation while all members hold miniature flags.*
*(bottom) Unity pose on the outside, upper Capitol steps with Governor Asa Hutchinson and the advisors (Byron holds the business proclamation).*

*Photo 23 2018: Governor Asa Hutchinson presents Byron, Phyllis, and the Carousel Fit 4 Life team the business proclamation.*

*Photo 24 The Capitol Citation is presented to Phyllis, Byron, and the advisors from Secretary of State Mark Martin in his office.*

*Photo 25 North Little Rock Mayor Joe Smith presents Phyllis, Byron, and the Carousel team a proclamation inside the North Little Rock City Hall, located in the Argenta district down the street from the Carousel.*

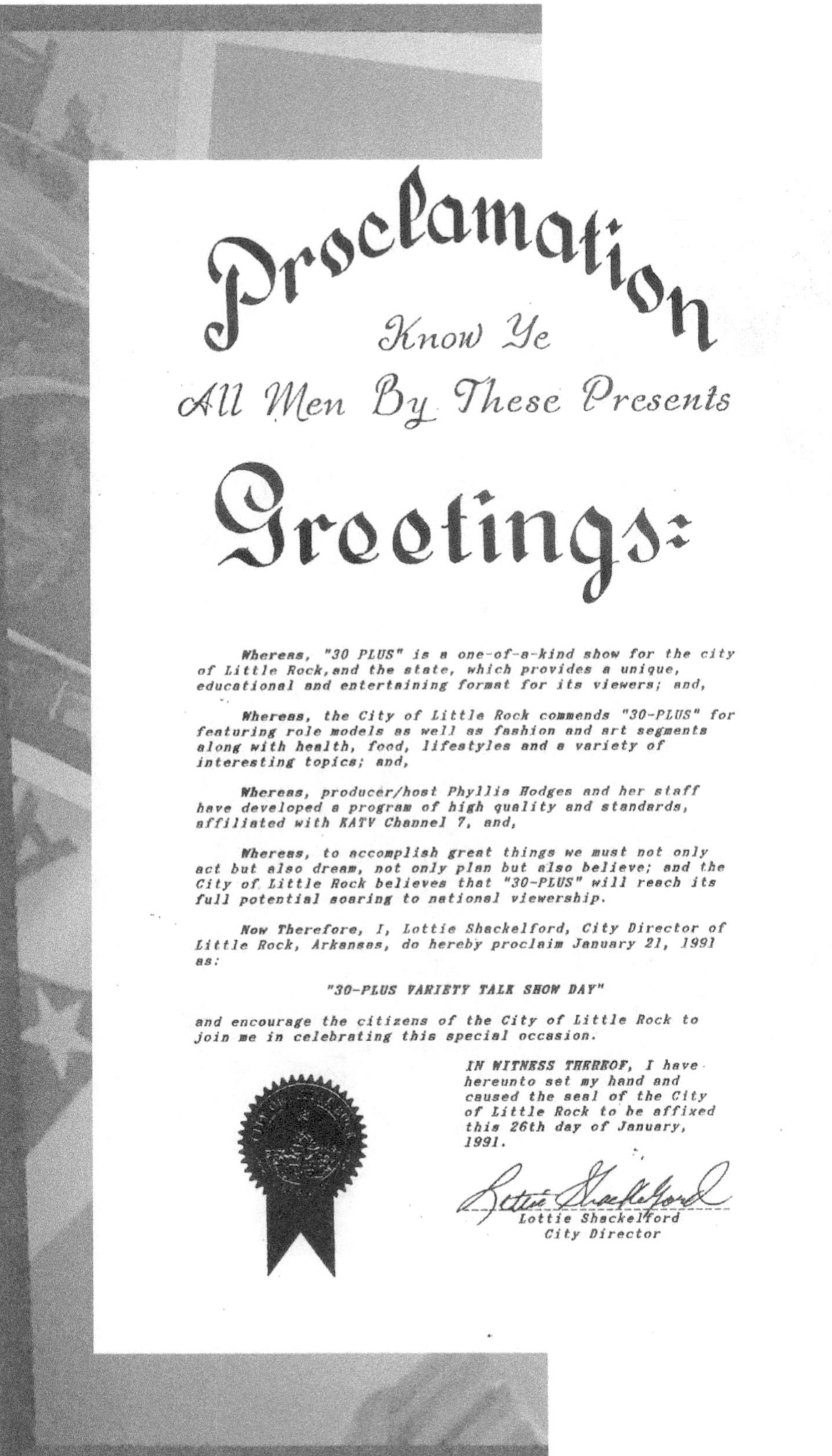

# Proclamation

*Know Ye*

*All Men By These Presents*

# Greetings:

*Whereas, "30 PLUS" is a one-of-a-kind show for the city of Little Rock, and the state, which provides a unique, educational and entertaining format for its viewers; and,*

*Whereas, the City of Little Rock commends "30-PLUS" for featuring role models as well as fashion and art segments along with health, food, lifestyles and a variety of interesting topics; and,*

*Whereas, producer/host Phyllis Hodges and her staff have developed a program of high quality and standards, affiliated with KATV Channel 7, and,*

*Whereas, to accomplish great things we must not only act but also dream, not only plan but also believe; and the City of Little Rock believes that "30-PLUS" will reach its full potential soaring to national viewership.*

*Now Therefore, I, Lottie Shackelford, City Director of Little Rock, Arkansas, do hereby proclaim January 21, 1991 as:*

***"30-PLUS VARIETY TALK SHOW DAY"***

*and encourage the citizens of the City of Little Rock to join me in celebrating this special occasion.*

*IN WITNESS THEREOF, I have hereunto set my hand and caused the seal of the City of Little Rock to be affixed this 26th day of January, 1991.*

*Lottie Shackelford*
*City Director*

*Photo 26 1991: A proclamation for Phyllis' talk show, "30 Plus" presented by City Director Lottie Shackleford.*

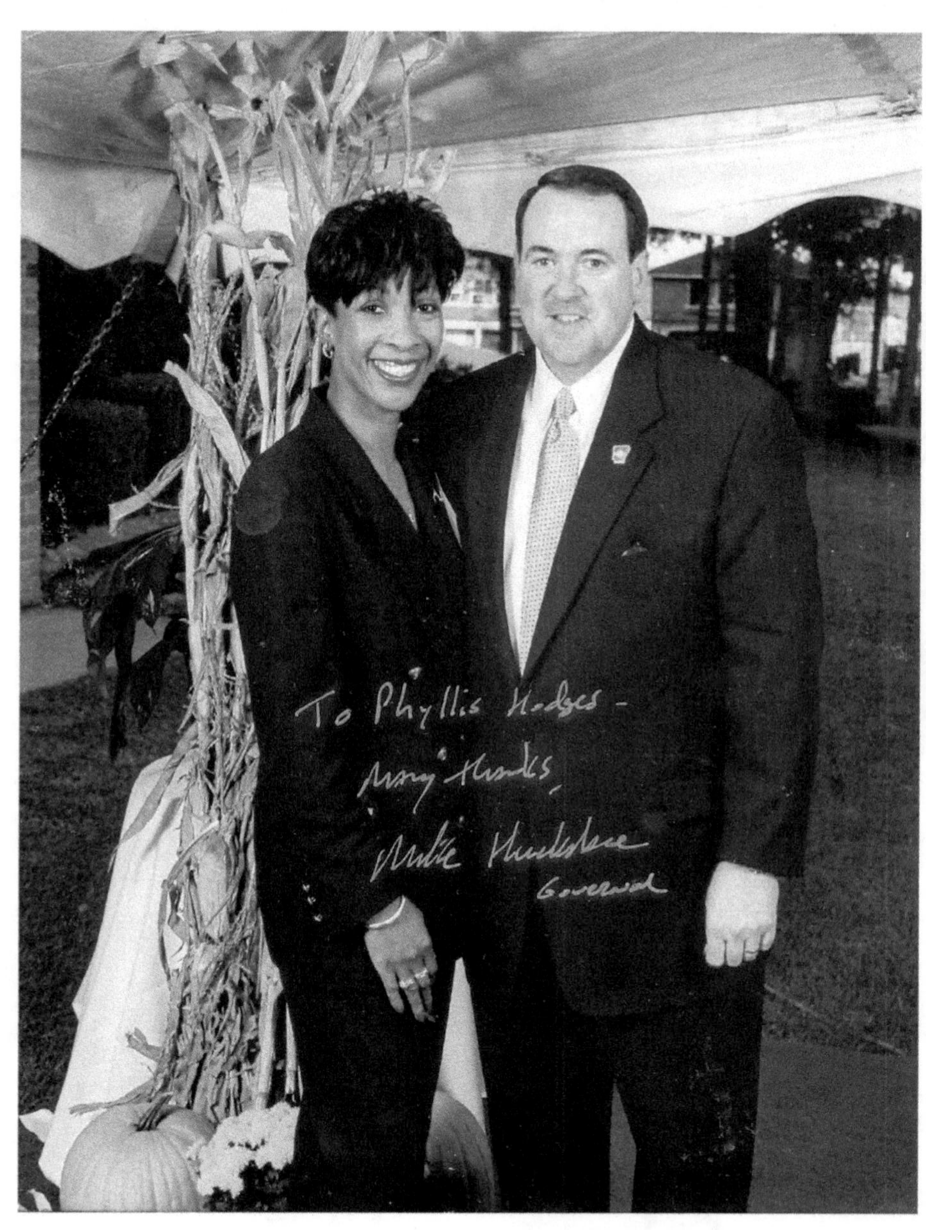


*Photo 27 At the Governor's Mansion for a special occasion with Governor Mike Huckabee.*

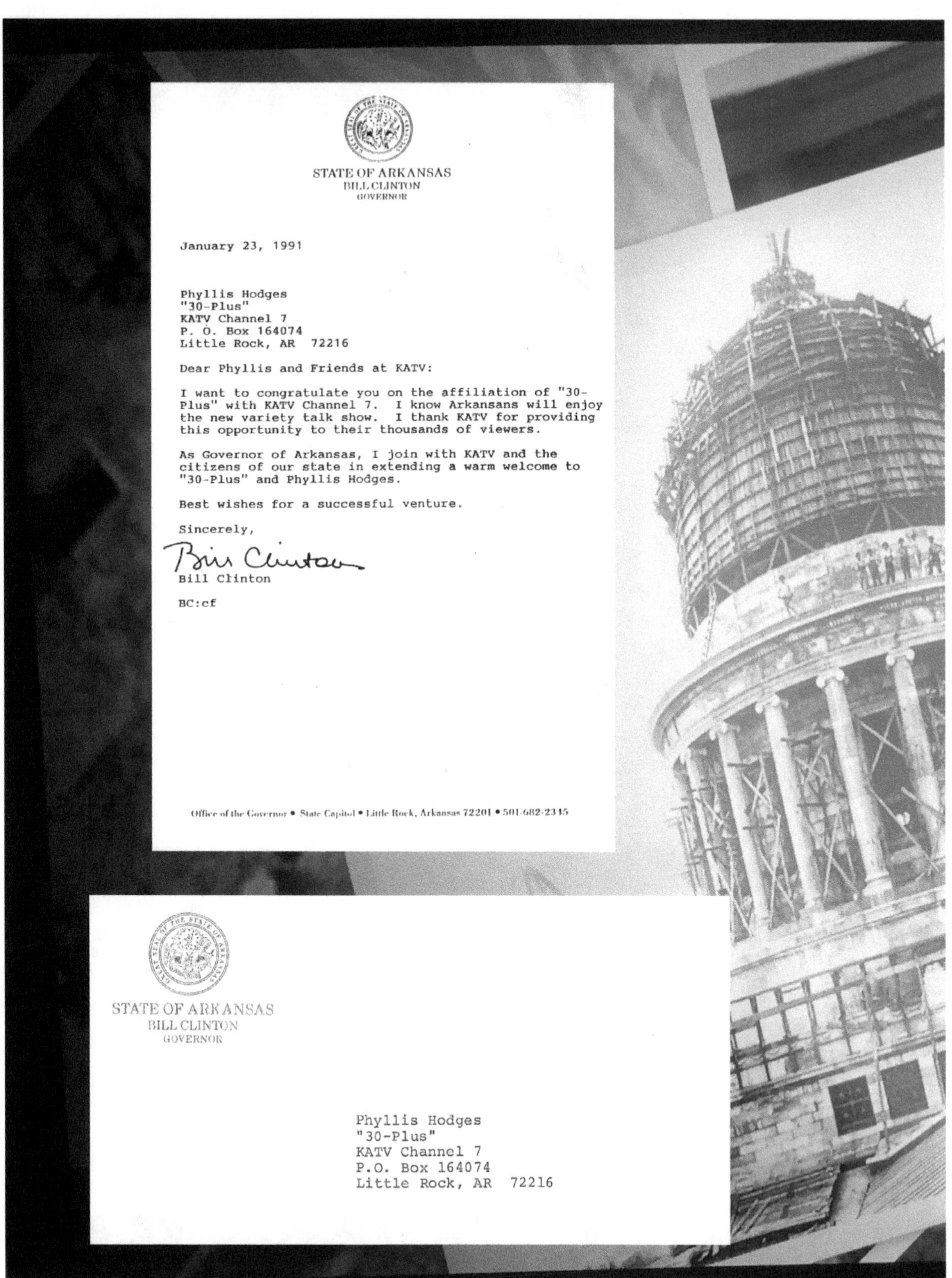
STATE OF ARKANSAS
BILL CLINTON
GOVERNOR

January 23, 1991

Phyllis Hodges
"30-Plus"
KATV Channel 7
P. O. Box 164074
Little Rock, AR 72216

Dear Phyllis and Friends at KATV:

I want to congratulate you on the affiliation of "30-Plus" with KATV Channel 7. I know Arkansans will enjoy the new variety talk show. I thank KATV for providing this opportunity to their thousands of viewers.

As Governor of Arkansas, I join with KATV and the citizens of our state in extending a warm welcome to "30-Plus" and Phyllis Hodges.

Best wishes for a successful venture.

Sincerely,

Bill Clinton

BC:cf

Office of the Governor • State Capitol • Little Rock, Arkansas 72201 • 501-682-2345

STATE OF ARKANSAS
BILL CLINTON
GOVERNOR

Phyllis Hodges
"30-Plus"
KATV Channel 7
P.O. Box 164074
Little Rock, AR 72216

*Photo 28 1991: Letter from Governor Bill Clinton congratulating Phyllis on her affiliation on her talk show, "30 Plus" which aired on KATV, Channel 7.*

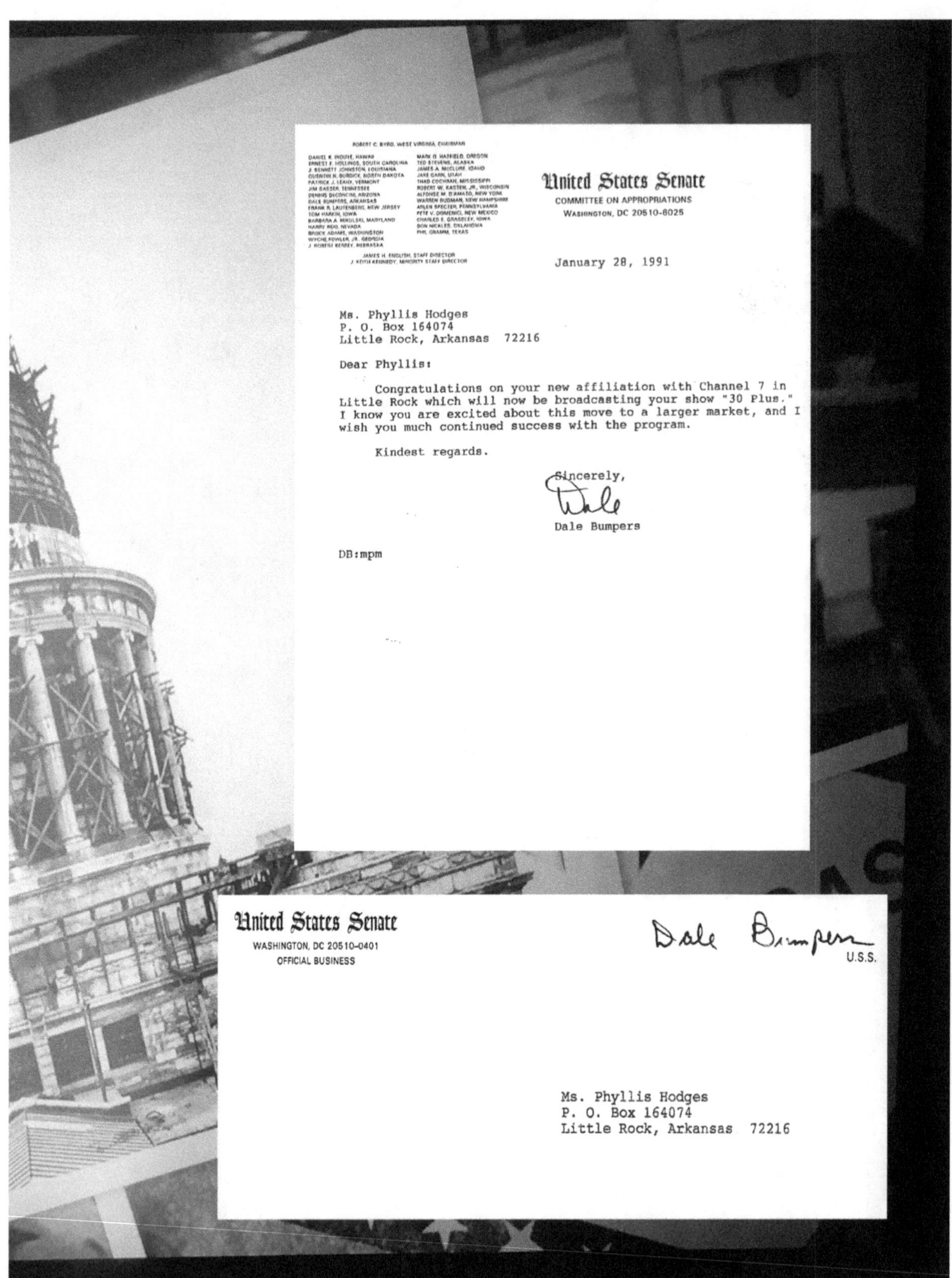



United States Senate
COMMITTEE ON APPROPRIATIONS
WASHINGTON, DC 20510-6025

January 28, 1991

Ms. Phyllis Hodges
P. O. Box 164074
Little Rock, Arkansas 72216

Dear Phyllis:

Congratulations on your new affiliation with Channel 7 in Little Rock which will now be broadcasting your show "30 Plus." I know you are excited about this move to a larger market, and I wish you much continued success with the program.

Kindest regards.

Sincerely,

Dale

Dale Bumpers

DB:mpm

United States Senate
WASHINGTON, DC 20510-0401
OFFICIAL BUSINESS

Dale Bumpers
U.S.S.

Ms. Phyllis Hodges
P. O. Box 164074
Little Rock, Arkansas 72216

*Photo 29 1991: Senator Dale Bumpers congratulating Phyllis on her "30 Plus" talk show affiliation.*

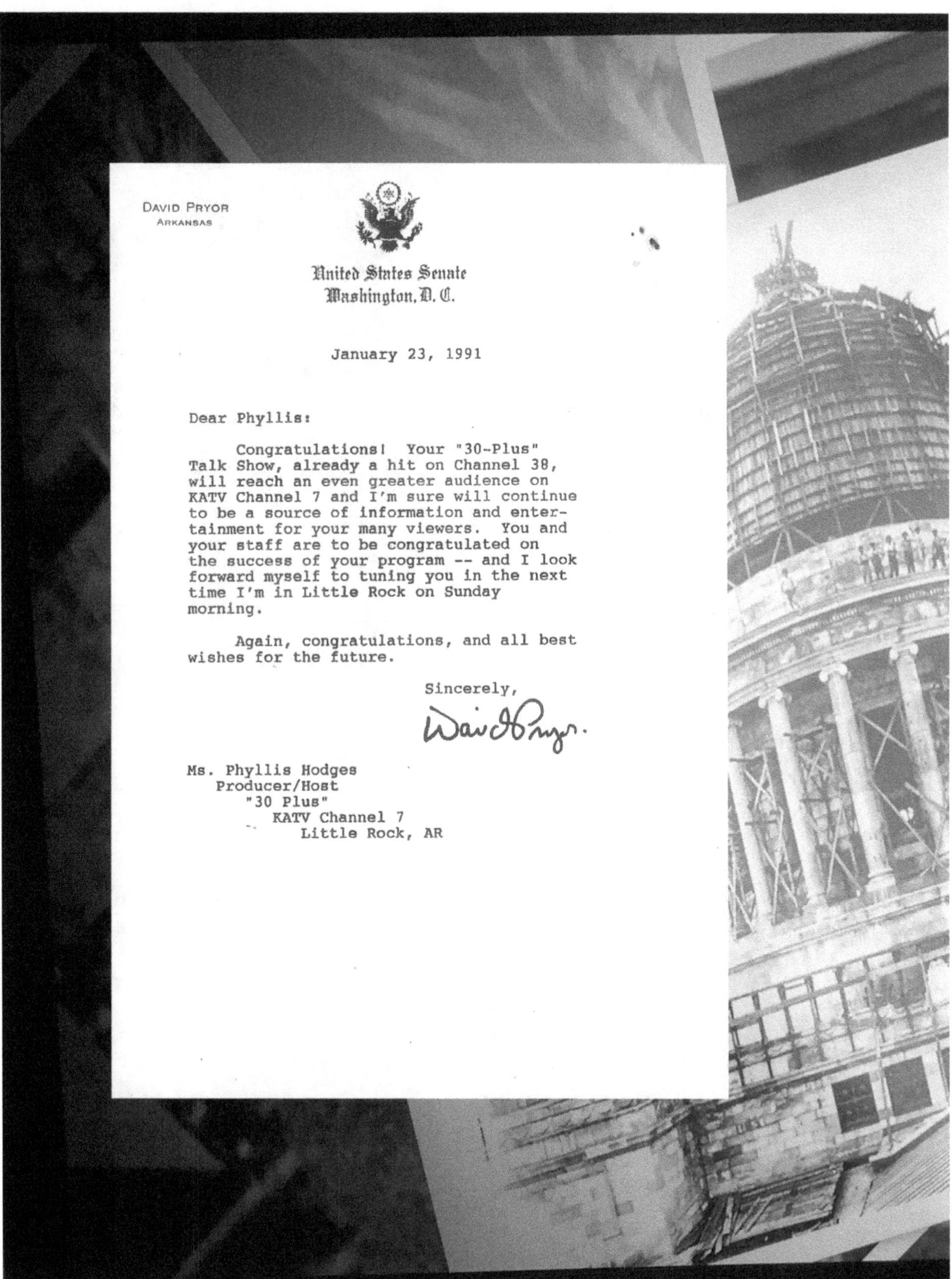

DAVID PRYOR
ARKANSAS

United States Senate
Washington, D. C.

January 23, 1991

Dear Phyllis:

Congratulations! Your "30-Plus" Talk Show, already a hit on Channel 38, will reach an even greater audience on KATV Channel 7 and I'm sure will continue to be a source of information and entertainment for your many viewers. You and your staff are to be congratulated on the success of your program -- and I look forward myself to tuning you in the next time I'm in Little Rock on Sunday morning.

Again, congratulations, and all best wishes for the future.

Sincerely,

David Pryor.

Ms. Phyllis Hodges
Producer/Host
"30 Plus"
KATV Channel 7
Little Rock, AR

*Photo 30 1991: Letter from Senator David Pryor congratulating Phyllis on her television move from Channel 38 to Channel 7. He mentioned looking forward to watching the show when he returned to Arkansas on Sundays.*

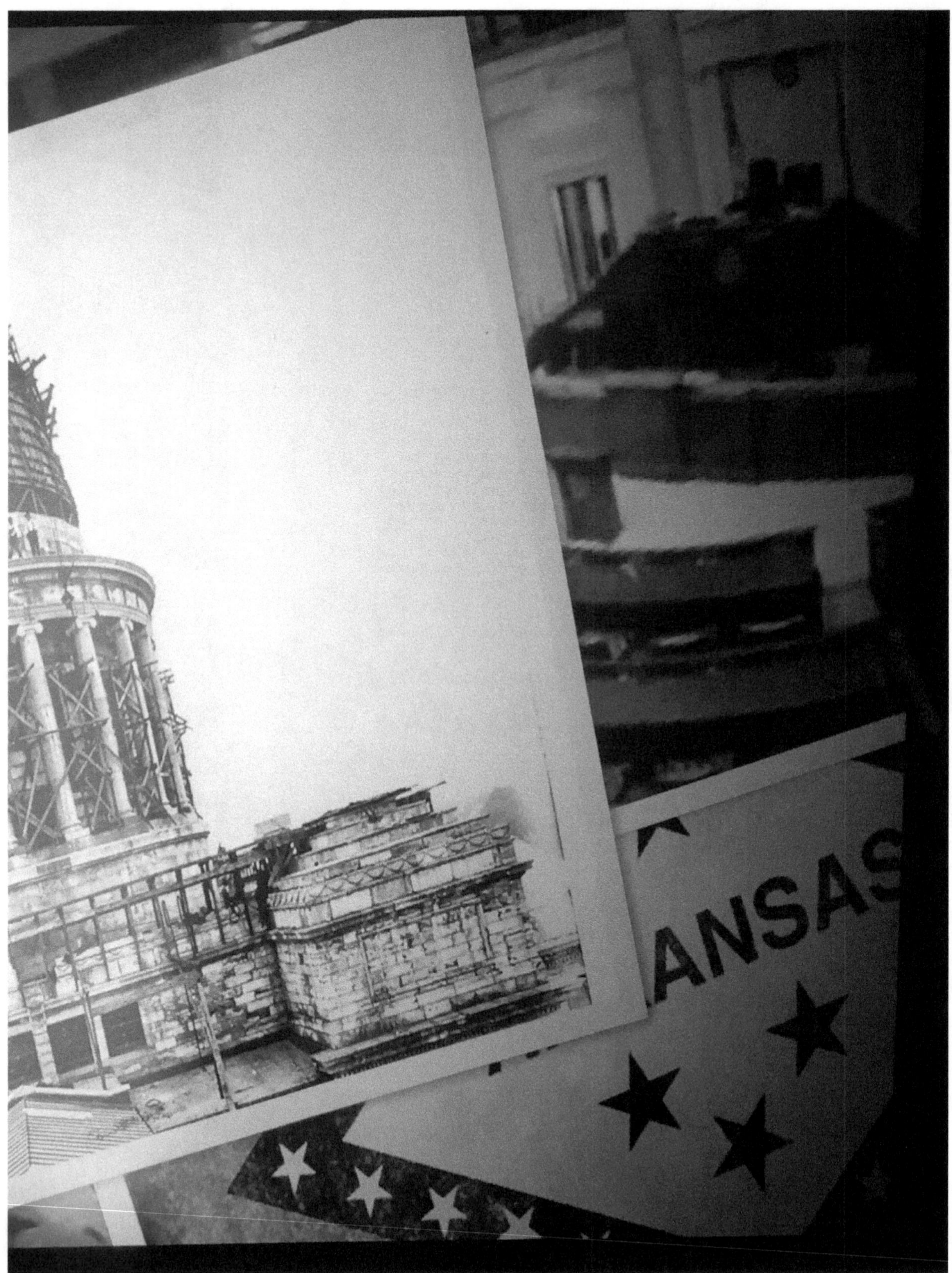

*Photo 31 Arkansas historical images.*

# Acclaim for 8 Years of Unforgettable History

"Those who don't know history are doomed to repeat it."
**Edmund Burke**

"It is imperative that young people know and understand critical movements throughout history, not only in this nation but around the world. We are living in a time of renewed apartheid in America when it has become fashionable to persecute anyone that is different from the norm. This is as dangerous to us as Hitler was to Germany in the early 20th century. Today's anti-intellectual movement is very dangerous when we encourage persons not to read, not to question, not to involve themselves in government by not voting. We have created the current situation we find ourselves in with a president who tweets from television without sound facts and logic. We must know our past so that we can chart our future."

Maxine Allen

Rev. Maxine Allen is the first African-American female to be ordained as an elder in The United Methodist Church in Arkansas (1999). She currently serves as the first female to serve as president of the Christian Ministerial Alliance of Little Rock, Arkansas.

---

"Taking a look back at the history of the African-American experience is crucial to promoting a deeper understanding of this country's past and prompts what should be an ongoing discussion as to what degree we have progressed as a society. Phyllis Hodges details the struggles and triumphs of notable African-Americans in her timely book!"

**Nichelle Brown Christian**
Columnist, Inside Perspective, The Lincoln Echo Newspaper
Co-Founder, Janis F. Kearney Writers Group

"It is extremely important for our youth to know their history. By reading, seeing, or hearing history, our youth can learn how their forefathers/mothers gave their lives so that we can live a free and abundant life which our Heavenly Father promised in His Word."

**Lencola Sullivan**
Miss Arkansas 1980
Miss American, 4th runner-up

---

"It is vitally important that our children learn Black History for the sake of establishing cultural identity and a pride within themselves. It's a glorious heritage that will change and alter their outlook in not only themselves, but the ever-changing world around them."

**Keyono Buck Cook**
Author of "Gutta"

---

"It's important to know your history because it defines your heritage and your roots."

**Curtis "JJ" Adams**
1968 Recruitment of the Original Black Panther Party

---

Dr. Hamilton was one of the first to integrate Little Rock University, now the University of Arkansas, and the first woman of color to integrate Governor Win Rockefeller's office after he became governor.

"It should be noted that history is history,
even when others fail to recognize or acknowledge it.
Therefore, we should all be accountable for knowing it as well as actively and positively contributing to it. Kudos to Phyllis Hodges for this beautiful book that does just that!"

**Dr. Wanda Hamilton**
Pioneer in Education & Government/Advocate for Children & Families

# News Worthy

# After the Great History-Making Moment...

*Everyone waited for:*

- ∂ Illinois governor heading for impeachment trial
- ∂ Afghanistan sends proposal to NATO
- ∂ Rwandan Troops enter Congo to find Hutu Militia leaders
- ∂ U.S. to be allowed new routes to supply troops in Afghanistan

# First Day as President

Obama and Michelle began their day at a prayer service which is traditional for new administration. The president talks about economy, wars, order ethics rules, and freezes some salaries.

The Athletic Profile is the new number one fan, Barack Obama who loves sports.

# Historic Moment Snapshots

All generations are there for the president. What's the conversation now on the ride back home from Washington DC? What about the cheers in the meeting rooms, even the conversations about all the newspaper articles, the many tweets, and people now talking about how big the crowds were. The Washington Post reported a crowd of 1.8 million; however, there was such a controversy over how many people attended the 1995 Million Man March. It was ordered by Congress to stop giving an estimated count. In 1981, President Ronald Reagan's inauguration drew about 500,000 people. In 1993, President Bill Clinton's inauguration drew about 800,000 according to the Park Service.

# Decent and in Order

Ministers from a variety of backgrounds opened and closed Tuesday's inauguration ceremonies.

Rev. Rick Warren was President Barack Obama's choice to give the invocation.

Rev. Joseph Lowery gave the benediction at the end of the swearing-in ceremony; his remarks started with the words from the Negro-National Anthem. Lowery brought some humor into his remarks which caused Barack to smile. The one and only, Aretha Franklin, was among some of the celebrities performing as part of the ceremonies at the Capitol.

# The Peaceful Transfer of Power

## Republican George W. Bush to Democrat Barack Obama

Obama stood on Capitol steps, placed his left hand on the Bible used by Abraham Lincoln, and repeated the inaugural oath (There was a false start and an awkward pause). Afterwards, the Obamas climbed out of the heavily armored presidential limousine and walked a few blocks along Pennsylvania Avenue. They were carefully watched by security agents while they waved at the crowds. They later put the day's formality behind them to begin the celebration of the ten inaugural balls. At the Commander in Chief ball, Barack announced, "Tonight we celebrate, tomorrow the work begins." That night, many announcements, speeches, waves, dances, and fellowshipping contributed to the 47-year-old former senator from Illinois' transformation into the president of the United States of America.

# The 4-Poets and the Presidential Inaugurations

1961 - The *first* poet, Robert Frost, invited by John F. Kennedy, but because of the weather, sun, and wind he was not able to deliver the poem.

1993 - President Clinton invited Dr. Maya Angelou.

1997 - President Clinton invited Miller William.

2009 - President-Elect Barack Obama invited Mrs. Elizabeth Alexander.

# TV Coverage

It all began here in front of my television at the Carousel Fit-4-Life Wellness Center. The morning of the inauguration, it was very quiet in the Carousel; there were only a few clients. I had both televisions on, one in the work-out room and the other one in my office. I would excuse myself from my clients and go to my office to see up-close shots and to make sure I wouldn't miss anything. I made sure I had my cell phone, so I could call my friends to make sure they were watching as well. I made sure my phone was charged because I wanted to be prepared to take many pictures.

Nobody could have told me I wasn't in Washington DC with the rest of the world at our incoming president's live coverage inauguration because most networks began coverage on Tuesday, January 20th, 2009 at 9:00 a.m. Central time, after special inaugural editions of their early morning programs. The swearing- in ceremony officially began at 10:30 a.m. on the west front of the Capitol. The inaugural parade down Pennsylvania Avenue kicked off at 1:30 p.m., with the inaugural balls starting around 7:00 p.m.

## *Network Coverage Included...*

CBS, ABC, NBC, PBS, Fox News Channel, CNN, MSNBC, C-SPAN, and the Disney Channel all covered the inauguration. There was a stampede of other networks (cable outlets) to cover the event as well including: Nickelodeon, BET, TV One, and QVC.

It's exciting to me to know that even QVC got in on the action! They sold everything from Obama stamps from Liberia to Obama-Biden coins, Obama throw blankets, lapel pins, and medallions. I thought this was a smart business move for QVC.

There was also continuous coverage of the inauguration on various websites, blogs, and video streaming.

# History Was Being Made

A special planned event, a free welcome concert, "We are one," on the steps of the Lincoln Memorial Historical Passages was to be read by Jamie Foxx, Martin Luther King III, Queen Latifah, and Denzel Washington. The performers included Beyoncé, Mary J. Blige, Bono, Garth Brooks, Sheryl Crow, Josh Groban, Herbie Hancock, John Legend, John Mellencamp, Shakira, Bruce Springsteen, James Taylor, Usher, and Stevie Wonder. I personally called this free concert the "Heavy Hitters," because so many people would never be able to afford to pay to see headliners like these in one place.

## *His Day in History: Obama Heads for D.C*

President-Elect Barack Obama stepped onto a vintage train car and traveled to Washington as part of a three-day prelude to his inauguration as the country's 44$^{th}$ president. Obama spoke from a presidential stage, with nine American Flags in the background. His wife Michelle and their daughters, Malia, 10-years-old, and Sasha, 7-years-old, joined him on stage. Malia held a digital camera, taking pictures of her father and the crowd of about 200 invited guests. I smile while I write this history book and think about my two granddaughters, Ca'Ron and Jade, taking pictures during special moments in our lives. All of which will go down in history!

A vintage train car, wow, I can only imagine! I've never ridden a train before, but my Granddad, John Henry Bolden, was a Missouri Pacific Train Oiler on the night shift. This was way back in the day. My mom had an opportunity as a child, being the youngest daughter, to remember plenty of train trips with her mother, my grandmother, and her brother. Granddad had a family pass, so the family could travel free at any time. I fantasize that the train the Obamas road on could've been one of the trains my granddad worked on.

# Commemorative Moments

It was estimated that at least 1.5 million people would be attending Obama's inaugural ceremony.

As Arkansans, we waited in line hoping and praying that we would receive a ticket to witness a moment in history; a silver-trimmed card made of heavy stock paper covered with fancy calligraphy that read, "The Favor of Your Presence is requested at the Ceremonies attending the inauguration of the President and Vice-President of the United States." On the opposite side of the invitation was a map of the U.S. Capitol grounds. There were 1,578 tickets allotted to Arkansas' congressional delegation. With all of this excitement in the air, everyone was talking about going to the inauguration. I had to remember that I had a family and being a small business owner these past few years had been very challenging financially, so I decided I was not going to add any other challenges to my life.

Instead, I made up my mind that I wasn't going to miss any television for the next few months. That's very rare for me because I'm not a fan of television; that's something my husband and son do, watching television all the time. However, because of this impending history-making moment, television and newspaper became my best friends.

Later, I would read the newspapers and find out that friends I knew (Bethania Gill, Margaret Preston, her grandson, and many others) were blessed to receive tickets. I found myself happy for them that they were about to attend the inauguration. There were several hundred Arkansans traveling to Washington D.C. on chartered tour buses. Many people had decided to carpool. Flights were being scheduled all over the world for this historic event!

The marching bands of the University of Arkansas at Pine Bluff and Siloam Springs High School were to attend. Both of these bands had the honor to be present and mark history. They would march along Pennsylvania Avenue, honoring President-Elect Barack Obama.

Former Vice President and Nobel Laureate Al Gore hosted a "kids" inaugural event held at the Verizon Center. Michelle Obama challenged the audience saying, "We are the future concert to serve our country." She encouraged the youth to serve their communities, volunteer in homeless shelters, visit the elderly, and write letters to U.S. Troops. Teen star Miley Cyrus was in attendance. She performed her inspirational song, "The Climb" then went into the audience to quiz kids on some history.

Comedian George Lopez joked with the crowd saying that although they were missing school, they were indeed having a quiz. He incorporated the "Yes, we can," slogan.

The guest of honor was the boxing legend Muhammad Ali, who was celebrating his 67th birthday. This was a party of 1,400 that included other celebrities, lawmakers, and native Kentuckians. It was stated that it was only befitting that both Obama and Ali were being saluted at the same time because Obama was the leader of the greatest nation on earth, and Muhammad Ali was the greatest boxer of all time.

I once had the opportunity to interview Muhammad Ali and take pictures with him. It was a dream come true. He was in Pine Bluff, Arkansas. My next dream is to give a copy of this history book to Former President Obama one day which would include an interview with him and a photo opt.

Reading about all of this and watching the events unfold on television caused such a feeling of gratitude within me. It confirmed how important history is and that our youth should know as much about their history as possible. My hope is that while reading this book that includes the histories of eight Arkansas Firsts, you will relate to their thoughts on why they think it's imperative that everyone (including our youth) know their history.

## The Washington Post

Special 38 Page Commemorative Section and Staff Writers

### *Obama celebrates*

The Obama family hosted about 100 friends at the Blair House. The guests included family, old friends, classmates from high school, former college professors, basketball buddies, and political mentors. There were also friends Obama made while working as a community organizer, as well as Obama's boss, Gerald Kellman.

Obama took his most extensive tour of Washington since moving there. He visited 14 wounded soldiers at Walter Reed Army Medical Center. Then, he went to the stock show Bruce Youth Work shelter for homeless teenagers. Later, Obama visited Calvin Coolidge Senior High School in the northwest.

Obama was very involved in all his stop - rolling up his sleeves painting while he was at the youth work shelter; then, he and Michelle both clapped and danced to the beat of the cheer during an impromptu cheer. He delivered a brief speech to 300 volunteers from local service organizations.

## Things most don't know about

President Obama, Hartford, and Mary Black Eagle adopted Barack Obama in a Native American ceremony in May. The candidate made a campaign stop at the Vast Crow Reservation. The adoption marked an unusually intimate intertwining of politics, history, and families. Obama's outreach to Native Americans was part of a political strategy during critical primary battles in western states. The adoption is no scam ordered campaign prop. It's a reverend compact that has linked the first family with five generations of first Americans. Obama daughters, Sasha and Malia, beamed as they met their adoptive grandparents.

Obama named his key team to positions. The new president, for the first time, assumed the responsibility for the Iraq War that he opposed from its inception and the series of international crisis. Obama instructed the Pentagon to prepare for a stepped-up withdrawal of combat troops from Iraq, to be completed within 16 months, and to hear proposals for turning around the deteriorating war in Afghanistan.

A variety of things happened during the history-making moment; President-Elect Barack Obama honors Americans whose lifetime of Public Service has been enhanced by a dedication to bipartisan achievement as well as Senator John McCain whom he defeated in November. Obama also paid tribute to former Secretary of State and retired General Colin Powell, and Vice President-Elect Joe Biden. It was a possibility that his work could be overwhelmed with calls and pictures being sent; people could anticipate delays. It was often stated that Barack was known as the Blackberry-toting president.

# Encore for the Obama's

# OBAMA 303 ELECTORAL VOTES- 270 NEEDED TO WIN! ROMNEY 206.

Obama wins the re-election. Republican Mitt Romney speaks on election night in Boston, Massachusetts. Romney conceded the election to President Barack Obama. During a second White House term, Obama tweeted to supporters as he celebrated four more years in the White House. The turnout was enormous but much lower than the 2008 totals.

## *Election Night 2012*

Supporters of President Obama turn out in abundance at the Chicago's McCormick Place Convention Center after hearing that Obama had won! The second term, President Obama acknowledges supporters after a bitterly fought campaign; his victory speech summoned some of the poetic flourishes of 2008. It's been stated that this election was the most expensive election in America.

A common quote the president found himself often saying was, "The Best Is Yet to Come." While I read enormous amounts of papers doing my research, I noticed in the Wednesday, November 7th, 2012, paper where pictures showed members of the Army National Guard stationed along the New Jersey coastline filling out absent voter ballots. All I could think was, there is no reason we, the people, could not vote. I found myself calling and encouraging my family and friends to vote early and not to wait for the election date just in case something came up or long lines would be a hindrance.

# 2012 Obama takes most Battleground States

## *"Four More Years..."*

Looking back, I'm contemplating the question many have asked, "Did blacks vote for President Obama?" The first time around, I believe it was out of a sense of pride that gave Obama the votes from most black people, but for the second term, the threats to rescind Obamacare and so many other negative promises from the other party brought blacks out again to vote!

# What's about to happen now?

## The Big Reveal

Arkansans reveal who got their tickets to the State of the Union speech. The biggest show in town is the State of the Union address and tickets are scarce and coveted. First Lady Michelle Obama sits next to an empty seat honoring victims of gun violence during President Barack Obama's State of the Union speech. While I watch this moment in history unfold, I was emotional. I started to recap all the feelings over the past eight years of how my life would never be the same and how much hope I felt others had gained through this process of watching history unfold before our eyes. Plus, witnessing change that had never been, I wondered would it ever be again!

## The Date is Set

The date for the inauguration, set in the Constitution, January 20th falls on a Sunday the year of 2013. Obama and Biden were to be sworn in for second terms in separate, private ceremonies today. Monday in the public ceremonies when Obama will take the oath of office at noon, he will deliver an inaugural address before a large crowd and a national television audience in the millions. A traditional lunch with lawmakers in the Capitol will follow, as will the inaugural parade along Pennsylvania Avenue toward the White House. Most Arkansans will be tuning in to see the Little Rock Central High School.

## Little Rock Central Inaugural Performance

The band, under the direction of Brice Evans, raised about $100,000. Financial help came from a donation from the city of Little Rock and the Little Rock Convention of Visitors Bureau. The Central High Group is to use the trip to see many of Washington's landmarks. It was so exciting to know many of the students and members of the Flag Line personally.

## Attendees

Workers spent a lot of time erecting lighting and stages for Obama's two official inaugural balls. They would be entertained by Stevie Wonder, Alicia Keys, and the cast of tv's "Glee."

It was estimated that as many as 800,000 people will attend Monday's public ceremonies, which is more than the number of people who live in the city, and far fewer than 1.8 million who were at the Obama's first inauguration in 2009. James Taylor performed "America the Beautiful." Kelly Clarkson sang "My Country Tis of Thee," and Beyoncé closed the inaugural ceremony singing "The National Anthem."

## A Private Affair

The private, swearing-in affair, attended only by First Lady Michelle and daughters, Malia and Sasha, was held at the White House on Sunday morning in advance to the public moment forced by a rare quirk of the constitutional calendar. This private but official swearing in of the 44th president at 10:55 am Central time was just the seventh such event in history to be held before the public ceremony and the first since Ronald Reagan's second inaugural, each one occurring because the constitutionally mandated date for inauguration fell on a Sunday. Michelle, holding the Robinson family Bible and their daughters, stood by while Chief Justice John Roberts officially swore in President Barack Obama in the grand blue room as he recited the oath. After they finished, Roberts congratulated Obama. Obama thanked him and embraced his wife and daughters. Sasha said, "Good Job, Daddy." And he replied, "I did it!"

## Presidential Influence

The president has often said Martin Luther King is one of two people he admires "more than anybody in American history." President Abraham Lincoln is the other. During the ceremonial oath of office on Monday January 21, 2013, using the two men's Bibles, Lincoln's which Obama also used in 2009 will rest on top of King's which is larger. A video was released by inaugural planners with Obama saying, "The movement they represent are the only reason that it's possible for him to be inaugurated!"

At the Inaugural Ball, President Obama and First Lady Michelle, danced as Jennifer Hudson sings Al Green's "Let's Stay Together."

## What Was Going On?

President Barack campaigned for Democrat Edward Marking ahead of the U.S. Senate special election June 25, 2013, in Massachusetts telling supporters in Boston that the veteran lawmaker will continue the state's legacy of sending "tough" and "smart" leaders to Washington.

President Barack Obama squeezed in a nine-hole round of golf in Southern California at the Sunny Lands Estate with two childhood friends from Hawaii and a White House aide, after wrapping up weekend talks with Chinese President Xi Jinping.

U.S. - China talks, a two-day summit with China's new leader Xi Jinping. Obama had a custom-made redwood bench made for his Chinese counterpart. They held more than eight hours of talks over the course of the two-day summit pertaining to climate change and cybersecurity.

Present Barack called on GOP leaders to stop "endless, fruitless" attempts to repeal the new healthcare law.

## The First Term Vs. the Second Term

- The economy deepening recession, is now recovering slowly as unemployment recedes and stocks are somewhat high.
- Courtesy of a split ruling by the Supreme Court, the healthcare legislation that President Obama urged Congress to enact in his first inaugural address is now the law of the land.
- Al-Qaeda leader Osama Bin Laden is dead at the hands of U.S Special Operation Forces.
- When Obama took office in 2009, his Democratic allies held control of Congress. The Republicans who control the house lead the way in insisting that the administration agree to spending cuts.
- Obama wants Congress to overhaul the nation's immigration laws and to take steps to reduce gun violence.

# Things Happening in The White House

## Petraeus Resigns

CIA Director David Petraeus meets with President Obama at the White House and asks to resign. President Obama accepts Petraeus' resignation.

## The President Receives an Encyclical from Pope Francis

During the first visit for President Obama and Pope Francis to discuss international conflict human rights along with religious freedom, they talked more of shared interests than differences. President Obama presented Francis with a custom-made seed chest which included a variety of fruit and vegetable seeds. The box is made from timber from the first Cathedral to open in the United States in Baltimore.

## Scalia's Death

Scalia's death leaves President Obama with the decision of when to nominate a successor. President Obama said he plans to fulfill his constitutional responsibility and nominate a successor.

## The Obama's Exit Plan

Their vacation as president and first lady is behind them; they arrive on Air Force One at Andrews Air Force Base on their way to the White House as they return from their annual vacation in Hawaii. Barack is entering the closing stretch of his tenure to complete his legacy before handing the reins to President-Elect Trump.

Obama must also prepare to become a private citizen for the first time in two decades. The Obama's family will be making arrangements to move into a rental home in Washington where they plan to stay until youngest daughter, Sasha, finishes high school.

Live streamed interview at Blair House, across the street from the White House, the president talks Friday with news site Vox's Ezra Elein and Sarah Kliff. He warns GOP against repeal with no replacement at hand. Friday was a day to remember because First Lady Michelle, gave her last speech as first lady during a ceremony for educators, where she said being first lady was the greatest honor of her life.

## Farewell, President Obama

Obama directed his team to craft an address that would feel "bigger than politics" and speak to all Americans. During the final state of the Union Address, President Obama pauses while Vice President Biden and House Speaker Ryan, stand and applaud his remarks. President Obama told Americans to rekindle their belief in the promise of change that first carried him into the White House, and if we give up now, then we forsake a better future.

In his hometown of Chicago, thousands came out in single digit temperatures to witness the last presidential address. As I sat in the warmth of my home watching Obama's farewell address on my television, I couldn't fight back the tears. When Barack acknowledged Michelle, you could feel the true everlasting love as he quoted "To Kill a Mockingbird."

I was reading the paper the next morning about what had just happened, and it was explained that this speech had gone through more than four drafts before Obama had what he wanted to say to the American people. His Chief Speechwriter, Cody Keenan, started writing it the previous month and was expected to stay at the White House all night to help perfect Obama's final message.

History, if we allow it, can afford each of us an opportunity to 'climb into the skin of others' and to learn from their triumphs as well as their mistakes. I have a newfound appreciation for it, and I pray that after reading this book, you will too.

# References

Special Courtesy of W3 Newspapers

African-American Newspapers - Online

A list of currently published African-American newspapers including Baltimore Afro-American, New York Amsterdam news, Philadelphia Tribune, and the Chicago Defender.

California

Los Angeles Sentinel

LA Black Post

Oakland Post Newspaper

Sacramento Observer

San Francisco Bay View

Delaware

Delaware Black (Newark)

Florida

Burning Spear

Florida Star (Jacksonville)

Miami Times

Pensacola Voice

Florida Sentinel Bulletin (Tampa)

Westside Gazette (Fort Lauderdale)

Georgia

Atlanta Daily World

Atlanta Voice

Metro Atlanta Black

Savannah Tribune

Illinois

Chicago Citizen

Chicago Crusader

Chicago Defender

Daily Tabloid format newspaper owned by Real Times Inc.

Final Call

Chicago based newspaper was founded in 1979 by Minister Louis Farrakhan

Indiana

Indianapolis Recorder

Iowa

Iowa Baystander

Louisiana

Louisiana Weekly (New Orleans)

Maryland

Afro-American (Baltimore)

Massachusetts

Bay State Banner

Daily newspaper published in Boston, Massachusetts for primarily African-American readers.

Michigan

Michigan Chronicle

Regional Weekly newspaper based in Detroit Michigan.

Mississippi

Jackson Advocate

Weekly newspaper headquartered in Jackson, Mississippi.

Missouri

Kansas City The Call

St. Louis American

Nebraska

Omaha Star (North Omaha)

New York

New York Amsterdam News

Founded in 1909 the Amsterdam news is one of the oldest African-American newspapers in the United States

North Carolina

Carolina Peacemaker (Greensboro)

Charlotte Post

African-American community newspaper based in Charlotte, North Carolina.

Ohio

Call and Post

Weekly newspaper published in Cleveland, Ohio. Most of its circulation in the predominantly African-American neighborhoods.

Oklahoma

Black Chronicle

Africa American Community Newspaper based in Oklahoma City. The newspaper owned by Perry Publishing and Broadcasting

Oregon

Skanner (Portland)

Pennsylvania

Philadelphia Tribune

African-American newspaper published in Philadelphia, Pennsylvania.

Pittsburgh Courier (Pittsburgh)

Afrophilly (Philadelphia)

Tennessee

Tennessee Tribune (Memphis, Jackson, Nashville, and Chattanooga)

Memphis-Tri-State Defender (Memphis)

Texas

African-American News and Issues

Most widely read African-American perspective newspaper published in Texas.

Dallas Weekly

Houston Forward Times (FT)

Houston Defender

Virginia

Richmond Free Press

Newspaper published in Richmond, Virginia

New Journal and Guide (Norfolk)

Washington

Seattle Medium

Featuring business, sports, religion, events, business, health and more

Washington D.C.

Washington Afro-American

Washington Informer

Weekly newspaper serving Washington D.C. Metropolitan area

Washington Sun

Weekly newspaper based in Washington D.C.

DC Black

Tod Perry, via Google search of Obama accolades, "28 of Barack Obama's Greatest Achievements as President of the United States", https://www.good.is/articles/obamas-achievements-inoffice

# About the Author

Phyllis Hodges is a woman of many talents, but perhaps her most significant contribution to those who know her (in my opinion) is her spirit. The first time I met her, I vividly remember thinking, "I don't know what she is doing, but I need to be doing it too!"

Phyllis' high energy is simply infectious. Being in her presence is truly an experience!

As I read this book compiled of history makers, noteworthy facts, and events, I can't help but realize that we are all living and making history each day. The thing that is so profound about Phyllis is that she seems to have always been aware of it. Have you seen her photo collection? Absolutely astounding!

You've read about Phyllis and her seemingly 'larger than life' life, and if you know her, you know that when she walks into a room, she takes up all the space with her huge heart, caring nature, and generous spirit.

Her smile and laughter are not only genuine, but like her energy, they too are infectious.

Her legacy (one of them) is connecting and recognizing history. This gift is evident by the caliber of authors who agreed to pour into this dream of hers.

To know her is to truly love her.

I love you lady!

*Iris M Williams*

# Contact Phyllis Hodges

**Address**
513 Main
North Little Rock, AR 72114

**Phone**
(501) 372-3348
Or
(501) 563-0861

**Email**
Carouselfit4life@gmail.com

**Website**
http://carouselprojects.weebly.com

**Social Media**

@CarouselFit4LifeWellnessCenter

# Butterfly Typeface Publishing

PO Box 56193

Little Rock AR 72215

(501) 823 - 0574

www.butterflytypeface.com

*We Make Good Great!*

# Your History!

**THE FAMILY REGISTER**

# Certificate of Marriage

**THIS CERTIFIES THAT**

______________________________________________

**AND**

______________________________________________

**WERE UNITED IN**

## Holy Matrimony

**ON THE** ____________________ **DAY OF** ____________________

**IN THE YEAR OF OUR LORD** ______________________________

**AT** ______________________________________________

**BY** ______________________________________________

**WITNESS** ______________________________________________

**WITNESS** ______________________________________________

# HUSBAND'S GENEALOGY

NAME ____________________

BIRTH ____________________
PLACE DATE

BAPTISM ____________________
CHURCH MINISTER DATE

CHURCH MEMBERSHIP ____________________
CHURCH MINISTER DATE

OFFICES HELD ____________________
CHURCH OFFICE DATE

SPECIAL EVENTS ____________________
DATE

MILITARY SERVICE ____________________
BRANCH ENTERED DISCHARGED RANK

## PARENTS

FATHER

____________________
NAME

____________________
DATE AND PLACE OF BIRTH

MOTHER

____________________
NAME

____________________
DATE AND PLACE OF BIRTH

# HUSBAND'S GENEALOGY

## GRANDPARENTS

**PATERNAL**

______________________________
**GRANDFATHER**

______________________________
**DATE AND PLACE OF BIRTH**

______________________________
**GRANDMOTHER**

______________________________
**DATE AND PLACE OF BIRTH**

**MATERNAL**

______________________________
**GRANDFATHER**

______________________________
**DATE AND PLACE OF BIRTH**

______________________________
**GRANDMOTHER**

______________________________
**DATE AND PLACE OF BIRTH**

# HUSBAND'S GENEALOGY

## GREAT GRANDPARENTS

**PATERNAL**

GRANDFATHER'S FATHER

DATE AND PLACE OF BIRTH

GRANDFATHER'S MOTHER

DATE AND PLACE OF BIRTH

GRANDMOTHER'S FATHER

DATE AND PLACE OF BIRTH

GRANDMOTHER'S MOTHER

DATE AND PLACE OF BIRTH

**MATERNAL**

GRANDFATHER'S FATHER

DATE AND PLACE OF BIRTH

GRANDFATHER'S MOTHER

DATE AND PLACE OF BIRTH

GRANDMOTHER'S FATHER

DATE AND PLACE OF BIRTH

GRANDMOTHER'S MOTHER

DATE AND PLACE OF BIRTH

# WIFE'S GENEALOGY

NAME ______________________________

BIRTH ______________________________
PLACE DATE

BAPTISM ______________________________
CHURCH MINISTER DATE

CHURCH
MEMBERSHIP ______________________________
CHURCH MINISTER DATE

OFFICES HELD ______________________________
CHURCH OFFICE DATE

SPECIAL EVENTS ______________________________
DATE

MILITARY
SERVICE ______________________________
BRANCH ENTERED DISCHARGED RANK

## PARENTS

**FATHER**

______________________________
NAME

______________________________
DATE AND PLACE OF BIRTH

**MOTHER**

______________________________
NAME

______________________________
DATE AND PLACE OF BIRTH

# WIFE'S GENEALOGY

## GRANDPARENTS

**PATERNAL**

GRANDFATHER

DATE AND PLACE OF BIRTH

GRANDMOTHER

DATE AND PLACE OF BIRTH

**MATERNAL**

GRANDFATHER

DATE AND PLACE OF BIRTH

GRANDMOTHER

DATE AND PLACE OF BIRTH

# WIFE'S GENEALOGY

## GREAT GRANDPARENTS

PATERNAL

GRANDFATHER'S FATHER

DATE AND PLACE OF BIRTH

GRANDFATHER'S MOTHER

DATE AND PLACE OF BIRTH

GRANDMOTHER'S FATHER

DATE AND PLACE OF BIRTH

GRANDMOTHER'S MOTHER

DATE AND PLACE OF BIRTH

MATERNAL

GRANDFATHER'S FATHER

DATE AND PLACE OF BIRTH

GRANDFATHER'S MOTHER

DATE AND PLACE OF BIRTH

GRANDMOTHER'S FATHER

DATE AND PLACE OF BIRTH

GRANDMOTHER'S MOTHER

DATE AND PLACE OF BIRTH

# CHILDREN'S RECORD

NAME ____________________

BIRTH ____________________
PLACE DATE

BAPTISM ____________________
CHURCH MINISTER DATE

CHURCH MEMBERSHIP ____________________
CHURCH OFFICE DATE

OFFICES HELD ____________________
CHURCH OFFICE DATE

MILITARY SERVICE ____________________
BRANCH ENTERED DISCHARGED RANK

MARRIAGE ____________________
NAME OF SPOUSE PLACE DATE

____________________
MINISTER BEST MAN MAID OF HONOR

CHILDREN ____________________
NAME DATE OF BIRTH PLACE

____________________
NAME DATE OF BIRTH PLACE

____________________
NAME DATE OF BIRTH PLACE

____________________
NAME DATE OF BIRTH PLACE

OTHER NOTEWORTHY EVENTS ____________________

DEATH ____________________
PLACE DATE PLACE OF BURIAL

# CHILDREN'S RECORD

NAME ____________________

BIRTH ____________________
PLACE DATE

BAPTISM ____________________
CHURCH MINISTER DATE

CHURCH MEMBERSHIP ____________________
CHURCH OFFICE DATE

OFFICES HELD ____________________
CHURCH OFFICE DATE

MILITARY SERVICE ____________________
BRANCH ENTERED DISCHARGED RANK

MARRIAGE ____________________
NAME OF SPOUSE PLACE DATE

____________________
MINISTER BEST MAN MAID OF HONOR

CHILDREN ____________________
NAME DATE OF BIRTH PLACE

____________________
NAME DATE OF BIRTH PLACE

____________________
NAME DATE OF BIRTH PLACE

____________________
NAME DATE OF BIRTH PLACE

OTHER NOTEWORTHY EVENTS ____________________

DEATH ____________________
PLACE DATE PLACE OF BURIAL

# CHILDREN'S RECORD

NAME ____________________

BIRTH ____________________
PLACE DATE

BAPTISM ____________________
CHURCH MINISTER DATE

CHURCH MEMBERSHIP ____________________
CHURCH OFFICE DATE

OFFICES HELD ____________________
CHURCH OFFICE DATE

MILITARY SERVICE ____________________
BRANCH ENTERED DISCHARGED RANK

MARRIAGE ____________________
NAME OF SPOUSE PLACE DATE

____________________
MINISTER BEST MAN MAID OF HONOR

CHILDREN ____________________
NAME DATE OF BIRTH PLACE

____________________
NAME DATE OF BIRTH PLACE

____________________
NAME DATE OF BIRTH PLACE

____________________
NAME DATE OF BIRTH PLACE

OTHER NOTEWORTHY EVENTS ____________________

DEATH ____________________
PLACE DATE PLACE OF BURIAL

# CHILDREN'S RECORD

NAME ______________________________

BIRTH ______________________________
PLACE DATE

BAPTISM ______________________________
CHURCH MINISTER DATE

CHURCH MEMBERSHIP ______________________________
CHURCH OFFICE DATE

OFFICES HELD ______________________________
CHURCH OFFICE DATE

MILITARY SERVICE ______________________________
BRANCH ENTERED DISCHARGED RANK

MARRIAGE ______________________________
NAME OF SPOUSE PLACE DATE

______________________________
MINISTER BEST MAN MAID OF HONOR

CHILDREN ______________________________
NAME DATE OF BIRTH PLACE

______________________________
NAME DATE OF BIRTH PLACE

______________________________
NAME DATE OF BIRTH PLACE

______________________________
NAME DATE OF BIRTH PLACE

OTHER NOTEWORTHY EVENTS ______________________________

DEATH ______________________________
PLACE DATE PLACE OF BURIAL

# CHILDREN'S RECORD

NAME ______________________________

BIRTH ______________________________
PLACE DATE

BAPTISM ______________________________
CHURCH MINISTER DATE

CHURCH MEMBERSHIP ______________________________
CHURCH OFFICE DATE

OFFICES HELD ______________________________
CHURCH OFFICE DATE

MILITARY SERVICE ______________________________
BRANCH ENTERED DISCHARGED RANK

MARRIAGE ______________________________
NAME OF SPOUSE PLACE DATE

______________________________
MINISTER BEST MAN MAID OF HONOR

CHILDREN ______________________________
NAME DATE OF BIRTH PLACE

______________________________
NAME DATE OF BIRTH PLACE

______________________________
NAME DATE OF BIRTH PLACE

______________________________
NAME DATE OF BIRTH PLACE

OTHER NOTEWORTHY EVENTS ______________________________

DEATH ______________________________
PLACE DATE PLACE OF BURIAL

# CHILDREN'S RECORD

NAME ____________________

BIRTH ____________________
PLACE DATE

BAPTISM ____________________
CHURCH MINISTER DATE

CHURCH MEMBERSHIP ____________________
CHURCH OFFICE DATE

OFFICES HELD ____________________
CHURCH OFFICE DATE

MILITARY SERVICE ____________________
BRANCH ENTERED DISCHARGED RANK

MARRIAGE ____________________
NAME OF SPOUSE PLACE DATE

____________________
MINISTER BEST MAN MAID OF HONOR

CHILDREN ____________________
NAME DATE OF BIRTH PLACE

____________________
NAME DATE OF BIRTH PLACE

____________________
NAME DATE OF BIRTH PLACE

____________________
NAME DATE OF BIRTH PLACE

OTHER NOTEWORTHY EVENTS ____________________

DEATH ____________________
PLACE DATE PLACE OF BURIAL

# CHILDREN'S RECORD

NAME ______________________________

BIRTH ______________________________
PLACE DATE

BAPTISM ______________________________
CHURCH MINISTER DATE

CHURCH MEMBERSHIP ______________________________
CHURCH OFFICE DATE

OFFICES HELD ______________________________
CHURCH OFFICE DATE

MILITARY SERVICE ______________________________
BRANCH ENTERED DISCHARGED RANK

MARRIAGE ______________________________
NAME OF SPOUSE PLACE DATE

______________________________
MINISTER BEST MAN MAID OF HONOR

CHILDREN ______________________________
NAME DATE OF BIRTH PLACE

______________________________
NAME DATE OF BIRTH PLACE

______________________________
NAME DATE OF BIRTH PLACE

______________________________
NAME DATE OF BIRTH PLACE

OTHER NOTEWORTHY EVENTS ______________________________

DEATH ______________________________
PLACE DATE PLACE OF BURIAL

# CHILDREN'S RECORD

NAME ______________________________

BIRTH ______________________________
PLACE DATE

BAPTISM ______________________________
CHURCH MINISTER DATE

CHURCH MEMBERSHIP ______________________________
CHURCH OFFICE DATE

OFFICES HELD ______________________________
CHURCH OFFICE DATE

MILITARY SERVICE ______________________________
BRANCH ENTERED DISCHARGED RANK

MARRIAGE ______________________________
NAME OF SPOUSE PLACE DATE

______________________________
MINISTER BEST MAN MAID OF HONOR

CHILDREN ______________________________
NAME DATE OF BIRTH PLACE

______________________________
NAME DATE OF BIRTH PLACE

______________________________
NAME DATE OF BIRTH PLACE

______________________________
NAME DATE OF BIRTH PLACE

OTHER NOTEWORTHY EVENTS ______________________________

DEATH ______________________________
PLACE DATE PLACE OF BURIAL

# EVENTS TO REMEMBER

## IN THE LIFE OF OUR FAMILY

# EVENTS TO REMEMBER

## IN THE LIFE OF OUR FAMILY

# EVENTS TO REMEMBER

## IN THE LIFE OF OUR FAMILY

# EVENTS TO REMEMBER

## IN THE LIFE OF OUR FAMILY